Crypto- A Practical Guide for Real-World Investors

Crypto- A Practical Guide for Real-World Investors

Cut through the hype and build a rational role for crypto in your wealth strategy

Daniel R. Hale

Mindful Pages

Published in 2025

ISBN: 9789371775069 (PB)
ISBN: 9789371779975 (eBook)

Published by

Mindful Pages
Imprint of Alpha Editions LLC
312 W. 2nd St #1834
Casper, WY 82601, USA

This book was developed using advanced writing tools to support the drafting and ideation process. All content has been thoughtfully curated, refined, and reviewed to ensure quality and relevance.

Content

Introduction Crypto Without the Noise viii

Chapter 1 The Cult and the Crash: Why Crypto Confuses Everyone 1

Chapter 2 A History of Value: Why Money Keeps Changing 30

Chapter 3 The Crypto Stack: What You're Actually Buying 57

Chapter 4 Risk, Volatility, and Why Most People Lose...84

Chapter 5 A Framework for Rational Exposure 110

Chapter 6 Beyond Buying: Earning, Yielding, and Using 133

Chapter 7 Digital Self-Custody: Why It Matters (and Scares People) 161

Chapter 8 Beyond Bitcoin: Stablecoins, CBDCs, and the Future of Money 187

Chapter 9 Regulation, Crackdowns, and What You Need to Know 216

Chapter 10 Smart Questions, Not Hot Takes 243

Chapter 11 Crypto as a Mirror: What This Space Teaches Us About Ourselves 270

Chapter 12 Designing Your Crypto Plan 295

About the Author 320

Introduction
Crypto Without the Noise

Crypto elicits some of the sharpest divisions in contemporary discourse. To certain enthusiasts, it represents a financial revolution, a pathway to a more decentralised, democratic, and digitally native economy. To others, it is little more than a speculative frenzy, dressed in techno-utopian rhetoric and inflated by human greed, seemingly destined for collapse. Depending on whom one asks, crypto is either the next evolution of money or a warning against irrational exuberance. In truth, it may be neither—at least in the way most narratives suggest.

What is undeniable is that crypto has moved far beyond its origins as a fringe internet curiosity. It now functions as a kind of cultural Rorschach test, reflecting the preconceptions, anxieties, and aspirations of each observer. For the hopeful, it promises liberation from traditional banking and governmental oversight; for the sceptical, it exudes the aroma of Ponzi schemes and regulatory blind spots. To many, however, it remains opaque and volatile—a realm easier to mock than to navigate. Yet for the discerning investor, who neither idolises crypto nor dismisses it outright, the central question persists: where, if at all, does crypto fit within a rational, long-term wealth strategy?

This book aims to provide clarity, not through predictions or ideology, but through structured, disciplined thinking. It does not seek to convince you that crypto is the future, nor to warn you off with alarmist rhetoric. Its purpose is to cut through the noise, enabling a reasoned understanding amidst the headlines, market hysteria, and ideological fervour.

The rise of crypto coincides with a deep erosion of trust in established institutions. Central banks have stretched monetary policy to unprecedented lengths. Political systems appear paralysed by polarisation. Tech giants wield power rivalling—or even surpassing—states. Within this context, it is hardly surprising that decentralised, programmable money has captured imaginations. Yet such an environment also distorts perception: when people feel betrayed by existing structures, they become more receptive to narratives promising both salvation and catastrophe.

Consequently, public discourse on crypto is dominated by extremes. On one side are the maximalists and evangelists, who view decentralised finance as a moral imperative. On the other are sceptics and traditionalists, who equate crypto with fraud or youthful folly. The balanced, rigorous voice—one willing to interrogate assumptions, demand clarity, and acknowledge both risk and potential—has been largely absent. This book seeks to fill that gap.

It is written for the pragmatic investor: grounded in financial reality, open to innovation, yet uninterested in tribalism or hype. Someone who understands that wealth is built through disciplined allocation under uncertainty, not chasing novelty or consensus. This audience recognises that innovation does not guarantee inevitability, but neither does tradition inherently ensure safety.

Why now? Because while the crypto market has matured, it has not necessarily become more intelligible. Concepts such as blockchain, DeFi, NFTs, and Web3 circulate widely—boardrooms, media panels, even family WhatsApp groups—often with more enthusiasm than comprehension. Prices swing wildly, new tokens appear overnight, regulation looms uncertainly, and genuine innovation continues in parallel—some promising, much untested.

Most investors are unsure how to respond. Buy Bitcoin as a hedge? Avoid entirely? Wait for clarity on regulation? Explore altcoins? Trust institutional custody or self-manage? And crucially, how much of a portfolio, if any, should be exposed to such a volatile and emerging asset class? This book provides a framework to address these questions with reasoned confidence.

Importantly, it does not rely on predicting which coin will soar or when the next bull run will occur. Instead, it emphasises enduring principles: assessing risk, sizing positions appropriately, thinking probabilistically rather than absolutistically, and integrating crypto into a wider, risk-aware investment strategy.

To do so, we must confront crypto honestly—both what it is and what it is not. The first chapter traces swings of public opinion, from utopian enthusiasm to regulatory panic, revealing why crypto has become so misunderstood. We then examine the narratives that grant it emotional power: myths of digital gold, fears over fiat collapse, and dreams of financial autonomy. While compelling, these stories can cloud judgment if unexamined.

Next, we examine the mechanics. What are you truly buying with a coin or token? How do Bitcoin, Ethereum, and the myriad subsequent assets differ? Which demonstrate credible use-cases, and which are speculation masquerading as innovation?

Understanding the product alone is insufficient; the environment in which it trades is equally critical. Crypto markets are volatile, sentiment-driven, and prone to behavioural pitfalls. Many participants lose not because the system is rigged, but because assumptions are flawed. We explore these traps—and how to navigate them.

Then comes the strategic question: how much should you own? For most, the answer lies in measured exposure, not extremes. A thoughtfully sized 1–5% position, integrated into a broader portfolio, provides optionality without jeopardising stability. This book will guide you in defining a personal "crypto thesis," rooted not in noise, but in goals, time horizon, and risk tolerance.

We also address practical use-cases. Beyond capital appreciation, crypto offers staking, lending, and yield farming; cross-border payments; and other functional applications. Some are genuinely innovative, others repackaged leverage schemes. We evaluate substance against spin.

Technical realities cannot be ignored. How should digital assets be stored securely? Hot versus cold wallets, self-custody versus institutional custody? Tax considerations, legal compliance, and protection from hacks and fraud must all be understood.

Finally, we widen the lens. Stablecoins, central bank digital currencies, and global monetary policy shape crypto's broader landscape. Legal and regulatory evolution will influence its future, not just as an asset class, but as a component of societal infrastructure. And introspectively, crypto offers insight into human psychology, bias, and our perennial desire for systems we can trust.

Ultimately, this book is less about markets and technology than about trust, uncertainty, and decision-making in an uncontrollable world. Crypto mirrors our hopes for freedom, our anxieties over collapse, and our wish to belong to something transformative.

It offers no simple answers—only better questions and the tools to explore them. It asks you not to believe, but to understand; not to follow hype, but to assess rationally; not to abandon caution, but to engage thoughtfully.

By the final chapter, you will possess a framework, not a forecast; principles, not predictions; clarity, in a landscape designed to confuse. Hype will fade, cycles will recur, yet the capacity to think clearly, act deliberately, and invest rationally will endure. Let us begin.

Chapter 1
The Cult and the Crash: Why Crypto Confuses Everyone

Crypto did not arrive quietly. From the outset, it thundered onto the global stage, carried as much by ideology as by technology. Bitcoin's genesis block, famously inscribed with a message referencing bank bailouts, was not merely a timestamp—it was a manifesto. Beneath the novelty of the code lay age-old sentiments: mistrust of institutions, a craving for autonomy, and a scepticism of authority. What began as lines of code swiftly morphed into culture, and from there, into doctrine. For early adopters, crypto was rarely just a new form of money; it became, in many ways, a belief system.

This belief system arrived with revolutionary fervour. Crypto was championed as the great equaliser, the instrument that would wrest power from governments, dismantle banks, and restore sovereignty to individuals. Terms like incorruptible, borderless, immutable, decentralised—once abstract concepts—were wielded as promises of a liberated future. It was no longer merely about value transfer; it was about freedom itself. Naturally, such grand narratives attracted fervent disciples and determined sceptics in equal measure.

Reality, however, proved more chaotic than the rhetoric. As crypto moved from obscure forums to front-page headlines, volatility became the norm. Fraudulent schemes proliferated, celebrities hyped and abandoned coins, and exchanges disappeared overnight, often taking user funds with them. Radical promise collided with human foibles, and public perception oscillated wildly. Today, crypto is less a single story than a hall of mirrors—innovation and chaos, utopia and scam, entwined.

This confusion is deliberate in a sense; it is baked into the way crypto has been communicated, marketed, and mythologised. Emerging technologies, particularly those challenging entrenched institutions, naturally attract narratives that outpace their substance. Crypto's stories became inseparable from its identity. This chapter seeks to strip away those layers of myth, panic, and promise to offer a clearer perspective.

The volatility of crypto markets is not purely technical; it is profoundly emotional. Market swings mirror cycles of collective euphoria and despair more akin to social movements than conventional finance. Take the crash of 2022: in a single year, total market capitalisation fell from over $3 trillion to under $900 billion. Institutions lauded as pillars of the "new financial order"—FTX, Celsius, Terra—imploded, exposing reckless leverage and internal rot. Yet, before the dust settled, new projects arose, capital returned, and narratives shifted toward recovery and regulation. That resilience, at once admirable and confounding, is part of crypto's enduring mystique.

The explanation lies in crypto's dual identity: it is both technology and narrative. Blockchains, smart contracts, and consensus mechanisms evolve logically, but human engagement with them is emotional, tribal, and often irrational. The gulf between technical potential and popular perception has become a theatre of cognitive dissonance.

Navigating this requires resisting simplistic binaries. Crypto is neither panacea nor snake oil—it is a toolkit. Its value is conditional on the problem being solved, the context of its use, and the competence of its user. Mistaking the tool for a cause—or, worse, an identity—is a common pitfall.

Many investors enter crypto through influence rather than understanding. Social media has become the principal conduit for tokens and ideas alike. Memes, influencers, and viral narratives often move markets faster than fundamentals. Communities coalesce around coins with the intensity of sports fandom or spiritual devotion. In this milieu, decisions frequently resemble ideological commitments more than rational appraisals.

Yet beneath the noise lies a quieter, practical reality. Not all users seek ideological purity or spectacular returns. Migrant workers leverage stablecoins for cheaper remittances. Residents of inflation-prone nations hedge savings with digital assets. Tech-savvy investors stake for modest yields. Developers build decentralised applications with real-world utility. These actors are pragmatic, measured, and often overlooked.

The real promise of crypto may reside in these understated applications rather than the grandiose claims. Like the early internet, its transformative effects often emerge quietly, addressing specific problems without upending entire systems.

Narrative shapes perception, and crypto thrives on metaphor: Bitcoin as digital gold, Ethereum as the world computer, DeFi as open finance. These analogies are compelling but imperfect. Bitcoin lacks industrial demand and physicality; Ethereum is not a singular machine; DeFi is not risk-free. Accepting these metaphors uncritically can lead to flawed assumptions.

Consider Bitcoin as digital gold. Its fixed supply and decentralised issuance invite comparison, yet it depends on electricity, internet infrastructure, and code integrity. Its value is consensus-driven, not intrinsic. Similarly, narratives of fiat collapse hold relevance in extreme contexts, but in stable economies, they are speculative at best. The freedom-tech argument—privacy, uncensorable transactions, and sovereignty—is nuanced. Public ledgers, KYC regulations, and state oversight complicate claims of absolute freedom.

Structural realities further distinguish crypto from traditional assets. Markets are fragmented, immature, and operate round-the-clock. Liquidity is volatile, insider knowledge prevalent, and conventional anchors—quarterly earnings, market hours—are absent. Behaviourally, this environment breeds reactive decision-making: buying high, selling low, following sentiment, and succumbing to emotional fatigue.

Long-term success demands more than conviction; it requires framework: risk awareness, strategic clarity, and psychological self-defence. Recognising patterns in volatility, separating myth from utility, and treating crypto on its own terms—not as an analogue to equities or bonds—are essential.

By chapter's end, readers should grasp why crypto bewilders so many, and how to avoid falling prey to that confusion. In this space, misunderstanding carries a tangible cost: overexposure, missed opportunity, emotional whiplash, or ideological capture. With the right lens, confusion yields to clarity—and in investing, clarity is everything.

The Promise and the Panic

Crypto has been called many things: revolutionary, fraudulent, decentralised salvation, environmental disaster. But perhaps its most defining trait is its volatility—not just in price, but in public perception. Few innovations in recent memory have swung so violently between idolisation and rejection. One moment it is the darling of Silicon Valley venture capital; the next, the target of regulatory crackdowns, media derision, and political scorn. The whiplash is not simply a reflection of asset prices, but of deeper cultural ambivalence. Crypto sits at the uncomfortable intersection of finance, technology, and ideology. This makes it not only misunderstood, but frequently misrepresented. Understanding this duality—its capacity to inspire and alarm—is essential to approaching it rationally.

At the height of its mania in late 2021, Bitcoin was valued above $65,000. Ethereum soared alongside it. Altcoins exploded in volume, meme coins like Dogecoin and Shiba Inu found cult followings, and non-fungible tokens (NFTs) became headline news. Crypto conferences turned into multi-day festivals; celebrities endorsed tokens; Super Bowl ads declared the future was being built on-chain. The space was thick with optimism, ambition, and cash. And then it collapsed.

By mid-2022, over two trillion dollars in market capitalisation had vanished. High-profile projects imploded. Terra, a much-touted algorithmic stablecoin, suffered a death spiral that obliterated $40 billion in investor value almost overnight. Celsius froze withdrawals. Voyager filed for bankruptcy. FTX—once the face of institutional crypto—collapsed in a spectacular display of mismanagement and alleged fraud. Media coverage shifted sharply: from breathless celebration to scathing takedowns. Governments called for action; regulators sharpened their tools. Trust evaporated.

These swings are not merely a by-product of speculative cycles. They are evidence of a deeper conceptual confusion: a failure to distinguish between the underlying promise of the technology and the mania that often surrounds it. Crypto's core innovation—decentralised, programmable, borderless value transfer—is not inherently fraudulent or miraculous. It is infrastructure. But infrastructure rarely captures attention. Narrative does.

Crypto's first mistake was its own marketing. From the outset, it sold not just utility, but utopia. It wasn't enough for Bitcoin to be an alternative ledger; it had to be "digital gold," a hedge against monetary collapse, a vehicle for sovereignty. Ethereum wasn't just a platform—it was "the world computer," a new substrate for global coordination. These narratives resonated, particularly in the wake of the

2008 financial crisis, which had left many questioning the credibility of traditional financial institutions. But utopian framing is a double-edged sword. When expectations are set sky-high, reality inevitably disappoints.

The result is a market defined by emotional extremity. Investors alternate between euphoric optimism and existential despair. When prices rise, crypto is freedom. When they fall, it is fraud. This binary obscures a more nuanced truth: crypto is neither a scam nor a saviour. It is a system of tools with varying degrees of maturity, tested in the open by participants of vastly different motivations, capabilities, and levels of understanding.

To understand how these swings have distorted public perception, it is instructive to look at the actors involved. Early crypto adopters were often technologists and libertarians, drawn by the ideological appeal of decentralisation. They were later joined by speculators chasing asymmetric returns, who in turn were followed by institutional investors seeking yield and diversification. Along the way came the influencers, the opportunists, the bad-faith actors, and the misinformed retail investors hoping not to miss out. This influx of competing agendas created a cultural stew in which clear communication became nearly impossible. Critics and proponents often talk past each other, referring not to the same technology, but to their respective mythologies.

And mythology matters. Bitcoin's status as "digital gold" is more than metaphor—it shapes how people understand its purpose, its risk profile, and its long-term potential. But the metaphor is imperfect. Gold has physical scarcity; Bitcoin's scarcity is digital and enforced by protocol. Gold is inert and requires no electricity to exist; Bitcoin's security model depends on ongoing energy expenditure. These differences are not trivial, yet they are often ignored in favour of rhetorical shorthand. When Bitcoin fails to behave like gold—as in times of macroeconomic stress—confidence is shaken, not because the technology changed, but because the narrative frayed.

Similarly, the myth of crypto as an escape from fiat currency collapses under scrutiny in stable economies. In the United States, the eurozone, Japan, and much of Asia, central banks maintain relative control over monetary systems. Inflation may fluctuate, but the prospect of hyperinflation is remote. Yet many investors in these regions base their crypto thesis on the eventual demise of fiat, an outcome not supported by evidence. This creates a mismatch between expectation and reality, setting the stage for disappointment.

Then there is the notion of decentralised freedom. Crypto is often described as censorship-resistant, anonymous, and sovereign. These attributes are real—but not absolute. Blockchain records are public and permanent. On-ramps like Coinbase or Binance are heavily regulated and comply with Know Your Customer (KYC) and Anti-Money Laundering (AML) laws. Governments can and do track wallet activity. Privacy-focused coins exist, but they remain niche and frequently face regulatory scrutiny. To invoke crypto as an unqualified freedom technology is to ignore the layers of trade-offs, constraints, and operational risks involved.

This is not to say the promises are empty. In unstable economies—Argentina, Venezuela, Zimbabwe—crypto offers a lifeline. Stablecoins provide dollar exposure in places where access to the banking system is restricted or untrustworthy. In Ukraine and Palestine, crypto has been used to fund humanitarian aid when traditional routes failed. In Nigeria, a growing youth population is using crypto to escape financial exclusion. These real-world applications underscore the value of digital assets when legacy systems falter. But they are rarely the focus of mainstream crypto discourse, which remains entranced by price movement and speculative fervour.

The disconnect between promise and panic is further amplified by the nature of crypto markets themselves. They operate continuously—24 hours a day, seven days a week—without central coordination. This creates a relentless feedback loop, where sentiment drives price, and price drives sentiment. Traditional investors accustomed to quarterly reporting and regulated exchanges find themselves unmoored. A tweet from a high-profile individual can move billions. A security vulnerability in a smart contract can cause cascading liquidations. The absence of circuit breakers or regulatory oversight compounds the volatility.

Moreover, the structural design of many crypto assets invites sharp cycles. Tokenomics often prioritise early adopters through mechanisms like initial coin offerings (ICOs), staking rewards, or emission schedules that create built-in inflation and deflation effects. These mechanisms can generate massive upside early on but often struggle to maintain long-term equilibrium. The result is a market that behaves less like equities and more like startup venture portfolios—high risk, high variance, low predictability.

In this context, emotional discipline becomes not just a virtue, but a necessity. Yet most participants are unequipped. The average investor approaches crypto as they would a stock: buy low, sell high, trust the chart. But charts in crypto are shaped not by earnings or cash flow, but by community sentiment, media cycles, and protocol upgrades. Success requires a fundamentally different mental model—one that incorporates not just financial analysis, but technological literacy and behavioural awareness.

The most dangerous aspect of crypto's volatility is not the asset price—it is what it does to the investor's mind. Rapid gains foster overconfidence; sudden losses induce panic. The space rewards impulsivity, punishes patience, and incentivises participation through manufactured urgency. To stay sane requires a framework: understanding what you own, why you own it, and what role it plays in your broader financial picture. Without that, crypto becomes not an investment, but a casino wrapped in the language of liberation.

The promise of crypto is real. But it is not inevitable, and it is not universal. The panic is also real—but it is not always justified. Most failures in crypto are not technological—they are human. Misaligned incentives, poor governance, inadequate risk controls, and misplaced belief. The technology is neutral. Its outcomes are not.

The task for the thoughtful investor is to escape the emotional extremes. Not by standing above them, but by seeing them clearly. To resist the siren calls of both utopia and collapse. To recognise that hype and fear are not opposites, but co-dependent forces. Crypto's wild swings will likely continue, because they are baked into its structure. But our understanding of it need not swing with them. Through clarity, discipline, and perspective, it is possible to evaluate crypto not as a cultural phenomenon or an investment fad, but as a set of tools with specific, evolving potential.

To do so is not to ignore the noise—it is to rise above it.

The Mythologies of Money

Money has always required a story. The metal in your pocket, the numbers in your bank account, the digits glowing on a screen—all are useless without shared belief. Trust, not tangibility, makes money work. This is not a flaw in the system; it *is* the system. From Mesopotamian ledgers to Venetian banking scripts to today's central bank reserves, money functions only because we agree to accept it as such. Yet this reliance on shared narrative also makes money vulnerable—to myth, metaphor, and the seductions of meaning. Crypto has amplified this dynamic, grafting a new set of ideologies onto an old human habit: telling stories about value to justify behaviour.

The digital asset world is not short on narratives. Crypto is "digital gold," a bulwark against inflation and fiat collapse. It's "freedom tech," emancipating users from corrupt banks and intrusive states. It's the next internet, the "Web3" revolution, a new layer of economic coordination. These are powerful metaphors—sticky, emotional, and persuasive. They confer purpose on complex systems. They transform technical architecture into moral cause. But they also distort judgment, especially when belief substitutes for scrutiny.

Consider Bitcoin as "digital gold." The analogy is both intuitive and misleading. Like gold, Bitcoin has a capped supply—21 million coins, ever. Like gold, it is mined, albeit digitally, through a proof-of-work mechanism. And like gold, Bitcoin is often presented as a hedge: against monetary debasement, geopolitical instability, or systemic risk. Yet the similarities end quickly. Gold has thousands of years of monetary history; Bitcoin has fifteen. Gold has industrial use, is held by central banks, and has relatively low volatility. Bitcoin's price can double—or halve—in weeks, and its valuation is driven by sentiment more than macro fundamentals. When central banks expand their balance sheets, gold may rise modestly; Bitcoin may soar—or plummet—depending on context.

And yet, for many investors, the gold metaphor justifies allocation. It implies stability, scarcity, and permanence. But Bitcoin is not a commodity. It is code. It relies on a network of miners, nodes, developers, and users for its continued function. Its scarcity is maintained not by geology, but by consensus—an agreement enforced by the rules of software and the commitment of a decentralised community. This is a different kind of trust: engineered, yes, but fragile in its own way. If the community fractures, the code can fork. If energy costs surge or regulation bites, miners can disappear. If the narrative weakens, demand evaporates.

The point is not that Bitcoin is worthless. It is that the metaphor of gold, while useful for framing, is insufficient for valuation. Investors who rely on the analogy without interrogating its limits are vulnerable to misjudging both risk and potential. They treat Bitcoin as a static asset in a dynamic system, ignoring the socio-technical complexity behind its operation. Myth comforts. But it also conceals.

A parallel mythology fuels the fear of fiat collapse. In this narrative, central banks are incompetent or malevolent. Governments are debasing currencies to fund deficits, social spending, or wars. Inflation is not a transient annoyance but a terminal illness. In such a world, crypto becomes exit—your own bank, your own money, immune to the whims of policymakers. There are historical echoes to support this fear: Weimar Germany, Zimbabwe, Venezuela. And recent bouts of inflation across developed economies have lent some credence to concerns about currency dilution.

But the leap from inflation to fiat extinction is vast—and usually unwarranted. Modern central banks, despite their flaws, still anchor economic systems that most people trust. The US dollar is not collapsing. The euro remains stable. The Japanese yen, while under pressure, is not in freefall. Policy mistakes happen, but institutional resilience remains strong. For all its volatility, fiat money still greases the wheels of global trade, capital markets, and everyday transactions. It is backed not just by decree, but by vast systems of taxation, enforcement, and liquidity support.

The fiat collapse narrative also overlooks the operational challenges of replacing a dominant currency. Crypto assets are not plug-and-play substitutes. They suffer from price instability, limited merchant adoption, regulatory uncertainty, and UX hurdles. Stablecoins offer a temporary workaround, but they remain tethered to the very fiat systems they claim to outlive. If one believes that fiat will collapse, one must also believe that the infrastructure built atop it—exchanges, banks, payment rails—will survive in isolation. This is not just unlikely. It's internally inconsistent.

Yet the myth endures, because it appeals to deeper instincts: distrust of authority, longing for autonomy, fear of systemic fragility. It transforms a technical investment into a political act. Buying Bitcoin becomes a vote against the system. Holding Ethereum is a hedge against collapse. These are not financial positions—they are existential ones. And as with all identity-based narratives, they are difficult to evaluate objectively.

The third great myth is that of "freedom tech." Crypto, in this framing, is the final answer to censorship, surveillance, and financial exclusion. You hold your own keys. No one can freeze your account. Transactions settle without intermediaries. This promise is not entirely false. Blockchains do enable forms of resilience and openness not available in centralised systems. Activists, dissidents, and marginalised communities have used crypto to bypass restrictions. In hostile regimes, access to stable digital assets can be a matter of survival.

But the reality is more complex. True freedom in crypto requires significant technical competence: key management, operational security, chain analysis awareness. The average user is not there. Most hold assets on centralised exchanges, subject to the same KYC rules and data surveillance they sought to escape. Wallets are lost. Phishing scams proliferate. Protocols can be hacked. Regulation is tightening. In practice, the freedom narrative often creates a false sense of security, leading users to underestimate real risks.

Moreover, freedom is not evenly distributed. Technical users can navigate decentralised ecosystems safely. Casual users cannot. Financial freedom in crypto is often conditional on education, time, and tooling. And when things go wrong, there is no helpline, no reversal mechanism, no recourse. Autonomy cuts both ways. The very features that make crypto resistant to external control also make it resistant to support. You are free, but you are also alone.

Still, freedom tech resonates because it offers a counterweight to rising concerns about surveillance capitalism, authoritarian drift, and data exploitation. It speaks to a broader unease: that the digital systems we rely on are opaque, unaccountable, and increasingly invasive. Crypto presents itself as the antidote—a network of transparency, user control, and cryptographic trust. That it sometimes fails to deliver on this promise does not negate the value of the aspiration. But aspiration must be tempered by realism. Ideals are not infrastructure.

What unites all these myths is their ability to simplify. They offer legibility in a chaotic landscape. They transform ambiguity into certainty, risk into virtue. They help non-specialists feel informed, insiders feel righteous, and sceptics feel vindicated. But simplification has a cost. It replaces critical thinking with loyalty. It discourages questioning. And it locks users into positions they may not fully understand.

This is particularly dangerous in a domain as fast-moving and unregulated as crypto. Projects launch and fail with extraordinary speed. Incentive structures mutate. Regulatory regimes shift. What made sense last year may be obsolete today. In such an environment, clinging to static narratives is risky. The only sustainable advantage is clarity—understanding the mechanics, evaluating the incentives, and asking: *What problem does this actually solve?*

To see crypto clearly requires stripping away the stories. Not discarding them entirely—narratives can still inspire exploration—but holding them lightly, interrogating their premises, and recognising their limitations. "Digital gold" may be a useful metaphor, but it is not an investment thesis. "Fiat collapse" may sell newsletters, but it is not a sound macro strategy. "Freedom tech" may guide design, but it is not a substitute for operational robustness.

Ultimately, the challenge is not just to see through the myths, but to understand why they persist. Money has always been more than medium—it is mirror. It reflects our values, our fears, our aspirations. Crypto, in inheriting this role, becomes a projection surface for all the unresolved tensions of the modern financial psyche. Its myths are not accidents. They are artefacts of meaning in a system that feels increasingly out of our control.

To engage with crypto effectively is not to reject its stories, but to recognise them as stories—and then to do the harder work of analysis. That is where sound investment begins: not with faith, but with frameworks. Not with metaphors, but with models. Not with certainty, but with structured doubt.

When we understand the mythologies of money, we begin to see crypto not as salvation or scam, but as a domain in which clarity is rare and judgment is everything. And that, perhaps, is its most enduring lesson.

Who Actually Uses Crypto—and Why

The public perception of crypto tends to gravitate towards extremes: evangelists preaching revolution on one side, and sceptics warning of scams on the other. Lost between these poles is a quieter, more pragmatic group of users—those who neither revere crypto nor reject it outright, but engage with it instrumentally. Their motives are practical, their actions grounded, their aspirations modest. These are not the loudest voices in the room, but they may be the most telling. Because while crypto's image is shaped by hype cycles and ideological spats, its substance—its actual utility—rests largely in how it is used by people who are not trying to change the world, but to navigate it.

The clearest window into this pragmatic usage appears in remittances. In much of the global South, traditional remittance systems are slow, expensive, and restrictive. Western Union, MoneyGram, and other money transfer operators charge fees that can consume up to 10–15% of the amount sent, particularly on low-volume corridors. Transactions can take days to settle, and both sender and recipient must often travel to physical kiosks, queue, and present identification. In contexts where documentation is scarce or infrastructure is weak, this becomes a serious obstacle.

By contrast, a stablecoin sent over a public blockchain can arrive within minutes, settle in real-time, and cost a fraction of a penny in network fees. It requires only a smartphone and internet access—both increasingly widespread, even in low-income regions. In Nigeria, for example, where the naira's value has sharply depreciated and capital controls make currency conversion difficult, young professionals routinely receive payments in USDT or USDC. They don't speculate; they spend or save. Their concern isn't decentralisation—it's dependability. For them, crypto is not a cause. It's a workaround.

This pattern repeats across geographies. In Argentina, where inflation has long eroded trust in the peso, stablecoins are used as synthetic dollars. On peer-to-peer platforms like Binance P2P or LocalBitcoins, buyers and sellers exchange digital dollars directly, often bypassing the formal banking system. In Ukraine during the early days of the Russian invasion, crypto was used to receive cross-border donations and pay for services when local systems faltered. In Afghanistan, a women's NGO reportedly turned to USDC to continue paying workers after the Taliban's restrictions crippled banking access. These are not theoretical use cases. They are examples of crypto functioning as financial infrastructure when traditional rails become unreliable, predatory, or politicised.

Yet most media narratives—especially in developed markets—pay scant attention to this middle layer. The noise centres on price action, regulatory battles, or startup funding rounds. But beneath the surface, a growing number of people are engaging with crypto not as believers, but as users. They do not need the asset to 10x. They need it to work. And for specific use cases—borderless payments, censorship resistance, basic dollar access—it often does.

A second cohort of quiet users comprises those seeking yield. This is more nuanced, because yield in crypto is a broad and frequently misunderstood concept. At one end is staking: the process of locking up assets in a proof-of-stake blockchain to help secure the network, in exchange for a reward. Ethereum, Solana, and many other chains offer this. For technically proficient investors, staking provides a modest return on otherwise idle assets, akin to earning interest on a savings account—except that the risks, particularly around slashing penalties or validator downtime, are non-trivial.

More controversially, there is decentralised finance (DeFi) lending and yield farming. Here, users deposit tokens into lending protocols or liquidity pools and earn returns from borrowers or trading fees. These systems can be powerful—but also opaque. Risks include smart contract bugs, market volatility, and systemic contagion. The yield can look attractive—sometimes double digits—but it is often subsidised by token emissions or unsustainable incentives. In 2021, for instance, users flocked to protocols offering high annual percentage yields (APYs), only to find their capital trapped when platforms collapsed or their tokens devalued.

Yet within this landscape, some rational users persist. They are not chasing triple-digit returns. They are allocating small portions of their portfolio to earn a diversified stream of income, while fully recognising the risks. They compare DeFi yields not to traditional savings accounts, but to frontier asset classes—venture capital, emerging market debt, commodities—with similar risk-adjusted expectations. They read audits, split exposure, and build contingency into their plans. For them, yield is not fantasy. It is experimental cashflow, approached with the caution it deserves.

Portfolio diversification represents a third key use case—and perhaps the most institutionally palatable. Bitcoin, in particular, is increasingly framed as a non-correlated asset: something that behaves differently from equities, bonds, or real estate. The empirical case for this remains mixed. Correlations between Bitcoin and tech stocks have spiked during market panics and receded during bull runs. But for long-term allocators, crypto offers what few other assets can: asymmetric upside with programmable constraints. It is volatile, yes, but also globally liquid, accessible 24/7, and relatively unconstrained by central authority. That makes it attractive as a high-risk, high-conviction satellite in a diversified portfolio—especially in an environment of financial repression, where real yields are thin and traditional hedges underperform.

Institutional players are beginning to reflect this view. Pension funds in Canada, hedge funds in the US, and sovereign wealth funds in Asia have begun allocating token exposure—often modestly, often through structured vehicles, but nonetheless seriously. These are not crypto evangelists. They are fiduciaries. And while many of their initial investments have suffered drawdowns, the rationale behind allocation remains: to gain early exposure to a potentially transformative financial infrastructure, while limiting downside through careful sizing.

Importantly, these users are not here for the memes or the maximalism. They are not declaring the death of fiat or the end of central banking. They are making a pragmatic bet: that crypto assets, as a category, may offer differentiated return streams worth monitoring—if not for conviction, then for optionality. This is the "buy-and-ignore" crowd. They don't stake. They don't farm. They hold small positions passively, check quarterly, and rebalance as needed. Their presence adds stability to the ecosystem, even if it rarely garners attention.

These use cases—remittances, yield, diversification—share one trait: they are unglamorous. They do not fit neatly into crypto's grand narrative of disruption and redesign. They are small, practical, and frequently invisible. Yet they represent the foundation of crypto's actual utility—the places where code meets constraint, where promises are tested against real-world friction. And they remind us of an essential truth: *technology is only as transformative as the problems it quietly solves.*

To centre the conversation on these users is not to abandon ambition. It is to ground it. Crypto's potential to reshape finance may still unfold—but it will not come from utopian dreams or speculative fervour alone. It will come from iterative improvement, regulatory clarity, and real people choosing crypto not because they believe, but because it works. That may not make for viral headlines. But it makes for lasting impact.

Understanding this quiet middle also shifts the question from "Is crypto good or bad?" to "Who is it good for, under what conditions, and at what cost?" That question demands more nuance, but yields better answers. Because crypto is not a monolith—it is a set of tools. And tools, when used with care, do not require belief to be useful. They require function. They require judgment.

And most of all, they require attention—not to the loudest voices, but to the most consistent use.

This Is Not the Stock Market

The biggest mistake traditional investors make when entering crypto is assuming they're still in familiar territory. Superficially, crypto markets resemble equity markets: there are tickers, exchanges, charts, order books, and volatility metrics. But beneath this visual symmetry lies a set of structural, behavioural, and psychological dynamics so distinct that applying equity-style thinking to crypto often leads to consistently poor decisions. This is not an evolution of the stock market—it is a fundamentally different environment governed by different rules, incentives, and rhythms.

The first and most obvious difference is volatility. Equity markets move in basis points; crypto markets move in percentage points. A 3% daily swing in the S&P 500 is front-page news. In crypto, it's a quiet Tuesday. Bitcoin has, at various points, gained or lost over 10% in a single day. Smaller-cap tokens can rise 400% in a week and fall 90% within a month. This volatility is not an aberration—it's structural. It reflects the underlying immaturity of the asset class: shallow liquidity, fragmented order books, limited institutional anchoring, and extreme reflexivity. In equities, price is loosely tethered to fundamentals—earnings, margins, macro trends. In crypto, price is often driven by belief, momentum, and social contagion.

This isn't to say that fundamentals don't exist in crypto—they do, but they are harder to quantify and often lag perception. What matters in the short term is not what a protocol *is*, but what the market *thinks it might become*. That distinction is critical. Many investors apply discounted cash flow models or value metrics borrowed from equities, only to find themselves lost in a landscape where narratives move faster than metrics, and product-market fit may not even exist yet. It's like using a stethoscope to predict a thunderstorm—misapplied tools in the wrong environment.

Liquidity in crypto is another key departure. In traditional finance, large-cap equities trade on highly regulated venues with deep liquidity pools, market-makers, and central clearinghouses. Order execution is predictable, slippage is minimal, and price discovery benefits from a wealth of publicly disclosed information. Crypto operates differently. Liquidity is fragmented across dozens of exchanges—some centralised (e.g. Binance, Coinbase), others decentralised (e.g. Uniswap, Curve). Spreads can widen dramatically during periods of stress. "Flash crashes" are common, especially in altcoins with thin order books. Liquidity can disappear at the exact moment investors need it most.

This asymmetry creates an environment where investors often overestimate their ability to enter or exit positions cleanly. A token that looks attractive on a price chart may be practically untradeable at size. Even large-cap assets like Ethereum have demonstrated how liquidity can vanish under duress—during the 2020 "Black Thursday" crash, cascading liquidations on DeFi platforms caused prices to nosedive as automated collateral auctions overwhelmed available bids. In such moments, what matters is not just what an asset is worth, but whether anyone is willing to stand on the other side of the trade.

The behavioural layer compounds this fragility. Traditional equity markets, for all their flaws, benefit from institutional participation, long-standing norms, and a rhythm of quarterly reporting. Crypto markets, by contrast, are largely driven by retail participants operating without institutional guardrails. They trade 24/7, without opening bells, earnings calls, or analyst downgrades. Price is continuously negotiated by a global, heterogeneous set of actors: developers, traders, influencers, bots, whales, and tourists.

This creates a uniquely combustible psychological environment. Investors are subject to constant noise: real-time price alerts, social media hype, Telegram pump groups, and algorithmically curated headlines. FOMO (fear of missing out) is persistent, magnified by the visibility of wealth creation that often appears overnight. When a token gains 300% in a weekend, restraint feels foolish. When it crashes the next week, panic sets in. This pattern fuels a vicious feedback loop: euphoric buying begets more buying, until it collapses under its own weight.

Traditional equity markets are built to dampen these cycles. Trading halts, analyst coverage, disclosure requirements, and regulatory oversight serve as circuit-breakers—mechanisms that inject friction and promote deliberation. Crypto has none of these. There are no quiet periods, no regulators moderating earnings guidance, no penalties for rumour-mongering. Information asymmetry is not just tolerated—it's integral to how the market functions. Token insiders, often anonymous or pseudonymous, hold vast sway over price direction. Retail investors are routinely front-run by better-informed actors, including miners, validators, or automated bots exploiting mempool data.

The result is a market more akin to a high-frequency game of narrative arbitrage than a sober exchange of future cashflows. Success in this environment requires not just financial analysis, but media literacy, technical fluency, and psychological fortitude. It demands that investors develop a tolerance for chaos and an ability to discern signal in a landscape dominated by noise.

Compounding this complexity is the fact that most crypto assets are not shares of companies. They don't represent equity, voting rights, or claims on cash flow in the way stocks do. Some are governance tokens, some are utility tokens, some are outright speculative shells. Legal frameworks are evolving, but murky. Is a token a security, a commodity, or a voucher? Often, no one—including regulators—can say definitively. This ambiguity makes it difficult to assess value or risk using traditional models. There is no P/E ratio for a governance token. There is no dividend yield on a stablecoin.

And yet, many investors persist in mapping equity paradigms onto this new terrain. They ask which token is the "Apple of crypto," or which chain will be the "Amazon of Web3." These analogies, while appealing, are often misleading. Apple operates in a mature ecosystem with defensible moats, regulatory clarity, and established distribution. A layer-one blockchain operates in a permissionless ecosystem where competitors can fork its code, users can migrate overnight, and protocol revenues are subject to governance votes or code changes.

This structural instability is part of what makes crypto innovative—but also treacherous. In equities, moat-building takes decades. In crypto, entire ecosystems can be replicated and redeployed in days. This fluidity rewards agility, not incumbency. It also punishes complacency. What worked last cycle may be irrelevant this cycle—not because the product failed, but because the narrative moved on.

That said, the volatility and unpredictability of crypto are not purely weaknesses. They are also the conditions that make experimentation possible. Crypto markets, unlike public equities, enable anyone to launch a project, list a token, and attract capital. This openness has led to profound innovations—automated market makers, flash loans, zero-knowledge proofs—all of which emerged not from institutions, but from permissionless experimentation. The same environment that spawns scams and speculative manias also enables breakthroughs at unprecedented speed.

The challenge for investors is to navigate this landscape without delusion. Treating crypto like equities doesn't just misjudge its risk—it misses its potential. Equities are about ownership in proven models. Crypto is about participation in emergent systems. That distinction has investment consequences. Equity frameworks reward patience, mean reversion, and fundamentals. Crypto rewards speed, timing, and adaptability. Misunderstanding that leads to category errors: overexposure to volatility, mispriced risk, and misplaced conviction.

Ultimately, success in crypto requires a new mental model. One that accepts that markets can be irrational longer than you can remain solvent. One that recognises that liquidity is a privilege, not a constant. One that respects the difference between speculation and investment—not as moral distinctions, but as strategic ones. And above all, one that sees crypto not as an extension of equities, but as an alternate system—faster, riskier, less mature, but potentially more generative.

To invest here is to enter a different game. Not necessarily better or worse, but undeniably different. And as with any game, the first rule is simple: *know what field you're playing on before you step in.*

Chapter 2
A History of Value: Why Money Keeps Changing

Most people give little thought to money—until it falters. We earn it, spend it, store it, worry over it, yet rarely pause to question what it truly is or why it takes the forms it does. Often, we mistake it for a static institution: the banknote, the coin, the digital ledger entry. But money is not fixed. It is a social construct, mutable across time, shifting as trust, power, and technology evolve. To grasp where crypto might—or might not—fit into the financial landscape, we must first trace money's long arc. Crypto is not an anomaly; it is a new manifestation of a pattern that stretches back millennia.

Money has never been merely metal, paper, or digits. It has always been an agreement—a collective fiction whose value exists because enough people believe in it. Whether cowrie shells, silver coins, or government-issued notes, acceptance has hinged less on intrinsic worth than on social consensus. Societies confer trust, and thus money functions; withdraw that trust, and the medium collapses. This principle has held true across civilizations and epochs, through every monetary collapse and reinvention.

Historically, money often began as objects that were scarce, recognisable, and hard to counterfeit. Cowries in East Africa, salt bars in Ethiopia, feathers in the Americas, beads in China—all circulated because they were practical, portable, and widely desired, not because rulers decreed them so. Trade systems emerged organically around these objects long before any central authority imposed standardisation. Eventually, states co-opted these practices, issuing coins stamped with royal insignia and centralising fiscal power. This shift—from object to instrument of governance—marked a pivotal transformation: money became political.

Once sovereigns controlled coinage, trust moved from peer consensus to institutional legitimacy. Roman emperors clipped coins to fund wars; medieval kings debased currency in times of fiscal strain; centuries later, central banks issued notes backed not by metal but by promises. These changes were messy, uneven, and often precipitated collapse—but they followed a pattern: as trust migrated—from community to empire, metal to paper, physical to digital—money evolved. Today's architecture is merely the latest iteration of that journey.

Viewed through this lens, crypto is not aberrant. It is the next candidate in a centuries-long experiment. Advocates argue it returns to monetary neutrality—a digital commodity money, constrained by code rather than decree. Critics call it speculative, untethered from fundamentals, and prone to manipulation. Both miss the deeper question: under what conditions do societies adopt new forms of money, and how does crypto align—or clash—with those conditions?

Historically, new monetary systems emerge when old ones fail. Hyperinflation in Weimar Germany drove citizens to barter or use foreign currencies. In late-2000s Zimbabwe, denominations reached 100 trillion, savings evaporated, and transactional life shrank to improvisation. India's 2016 demonetisation invalidated 86 per cent of cash overnight, exposing systemic fragility and disrupting livelihoods. Such crises reveal a consistent insight: when institutional trust erodes, people seek alternatives that function—any that function.

It is precisely in these moments of instability that crypto gains traction. Adoption is rarely ideological at first; it is pragmatic. In Venezuela, surging inflation rendered the bolívar unusable, and Bitcoin and stablecoins became lifelines—not for speculation, but for survival. Similar dynamics appear in Argentina, Nigeria, Lebanon, and parts of Ukraine. Here, crypto is not a luxury, but a tool of last resort.

Necessity alone does not guarantee adoption. Trust infrastructure is equally crucial. For money to scale, it must not merely work; it must be believed. Belief is constructed through legal frameworks, enforcement mechanisms, cultural norms, and institutional backing. Fiat currencies function because they are embedded in governance, taxation, and recourse systems. Crypto, by contrast, asks trust in code, cryptography, and decentralised consensus. For some, that is an upgrade; for others, alien. The challenge is as cognitive as it is technical.

The leap from central-bank-backed currency to blockchain-based assets is non-trivial. Generations accustomed to sovereign guarantees may find it foreign; younger digital natives, sceptical of institutions and accustomed to decentralised services, may find it intuitive. Adoption, in this sense, is as much cultural and generational as it is financial.

Even cultural readiness is insufficient without usability. Blockchain wallets, gas fees, seed phrases, and protocol risks present barriers. Compare this with the ease of tapping a card or sending a bank transfer. Until crypto achieves similar convenience and reliability, its role as everyday money will remain marginal. Yet as wallets become user-friendly, layer-two solutions expand, and institutional custody grows, barriers gradually fall. The question is not whether crypto can function as money, but when, and for whom.

An evolutionary perspective is instructive. Rather than asking if crypto will replace existing currencies, it is more useful to see it as part of a continuum. Money has evolved—from shells to coins, paper to digital balances. Crypto may represent the next iteration: programmable, global, permissionless. Not a replacement, but an augmentation. Not the demise of central banks, but a move toward monetary plurality.

Monetary history demonstrates that multiple forms of value can coexist. Gold persisted alongside banknotes; mobile money in Kenya did not erase the shilling. Hybrid systems, blending legacy structures with emergent forms, often prove most resilient. Crypto's future may lie in interoperability—serving specific functions in specific contexts, coexisting with sovereign money, commercial bank deposits, and other digital assets.

This historical perspective equips the thoughtful investor. It provides clarity amid volatility and situates crypto within the ongoing negotiation between trust, technology, and authority. Money is not merely a medium of exchange; it is a system of belief, a record of obligation, and a map of political power. Engaging seriously with crypto demands asking not only what it is, but what it challenges—and what it could become if those challenges endure.

This chapter traces money's evolution, explaining why it changes, how trust underpins its function, and where crypto may fit. It differentiates transient fads from structural shifts, reminding us that while forms fluctuate, core functions endure: store of value, medium of exchange, and unit of account. Innovation arises in the tension between form and function.

Crypto is neither the first nor the last attempt to reinvent money. But it is the first to do so on a global, real-time scale, with open infrastructure. Whether it becomes systemic or marginal will hinge on technology, trust, context, and utility—and understanding those forces begins not with speculation, but with history.

From Shells to Sovereigns

Money did not begin with states, banks, or financial systems. It began with trust—small, personal, and improvised. Long before coins or paper notes, human communities exchanged objects not for their intrinsic worth, but for their perceived acceptability. Cowrie shells in the Indian Ocean, obsidian blades in Mesoamerica, salt bars in the Sahel, and whale teeth in Fiji were all used as money. These objects functioned not because they had legal tender status, but because they were *recognisable, scarce, and agreed upon*. The first monetary systems were not imposed—they emerged.

This decentralised, organic form of money had two critical properties: *social validation* and *practical constraints*. The objects were valued not because they could be consumed, but because they could be exchanged reliably within a defined community. Their scarcity was naturally enforced—cowries were difficult to forge; salt was hard to transport; feathers had ceremonial meaning. This created a form of distributed trust that required no central authority, but rather a repeated consensus among peers. In that sense, early money bore a striking philosophical resemblance to decentralised systems like Bitcoin: sustained by belief, not by decree.

The transition from these informal objects of exchange to state-issued currency marked a profound reconfiguration—not just in form, but in purpose. The earliest coins, minted in Lydia around the 7th century BCE, were not simply tools for trade. They were *assertions of sovereignty*. Each coin bore a symbol—typically of a ruler, deity, or city-state—not merely to certify its metal content, but to communicate authority. The coin became a political instrument as much as a medium of exchange. It standardised units of value, enabled taxation, and embedded money within the logic of state control.

The evolution of coinage introduced two critical innovations: *standardisation* and *scalability*. With consistent weights and state-backed legitimacy, coins could circulate beyond local trust networks. They allowed empires to govern at distance, collect taxes, pay armies, and lubricate commerce across geographies. The Roman denarius, Chinese spade money, and Islamic dinar all functioned as both economic tools and cultural exports. To use the coin was to participate in the empire's order. But with these advantages came a new vulnerability: *monetary control now lay in the hands of rulers.*

Control, of course, invites manipulation. Debasement—reducing the precious metal content of coins while maintaining their face value—became a common fiscal strategy. It allowed emperors and kings to finance wars, public works, or personal excess without raising taxes. But it also eroded trust. As silver was cut with copper and gold stretched thinner, inflation followed. Trust in the currency declined, and people reverted to barter, hoarded foreign coins, or demanded payment in kind. The lesson was clear: *money's value depends not just on what it is, but on who guarantees it—and how credibly they do so.*

Paper money amplified this dynamic. Originating in Tang and Song dynasty China as promissory notes, paper currency became widespread when states promised that it could be redeemed for metal. This promise enabled convenience—carrying notes was easier than hauling gold—but it introduced a new layer of abstraction. Now, money was not a thing of value, but a *claim* on value. As long as redemption was honoured, the system worked. When confidence faltered, it broke.

The European experience followed a similar arc. In the 17th century, Sweden and the Netherlands experimented with bank-issued notes. In England, the Bank of England was granted the exclusive right to issue notes in 1694, backed by government bonds and reserves. Over the next two centuries, central banks emerged as the architects of monetary policy—controlling issuance, managing inflation, and maintaining the value of national currencies. Trust shifted again: no longer in metal, but in institutions.

The final rupture came with the decoupling of money from gold. In 1971, the United States suspended the dollar's convertibility to gold, effectively ending the Bretton Woods system and ushering in the modern fiat era. Today, nearly all national currencies are fiat: they have no intrinsic value, are not backed by commodities, and rely entirely on the credibility of the issuing government. This shift made money more flexible—central banks could respond to crises with monetary tools—but also more fragile. With no anchor, trust became the only foundation. When trust cracks, currency crises follow.

The 20th and 21st centuries have witnessed repeated examples of this fragility. From Argentina to Zimbabwe, Turkey to Venezuela, governments have printed money in excess, inflated away savings, and broken public confidence. In such cases, people revert—once again—to alternative stores of value: foreign currencies, commodities, barter, and now, increasingly, *crypto*. What was once local improvisation is now global experimentation.

This brings us to a crucial insight: *money is not a linear story of progress—it is a pendulum between centralisation and decentralisation, between institutional trust and distributed consensus*. The modern state monopolised money not because it was inevitable, but because it solved key problems: standardisation, taxation, scale, and governance. But its monopoly was not always earned. It was enforced through law, infrastructure, and, often, violence.

Crypto presents a reversal—not a full rejection of state money, but a decentralised alternative that draws from the logic of early money. Bitcoin, for instance, mimics commodity scarcity through code. It cannot be debased, inflated, or unilaterally altered. It offers finality of settlement, global accessibility, and a transparent issuance schedule. But it lacks the embedded legitimacy, tax authority, and legal finality that sovereign currencies wield. In other words, it is not *yet* a replacement—but it *is* a return to a pre-sovereign logic: *money as mutual agreement, not sovereign fiat*.

To evaluate crypto's legitimacy, then, we must ask: what makes money work? History suggests three enduring criteria—*scarcity, recognisability, and institutional or social trust*. Shells had scarcity and recognisability. Coins added state legitimacy. Banknotes introduced abstraction and convenience. Fiat currencies centralised control. Crypto offers scarcity and transparency, but is still building recognisability and trust at scale. Whether it succeeds will depend not just on code, but on its ability to earn consensus in the same way money always has—through use, stability, and confidence.

The debate over crypto often misses this context. It is not just about technology, or volatility, or environmental impact. It is about *the story of money itself*—a system that has changed shape many times, each change born of friction in the previous one. Crypto is not the first challenger to the monetary status quo. But it is the first to do so with code, at global scale, in an age of declining institutional confidence.

From cowries to coins to central banks, the history of money is the history of shifting trust. Crypto does not rewrite that history. It continues it—raising new questions about what trust looks like in a world where it can be programmed, verified, and distributed without permission. Whether crypto becomes part of the monetary mainstream or remains a parallel system will depend on how convincingly it answers those questions—not in theory, but in use. That is how money has always proved itself. And crypto, for all its novelty, will be held to the same test.

The Invention of Trust

Money has no inherent value. It is not edible, sheltering, or warm. It does not heal, build, or nourish. Its power lies entirely in belief—the shared, often unspoken agreement that it *can* be used to obtain those things. This makes money one of the most remarkable inventions in human history: a tool that works only if everyone believes it will. And yet, for something so essential and omnipresent, few stop to consider how such belief is formed—or what happens when it breaks. Trust is not a given. It is manufactured, maintained, and sometimes manipulated. Understanding how societies have historically come to accept certain forms of money—and reject others—reveals what crypto is truly up against.

Trust in money is rarely built from scratch. It is typically piggybacked on existing structures: religious symbols, sovereign power, precious materials, or institutional guarantees. Early currencies succeeded not just because they were scarce or shiny, but because they were *familiar*. The cowrie shell, used across vast regions of Africa, Asia, and the Pacific, was already valued in spiritual and decorative contexts before it became currency. When the Lydians first minted coins in the 7th century BCE, they stamped them with images of lions—symbols of royal authority. The coin's acceptance was not purely about the metal; it was about the *issuer*. The object was trusted because the power behind it was.

Later, as currencies abstracted further from commodities, trust had to be constructed through more deliberate means. Paper money required the leap from tangible to representational value. This shift was not instantaneous. In medieval China, when the Song dynasty issued some of the first government-backed banknotes, they did so alongside edicts that mandated their acceptance, imposed penalties for refusal, and promised eventual redemption in coin or goods. These were not mere economic tools; they were instruments of statecraft. Their credibility rested on the state's capacity to enforce the fiction.

In the modern world, fiat money extends this fiction to its logical extreme. Today's currencies are backed not by gold or silver, but by legal systems, tax regimes, and central bank policies. The trust they command is contingent and contextual. A dollar works because it is widely accepted, backed by a functioning legal system, and embedded in global commerce. A Venezuelan bolívar fails, despite being a legal tender, because its institutions no longer command belief. *Utility without trust is powerless. Trust without utility is fragile.*

Consensus emerges when both exist. A useful form of money must not only be accepted in practice; it must be *expected* to be accepted. This expectation is what gives money its velocity—its willingness to circulate. If you believe others will accept a token in the future, you are more willing to accept it today. This circularity is not a flaw. It is the foundation. But it also creates a precarious dependence on collective perception. When consensus frays—due to inflation, political instability, or poor monetary governance—the whole edifice trembles.

This is the dynamic crypto must navigate. Bitcoin does not derive its value from a state. Ethereum is not enforced by law. Stablecoins, while pegged to fiat, are ultimately only as reliable as their collateral mechanisms and issuing institutions. In short, crypto seeks to build trust *without traditional scaffolding*. It proposes a new trust architecture—based not on political authority or historical precedent, but on transparency, code integrity, decentralised governance, and distributed consensus. This is ambitious, and in some cases, profoundly appealing. But it is also vulnerable in new and underappreciated ways.

The crypto ecosystem relies heavily on *procedural trust*. Instead of trusting people or institutions, one is asked to trust processes—open-source code, publicly auditable ledgers, algorithmic issuance schedules. Bitcoin's 21 million coin cap is not a promise; it is a protocol. Ethereum's transactions are not intermediated by banks, but validated by a global network of nodes. This system, when functioning correctly, is radically transparent. You can inspect it, replicate it, or fork it. But transparency alone is not sufficient. Users must also trust that the system will continue to operate as expected—and that bad actors cannot exploit its edges.

This introduces new complexities. Traditional money fails when governments mismanage policy. Crypto can fail when developers push buggy updates, validators collude, smart contracts are exploited, or governance is captured by plutocratic voting structures. These are not abstract risks. The 2016 DAO hack on Ethereum, which led to a controversial chain split, demonstrated how even well-intentioned decentralisation can fracture under stress. More recently, algorithmic stablecoins like Terra/Luna collapsed catastrophically, exposing the dangers of trusting automated financial engineering without sufficient resilience. In both cases, the failure was not in the vision, but in the *execution of trust mechanisms*.

Moreover, crypto's decentralised structure introduces coordination challenges. There is no single issuer to take responsibility when things go wrong. No lender of last resort. No regulator ensuring solvency or investor protection. For some, this is a feature, not a bug. But for the average user—accustomed to reversible payments, fraud protections, and centralised accountability—it is a steep learning curve. The loss of a seed phrase can mean irrevocable loss of assets. A poorly executed smart contract can drain millions. In this environment, trust must be paired with *competence*. And competence, unlike code, is not evenly distributed.

Still, crypto has succeeded—against considerable odds—in building partial trust at global scale. Tens of millions of people now hold crypto assets. Entire ecosystems of applications, lending protocols, payment platforms, and custodians have emerged. Major financial institutions have begun offering crypto exposure. Governments are experimenting with blockchain infrastructure. These developments suggest that *crypto's trust gap is narrowing*—but it is not closed.

Closing it requires more than improved UX or regulatory clarity. It demands a reframing of what trust means in a decentralised world. In traditional systems, trust is top-down: granted to institutions, enforced through law, and stabilised by reputation. In crypto, trust is *bottom-up*: constructed through incentive alignment, code audits, community governance, and economic game theory. Both models have strengths and weaknesses. The future of money may not belong exclusively to either. Instead, we are likely to see *hybrid trust systems*—where decentralised infrastructure interacts with centralised services, and where users choose systems based on context, need, and preference.

This pluralism does not undermine the importance of trust. It reinforces it. If anything, the rise of crypto makes explicit what traditional money has long obscured: that trust is not an abstract value, but a constructed, maintained, and contested reality. It can reside in a government, a brand, an algorithm, or a community—but it must reside *somewhere*. The challenge for crypto is to demonstrate that this "somewhere" can be engineered in open networks, sustained without coercion, and extended to those who have historically been excluded from trustworthy institutions.

Whether crypto can scale trust beyond niches and into mainstream economic life remains uncertain. But the very attempt compels us to think more clearly about what trust entails—and who gets to build it. In doing so, crypto has already contributed something valuable: it has reminded us that money is not neutral, not inevitable, and not above scrutiny. It is a human invention, and like all inventions, its legitimacy depends on the systems that sustain it—and the people who believe in it.

When Money Breaks Down

Money is assumed to be stable. That assumption underpins everything from wages and contracts to the price of bread and the value of pensions. But when money fails—when it ceases to hold value, command trust, or function predictably—society does not simply pause; it fractures. The breakdown of a currency is not an abstract macroeconomic event. It is a rupture in the daily rhythms of life. Savings become worthless, transactions stall, barter returns, and faith in institutions disintegrates. And in that vacuum of reliability, people search for substitutes—anything that offers even a semblance of consistency. This is where crypto begins to find a foothold: not as a utopian ideal, but as an alternative during collapse.

The history of money is not a history of continuous trust. It is punctuated by episodes of failure, often driven by a toxic mix of political instability, poor governance, and unaccountable monetary expansion. One of the most well-documented examples is the Weimar Republic in the early 1920s. Germany, burdened by reparations and fiscal deficits, began printing money at scale. The result was one of the most extreme cases of hyperinflation in modern history. In 1923, prices doubled every few days. A loaf of bread that cost 250 marks in January was priced at 200 billion by November. People were paid twice daily and spent their wages immediately. Currency was used as wallpaper or kindling. But what's often overlooked is that, even amid this chaos, *money did not vanish—it changed form.*

Foreign currencies, gold, barter items, and informal IOUs replaced the mark in everyday life. The monetary function persisted. The medium had failed.

A more recent—and ongoing—example is Venezuela. From 2014 onwards, the country's currency, the bolívar, entered a death spiral. Mismanagement of oil revenues, widespread corruption, and the central bank's unchecked money printing eroded its value to the point of absurdity. At its peak, inflation was measured in millions of percent annually. Basic goods were priced in foreign currency, and shopkeepers carried calculators to adjust prices by the hour. In this context, citizens turned not to banks or state reforms, but to parallel monetary systems. The US dollar became the de facto medium of exchange. But so too did crypto—particularly Bitcoin and later stablecoins like USDT and USDC. The appeal wasn't ideological. It was functional. With access to an internet connection and a phone, users could receive remittances from abroad, preserve value, and—crucially—escape the state-controlled monetary framework that had betrayed them.

India offers a different kind of crisis: not inflationary collapse, but sudden demonetisation. In 2016, the Indian government announced—without prior warning—that all ₹500 and ₹1,000 notes (comprising nearly 86% of the cash in circulation) would no longer be legal tender. The stated goals were to combat corruption and counterfeit money. The immediate impact was confusion, panic, and logistical paralysis. Millions of people who relied on cash—especially in rural areas—were suddenly cut off from economic participation. Queues formed at banks. Small businesses shuttered. Daily labourers were left unpaid. While the economy eventually stabilised, the episode highlighted a core vulnerability: *money is not just value—it is access*. When that access is revoked, even temporarily, the economic effects ripple far beyond balance sheets.

In such moments, the fragility of fiat systems is laid bare. State-issued money functions because people believe it will continue to function. But that belief is contingent. When institutions lose credibility, the currency they issue becomes suspect. And because fiat money has no intrinsic value—its worth lies solely in trust—the collapse of confidence is often more damaging than any underlying economic condition. This is why monetary crises are rarely contained to markets. They become social crises, political crises, and ultimately legitimacy crises. People stop asking how much a currency is worth. They start asking whether it is worth *anything* at all.

Against this backdrop, the rise of crypto as a monetary alternative becomes more intelligible. It is not that Bitcoin or stablecoins are better in every respect. In fact, they are often less convenient, more volatile, and harder to understand. But they offer something failing fiat cannot: *an exit*. Crypto is not necessarily trusted more, but it is *distrusted differently*. That difference matters. When your national currency is devaluing by the hour and your bank imposes withdrawal limits, even an imperfect alternative gains appeal. The threshold for adoption lowers. Functionality, not ideology, becomes the driver.

Lebanon illustrates this pattern vividly. In the aftermath of a prolonged financial crisis, Lebanese banks imposed strict capital controls. Depositors could not withdraw their savings. The lira collapsed against the dollar, and official exchange rates diverged wildly from black market prices. As a result, some Lebanese citizens began using crypto to store savings, receive foreign payments, and escape capital restrictions. It was not widespread. It was not frictionless. But it was *possible*. And in times of breakdown, possibility is currency.

This trend is not confined to authoritarian or failed states. In 2013, Cyprus experienced a banking crisis that led to the unprecedented decision to impose a levy on bank deposits. Overnight, depositors with more than €100,000 lost a significant portion of their savings. The policy—effectively a state-sanctioned seizure—shattered the assumption that banked money was inherently safe. In response, interest in Bitcoin surged. It wasn't yet mature, but it was *sovereign-resistant*. It offered custody without counterparty risk, and settlement without permission. The lesson stuck: when traditional financial systems become unreliable, decentralised alternatives gain attention, not just from the margins, but from the centre.

It is important to stress that crypto does not always function well under stress. Its volatility, regulatory uncertainty, and technical complexity can limit adoption when users are most vulnerable. The infrastructure may not be sufficiently resilient, especially in regions with weak internet connectivity or low digital literacy. But these are constraints of maturity, not of principle. The deeper point is that crypto *invites a different form of monetary imagination.* It allows individuals to participate in systems that are not governed by central banks, dependent on local institutions, or tied to the political fate of a single nation.

This raises a broader question: if fiat currency is a political artefact, and crypto is a technological one, what happens when the two intersect during crisis? The answer is still unfolding. In El Salvador, Bitcoin has been declared legal tender. In Ukraine, the government has accepted crypto donations for defence funding. In Argentina, dollar stablecoins are increasingly used as de facto savings accounts. These developments suggest not a wholesale replacement of fiat, but a diversification of monetary instruments. In times of peace and stability, crypto may remain speculative. In moments of breakdown, it becomes *adaptive.*

What's emerging is a world in which monetary sovereignty is no longer absolute. Governments still control currency issuance, taxation, and legal frameworks. But individuals, increasingly, can choose alternatives—outside borders, beyond institutions, and beneath the radar. This choice is most visible in crisis, but its implications reach further. It changes the calculus of trust, reshapes the boundaries of capital mobility, and challenges the monopoly of money as a state function. For crypto to matter, it doesn't need to replace the dollar. It needs only to remain a credible *plan B*.

Monetary crises will continue. History guarantees it. Whether triggered by war, mismanagement, corruption, or sheer misfortune, there will always be moments when official money stops working. What changes now is that people have options. And options, when trust erodes, are everything. Crypto's future will not be decided by bull runs or institutional adoption alone. It will be shaped by how effectively it functions when fiat falters—when people are not looking to get rich, but simply to *survive*. That is the true test of monetary utility. And that is where crypto may prove itself most relevant.

The Evolutionary Lens

If money is a technology—something humans have invented, iterated upon, and adapted over millennia—then it must evolve. It cannot remain static, because the environments in which it operates do not remain static. Trade routes shift, institutions rise and fall, and technological paradigms reshape how trust, value, and exchange are conceived. To understand crypto not as an anomaly but as a logical extension of this arc, one must approach it not through the lens of disruption, but through the lens of evolution. The question is not whether crypto will replace traditional money, but whether it represents the next stage in its functional development: decentralised, programmable, and globally portable.

Every form of money in history has emerged in response to specific contextual pressures. Cowrie shells became popular in parts of Africa and Asia because they were scarce, portable, and difficult to counterfeit. Roman coinage allowed a sprawling empire to standardise taxes, payments, and military wages across vast distances. Paper money in medieval China reflected a need to simplify commerce in a society increasingly dependent on complex trade routes. Central banking arose in the context of industrialisation, war finance, and economic nationalism. None of these innovations was inevitable. Each was contingent. But they all reflect a core pattern: money adapts to the constraints and affordances of its time.

In the twenty-first century, the dominant pressures are increasingly digital. Value moves at the speed of light. Financial infrastructure is deeply intermediated, and yet shockingly fragile in crisis. Institutional trust is strained. And data—arguably the most valuable economic resource today—flows globally with almost no friction. Against this backdrop, it is no surprise that the old architecture of money feels outdated. Bank hours, jurisdictional borders, correspondent networks, and even central clearing mechanisms increasingly resemble artefacts of an analogue age. Crypto, then, enters not as a revolution to be celebrated or feared, but as an adaptation to these pressures—a new species in the monetary ecosystem.

Consider programmability. Traditional currencies are inert. A pound or dollar does not contain rules about when or how it can be spent. Those rules must be enforced by external legal and institutional systems—contracts, courts, regulators, compliance departments. Programmable money, by contrast, embeds logic directly into the asset. With smart contracts, one can encode conditionality into transactions: only execute if both parties sign, if a delivery is confirmed, or if certain market conditions are met. This shifts trust away from intermediaries and towards code. The implications are vast—not because human institutions will disappear, but because they may no longer be the exclusive guardians of economic coordination.

Next is portability. Traditional financial assets are portable within narrow frameworks—banking networks, payment rails, card schemes. Moving funds across borders involves friction: currency conversion, settlement delays, compliance checks, and fee layers. Crypto, by contrast, is inherently borderless. It exists on distributed networks that are accessible from any internet-connected device. This changes the cost structure of international remittances, the mechanics of global fundraising, and the feasibility of cross-border entrepreneurship. When a small business in Kenya can raise capital from a buyer in Brazil without routing through five intermediaries, the monetary playing field shifts subtly, but decisively.

Decentralisation, perhaps the most contested dimension, is often misunderstood. It does not mean the absence of governance. Rather, it means governance by network consensus rather than institutional decree. In traditional systems, monetary policy is enacted by central banks. In crypto, monetary rules are hard-coded or community-governed. Bitcoin's supply schedule, for instance, is fixed and transparent. Ethereum's transition to proof-of-stake emerged through a distributed upgrade process. These systems are not apolitical or immune to capture. But their legitimacy is earned differently. It is less about hierarchical control, and more about credible neutrality—a notion increasingly salient in an era where economic policy is polarised and institutional trust is uneven.

Importantly, crypto's evolutionary logic does not negate the utility of fiat currencies. Nor does it imply that decentralised assets are superior in all contexts. Central bank money remains indispensable for taxation, public spending, monetary stability, and national sovereignty. What crypto offers is not a substitute, but a supplement: an additional layer in the architecture of money. Much like email did not replace face-to-face conversation but transformed how and when we communicate, crypto reshapes the margins of financial interaction—use cases that are underserved, overregulated, or simply incompatible with existing systems.

Take stablecoins as a case study. These are digital tokens pegged to fiat currencies, but issued on decentralised networks. Their growth reflects a clear market signal: users want the familiarity of dollars with the flexibility of crypto. In 2022, daily stablecoin volumes exceeded that of Visa's network. While much of this activity is driven by trading and speculation, a growing portion involves real economic use: payroll for remote workers, collateral in decentralised finance, cross-border commerce, and even treasury management for start-ups in volatile economies. Here, evolution is not theoretical—it is operational.

What distinguishes this evolutionary moment is not just the technology, but the meta-institutional shift it represents. Historically, monetary innovation was state-led or at least state-sanctioned. Today, it is emerging from open-source communities, start-ups, and decentralised networks. This challenges our categories. Who decides what money is? What legitimacy does non-state money possess? Can trust be manufactured outside of institutional hierarchies? These are not merely technical questions. They are philosophical, political, and strategic. And they cannot be answered by analogy alone. Crypto is not the internet of money, nor the digital version of gold. It is a new category, demanding new frameworks.

To navigate this shift, evolutionary thinking is critical. It allows us to move beyond binary debates—crypto good or bad, disruptive or irrelevant—and instead ask how, where, and why new monetary forms are gaining traction. Evolution does not reward perfection. It rewards adaptability. And crypto's strength lies not in its ideological purity, but in its capacity to adapt to different needs: censorship resistance in authoritarian regimes, financial inclusion in underbanked regions, capital efficiency in high-frequency markets, and asset diversification for institutions hedging systemic risk.

This adaptability is mirrored in the diversity of crypto itself. Bitcoin and Ethereum differ not just in code, but in philosophy. Bitcoin is conservative, focused on monetary immutability and decentralised security. Ethereum is experimental, prioritising expressiveness and decentralised applications. Other networks, from Solana to Avalanche to Cosmos, explore trade-offs around speed, interoperability, and governance. This pluralism reflects a core evolutionary principle: variation precedes selection. Not every protocol will survive. Many will fail. But the ecosystem, as a whole, learns.

What's emerging is not a singular new form of money, but a layered, modular monetary landscape. At the base are state currencies and central bank infrastructure. Above that, fiat-backed stablecoins and digital banking rails. Further out are crypto-native assets—some serving as stores of value, others as mediums of exchange or units of account within specific networks. Layered atop all this are protocols, smart contracts, and decentralised applications that create new forms of coordination, credit, and capital formation. Each layer speaks to different needs. Each evolves on its own trajectory.

The challenge for investors, policymakers, and everyday users is not to predict which asset will win, but to understand the evolutionary pressures at play. What problems are these assets solving? What new trade-offs are they introducing? And how might their utility shift as context changes? A decade ago, crypto was a curiosity. Today, it is a frontier. Tomorrow, it may be infrastructure. The pace of this transition is uncertain. Its direction, however, is no longer ambiguous.

To treat crypto solely as an investment class is to miss its deeper significance. It is an ongoing experiment in how value can be stored, transferred, and governed without central authority. It is a test case in monetary evolution—one that may prove flawed, incomplete, or even dangerous in parts, but which reflects genuine pressures in the modern economy. And as with all evolutions, the outcome will not be dictated by theory, but by what survives, scales, and adapts to human need. Crypto is not the end of money. But it may be one of its most consequential mutations.

Chapter 3
The Crypto Stack: What You're Actually Buying

Most newcomers to crypto assume they are simply buying a "coin." The terminology, often loose and at times deliberately obfuscatory, implies a simplicity that is misleading. Behind the click of a purchase lies a lattice of complexity: networks masquerading as currencies, tokens masquerading as equity, decentralised infrastructures that straddle the line between utility and speculation. If you cannot identify the layer in which you are participating—what claim, exactly, you hold—then you cannot truly know what you own. And without that knowledge, evaluating risks, narratives, and the durability of your position becomes guesswork. This chapter aims to restore that clarity.

The crypto ecosystem is not a single entity. It is a multi-layered stack, technical, economic, and ideological. At the foundation are protocols: decentralised networks coordinating computation, storage, and consensus. Native assets—"coins"—live atop these protocols, often functioning as incentives to secure the network. Tokens layer above, representing rights, assets, or functionalities. Surrounding all this are decentralised applications, centralised wrappers, cross-chain bridges, and a cacophony of marketing claims, investment theses, and tribal allegiances. Each layer carries distinct risk exposures, governance models, and return profiles, and each reflects a different conception of what crypto is meant to accomplish.

To navigate this, one must first ask: is this asset digital money, a stake in infrastructure, a speculative instrument, or merely hype in a new wrapper? Is the project genuinely building functionality, or primarily extracting capital from unwary participants? This is no trivial distinction. The 2021 bull run—much like the dot-com frenzy two decades prior—was driven not by fundamentals, but by fear of missing out. Tokens with slick websites and opaque whitepapers raised millions overnight. Many no longer exist. They were never investments; they were lottery tickets dressed as innovation.

Bitcoin and Ethereum exemplify the divergence within crypto. Bitcoin is a protocol-based monetary asset with a fixed supply and a narrow remit: decentralised, non-sovereign value storage and transfer. It offers no smart contracts beyond limited scripting, no central leadership, and is valued for ideological fidelity: money without masters. Ethereum, in contrast, is a general-purpose platform—a decentralised world computer enabling programmable logic, decentralised finance, tokenised assets, and digital identity. It trades simplicity and predictability for flexibility, evolving through governance proposals, consensus changes, and protocol upgrades. These ecosystems are not two iterations of the same thing; they embody distinct visions of decentralisation.

Beyond these pillars lies a chaotic frontier: assets promising faster transactions, lower fees, novel consensus mechanisms, privacy enhancements, or ambitious applications. Some, like Solana or Avalanche, occupy plausible niches. Others are recycled templates, repackaged for retail speculation. Here, the challenge is epistemological as well as technical: what are the network's security assumptions? How centralised is its validator set? Who controls its treasury? Is there a genuine user base, or merely circular demand sustained by incentives and liquidity schemes? Investing here resembles venture capital more than public equities: it is a probabilistic wager on network effects, adoption, and protocol credibility, rather than a claim on cash flow.

Distinguishing use-case from speculation is a matter of durability, not morality. Assets solving real problems—cross-border remittances, permissionless lending, decentralised exchanges—are more likely to endure market cycles. Assets that exist solely to be traded, whose only utility is price movement, are structurally fragile, reliant on a continuous inflow of new capital. When the music stops, collapse follows. Discernment must therefore go beyond charts and Twitter sentiment: what problem does this asset solve, for whom, and why is crypto uniquely suited to address it?

Evaluating whether a project is product or Ponzi can be subtle. A legitimate token may accrue value from protocol usage; a Ponzi may mimic this, offering no actual utility and depending entirely on new entrants. Yield platforms can appear sustainable until scrutiny reveals circular economics. Token emissions purporting to incentivise liquidity may merely subsidise temporary inflows. Packaging can be identical; economic coherence—does value genuinely flow or merely shuffle?—is the distinction.

Traditional due diligence relies on balance sheets and filings. In crypto, these are rare. Investors must synthesise evidence from open-source code, Discord communities, audit reports, on-chain analytics, and reputation. Technical literacy alone is insufficient; sceptical reasoning is essential. Who benefits if the token succeeds? Who bears the downside? Are incentives front-loaded or aligned over time? Is governance credible or theatrical? Are claims testable or deliberately vague?

At its best, crypto is a new economic design space, a chance to rethink value creation and coordination without centralised gatekeepers. At its worst, it mirrors ancient human instincts: greed, fear, and the desire for easy gains. The prudent investor must distinguish signal from noise, architecture from narrative, substance from theatre. Achieving this requires a mental map of the ecosystem: understanding what is being bought, what layer it occupies, and what logic underpins its design.

This chapter provides that map—not as dogma, but as orientation. You do not need to be a developer to differentiate protocol from token. You do not need to be an economist to evaluate supply dynamics or incentive structures. But you do need to ask better questions than most do. The default in crypto is herd-driven FOMO; the aim here is informed discernment.

Just as no one would buy a company's shares without understanding its business, no one should hold a crypto asset without knowing whether it represents infrastructure, governance rights, payment rails, or empty promise. Clarity is protection and a source of conviction when markets turn volatile—which, in crypto, they always do.

Investing intelligently requires fluency across technical, economic, social, and psychological layers. It separates the tourist from the builder, the punter from the allocator.

Crypto does not reward faith. It rewards understanding. And that understanding begins with knowing what you are actually buying.

Coins, Tokens, Protocols—What's the Difference?

An investor who confuses a token with a coin, or a coin with a protocol, is not just engaging in semantic sloppiness—they are stepping into a marketplace blindfolded. The language of crypto is deceptively casual. Projects use the terms interchangeably, marketing teams blur distinctions, and even some analysts lump assets together under the vague banner of "crypto." But if you intend to allocate capital in this domain with rigour, clarity begins at the foundation: understanding *what* you're buying. Is it infrastructure? A utility right? A governance mechanism? A store of value? A speculative placeholder? The answer makes all the difference—not just in theoretical design, but in risk exposure, valuation, and survivability.

Start with protocols. These are the foundational systems upon which entire blockchain ecosystems are built. A protocol is not an asset; it is a rule set, an agreed-upon logic that governs how transactions occur, how consensus is achieved, and how new data is added to the blockchain. Bitcoin is a protocol. So is Ethereum. So are Avalanche, Solana, and dozens of others. These systems define how computers (or "nodes") interact to validate data without a central authority. Crucially, protocols operate with incentive mechanisms—usually native coins—that align the interests of users, validators, and developers. Without these incentives, decentralised systems wouldn't sustain themselves. In this sense, a protocol is *infrastructure with embedded economics*.

Coins are the native digital assets issued directly by a blockchain protocol. They are integral to the protocol's function—not layered on top of it. Bitcoin (BTC) secures the Bitcoin network. Ether (ETH) pays for computation on Ethereum. These assets typically serve one or more core purposes: payment for services, staking for security, and sometimes governance. Coins are not merely speculative instruments. They're a protocol's lifeblood, aligning incentives across decentralised actors. Importantly, their scarcity, issuance schedule, and governance parameters are usually hard-coded and publicly auditable—though not always immutable.

Tokens, by contrast, are issued *on top of* a protocol. They do not run their own blockchains. Instead, they use an existing protocol's infrastructure—typically via smart contracts. Most tokens today are issued on Ethereum using ERC standards, but they can also exist on Solana, Avalanche, BNB Chain, and others. Tokens can represent virtually anything: voting rights in a decentralised autonomous organisation (DAO), access to a decentralised application (dApp), a claim on future cash flows, even synthetic exposure to off-chain assets. Their flexibility makes them attractive—but also fraught with confusion. Many tokens masquerade as currencies or equity-like assets, but with none of the legal clarity or investor protections those categories imply.

Consider the structural implications. When you hold BTC, you're holding the protocol's foundational asset—it exists nowhere else. When you hold a DeFi governance token issued on Ethereum, you are two layers removed from the infrastructure. Your asset derives its value from the adoption of a specific application, not from the network that hosts it. If Ethereum failed tomorrow, your token would be functionally worthless. This stacking of dependencies matters enormously when evaluating risk. It's the difference between owning the road and betting on a shop built next to it.

The terminology becomes even more consequential when you realise how these layers affect liquidity, regulation, and market psychology. Coins like BTC and ETH are highly liquid, with mature trading pairs, institutional custody solutions, and growing derivative markets. They are increasingly treated as commodities or non-sovereign assets by regulators. Tokens, however, occupy murkier ground. Some resemble securities in function, others in distribution. Many are launched without formal disclosures, without underlying economic models, or without clarity around how—and whether—holders derive value. For the investor, this isn't merely a question of nomenclature. It determines whether you are exposed to protocol risk, platform risk, regulatory risk, or all three simultaneously.

The behavioural dynamics also differ. Protocol coins attract ideologically committed holders who often see themselves as participants in a new monetary or computational paradigm. These communities—however tribal—tend to support long-term adoption, code robustness, and decentralised governance. Token holders, on the other hand, often behave more like early-stage venture capitalists or short-term speculators. Many tokens are launched with aggressive incentives—airdrop farming, liquidity mining, staking rewards—designed to create momentum rather than value. The resulting boom-and-bust cycles erode trust, especially when projects fail to deliver product-market fit beyond tokenomics theatre.

This structural distinction also changes how we value assets. Coins like Bitcoin can be approached with monetary metaphors: scarcity, issuance curve, network effects. Tokens often require an equity-like or utility-based lens. What are the sources of demand? What is the burn rate of incentives? Is there a flywheel between token use and protocol adoption? Unfortunately, most crypto projects today still collapse into circular logic: demand is driven by expectation of price appreciation, which itself is driven by marketing and listing velocity rather than utility. Knowing the difference between a native coin that sustains a network and a token whose value rests on perpetual hype cycles is not just helpful—it is indispensable.

Take the example of Ethereum and Uniswap. Ethereum is a base-layer protocol; its coin (ETH) secures the network and pays for computation. Uniswap is a decentralised exchange built on Ethereum. Its token (UNI) governs decisions about the protocol's treasury and upgrades. Owning ETH means holding a stake in general-purpose infrastructure that supports thousands of applications. Owning UNI means betting on the governance value and adoption of one specific application. The correlation between the two may be high during bull markets, but the risk profiles are entirely distinct. Regulatory clarity, smart contract risk, governance inertia, and token emission schedules—these are materially different forces.

This complexity deepens when you consider wrapped assets, synthetic tokens, and cross-chain representations. For instance, Wrapped Bitcoin (WBTC) is an ERC-20 token that represents Bitcoin held in custody. It allows BTC to be used in Ethereum's DeFi ecosystem, but it introduces custodial risk and smart contract dependencies. Similarly, synthetic tokens can track the value of real-world assets, such as stocks or commodities, but rely on oracles and counterparty guarantees. These derivatives might be structurally fragile, yet they often trade at par with their underlying—until they don't.

The upshot is this: crypto assets do not belong to a single taxonomy. They are not monolithic financial instruments, nor can they be evaluated through the lens of traditional asset classes. A coin may behave like money, a token like a startup equity, a protocol like a software platform. What they share is programmability, permissionless issuance, and exposure to technological evolution. But their mechanics, use-cases, and risk surfaces diverge sharply. To allocate responsibly, one must move beyond the retail investor's default posture—price chasing—and towards architectural fluency.

This fluency is not reserved for coders or insiders. It is entirely within reach for thoughtful investors who treat crypto not as a casino, but as a new layer of the financial stack. It begins with language. A coin is not a token. A protocol is not a product. Marketing does not equal utility. And decentralisation, often invoked as a virtue, is a spectrum—not a binary state.

By internalising these distinctions, investors not only avoid obvious missteps—they gain strategic leverage. They can ask better questions, build portfolios with layered exposure, and spot red flags early. They become less susceptible to the narrative churn of the crypto cycle, where yesterday's darling token becomes tomorrow's cautionary tale. They shift from reactive to proactive engagement. In a space built on open architecture, those who understand the plumbing—not just the packaging—will navigate most effectively.

Crypto's technical scaffolding is not optional knowledge. It is the difference between buying into a network and buying into noise. And as the industry matures, the line between the two will only grow sharper. For those willing to think carefully, the distinctions are not barriers—they are signals.

They tell us what matters, what lasts, and what merely pretends. And that is where intelligent investing begins.

Bitcoin vs Ethereum vs Everything Else

If investing in crypto assets feels like stepping into a war of allegiances rather than a search for value, you're not imagining it. Crypto doesn't merely present a new asset class—it presents competing ideologies, architectural models, and economic philosophies. Bitcoin maximalists dismiss all other projects as distractions or scams. Ethereum advocates argue they're building the future of decentralised applications. Supporters of newer Layer 1s or exotic token ecosystems often promise superior speed, scale, or adaptability. But buried beneath the noise lies a far more useful question for the pragmatic investor: *What exactly am I buying, and what function does it serve in the broader digital economy?*

To navigate this terrain wisely, one must abandon tribalism and adopt analytical clarity. Strip away the Twitter flame wars, the speculative mania, and the marketing gloss, and you're left with three overlapping but fundamentally distinct investment profiles: Bitcoin as a trust-minimised monetary asset, Ethereum as a programmable economic layer, and "everything else" as an experimental frontier of possibility—with all the risk that entails.

Bitcoin: The Institutional Heretic

Bitcoin is often described as digital gold, and while the analogy is imperfect, it captures a core truth: Bitcoin is not designed to be flexible, fast, or feature-rich. It is designed to be hard. Hard to change, hard to inflate, hard to corrupt. Its fixed supply of 21 million coins, its decentralised consensus model, and its deliberately constrained scripting language reflect a narrow but powerful design goal—to serve as a censorship-resistant, self-sovereign store of value.

This rigidity has earned Bitcoin both reverence and critique. Supporters view it as the world's first incorruptible asset—a monetary system free from central banks, fiscal policy, or political tampering. Its monetary policy is auditable and known in advance. This predictability, combined with its security through proof-of-work mining, gives Bitcoin a singular role: a hedge not against market volatility per se, but against monetary debasement and institutional distrust.

Critics argue that Bitcoin's simplicity makes it obsolete as a platform for innovation. It lacks built-in programmability. Its transaction throughput is low. Its energy consumption is high. But these are not accidental oversights—they are trade-offs in service of a specific design philosophy. Bitcoin is not trying to be a Swiss Army knife; it is trying to be a vault. Whether or not that is valuable depends on what you are trying to protect.

Ethereum: The Modular Economy

Ethereum emerged not to challenge Bitcoin's role as sound money, but to expand what blockchain technology could do. Where Bitcoin offers finality and simplicity, Ethereum offers flexibility. It introduced the idea of "smart contracts"—programmable agreements that execute automatically when conditions are met. This turned Ethereum into a decentralised computing platform, not just a payments layer.

Ethereum is, in essence, an economic operating system. It powers decentralised finance (DeFi), NFT platforms, decentralised autonomous organisations (DAOs), and increasingly complex applications ranging from insurance to identity. It also embraces change: Ethereum has undergone major upgrades, including the transition from proof-of-work to proof-of-stake in the "Merge," and it continues to evolve through proposals like sharding and rollups aimed at increasing scalability.

With this innovation comes complexity and risk. Ethereum's supply is dynamic, governed by fee-burning mechanics and staking incentives. Its applications can be exploited via code vulnerabilities. Its consensus design, while less energy-intensive post-Merge, remains economically experimental. And yet, Ethereum's openness to experimentation makes it a leading platform for economic creativity. Investors in Ether are not just betting on a monetary narrative—they are buying into a programmable, evolving infrastructure layer.

Everything Else: Innovation or Imitation?

Beyond Bitcoin and Ethereum lies a sprawling ecosystem of alternatives: Solana, Avalanche, Cardano, Polkadot, Cosmos, and thousands more. Some offer high throughput and low fees. Others promise modular interoperability. Many repackage existing ideas with different branding or incentive structures. A few have carved out niche use cases or developed genuinely novel architectures.

Yet the investor must remain sober. Most of these projects, even if technically impressive, lack meaningful adoption. Many have inflated tokenomics designed to attract short-term capital rather than long-term users. Some are outright schemes that exploit complexity to obscure Ponzi-like dynamics. Others aim to be Ethereum killers but rely on centralised validators or opaque governance to achieve their throughput.

That is not to say all non-Bitcoin, non-Ethereum assets are unworthy. But their investment case must be treated as venture-style risk: you are not buying established infrastructure, you are buying *potential*. Valuation must be forward-looking, technology-focused, and brutally honest about the fragility of network effects. Unlike Bitcoin and Ethereum, whose Lindy effect (the idea that things that have lasted tend to last) provides some resilience, the rest of the market is, for now, a sea of unproven bets.

Philosophy as a Differentiator

What truly separates these ecosystems isn't just their technology—it's their worldview. Bitcoin is fundamentally adversarial: it assumes institutions will fail, power will be abused, and only decentralisation can preserve freedom. Ethereum is technocratic: it believes in open coordination, composability, and iterative improvement. Many other projects adopt a startup mentality: move fast, optimise user experience, and capture market share before the next cycle resets the landscape.

Understanding these philosophies is critical, because they shape everything from community norms to governance structures to risk profiles. An investor in Bitcoin is buying into scarcity and security. An investor in Ethereum is buying into flexibility and innovation. An investor in altcoins may be buying into speed, niche utility, or sheer speculative momentum. But what they are *not* buying—despite the marketing—is a standardised financial product akin to a stock or bond.

Implications for Portfolio Construction

Treating crypto assets as interchangeable is a recipe for confusion. Bitcoin, Ethereum, and "everything else" require distinct mental models. They respond to different catalysts. They carry different tail risks. They interact differently with traditional assets. Bitcoin, for instance, may act as a long-duration hedge against fiat devaluation. Ethereum may serve as exposure to the decentralised app economy. Other assets may offer asymmetric upside with venture-like failure rates.

Diversification within crypto is not just about asset count—it is about function. A portfolio tilted entirely towards speculative altcoins is not diversified, even if it holds dozens of tickers. Likewise, holding only Bitcoin may miss exposure to emerging digital economies. The real task is to match asset role to investment thesis: What is this token *for*? What gives it staying power? Who are its users, and what problems does it solve?

In a space fuelled by narratives, clarity is rare and valuable. The goal is not to pick sides in a digital turf war. The goal is to build an architecture of understanding that filters signal from noise. To invest in crypto is not to "believe in crypto"—it is to interrogate claims, decode functionality, and make informed bets on systems that, despite their volatility, may yet shape how value flows in the 21st century.

Use-Case vs Speculation

A startling proportion of the assets traded in crypto markets today exist not to serve a practical function, but to be traded for their own sake. This phenomenon—where price action supersedes product utility—has not only inflated the size and volatility of the digital asset space but has also obscured its genuinely useful innovations. For investors seeking clarity, the critical task is to distinguish between assets that deliver value through real-world application, and those that merely feed on momentum, belief, and market reflexivity. This distinction, though conceptually straightforward, is operationally complex, as the line between utility and speculation is often blurred by branding, hype, and evolving use cases.

Cryptocurrencies were not originally designed as speculative instruments. Bitcoin emerged in 2009 with a stated purpose: a peer-to-peer electronic cash system. Ethereum followed in 2015, promising a decentralised computing platform for running tamper-proof applications. Both were conceived in the context of *use*. Yet ironically, the most visible and liquid cryptocurrencies are now primarily treated as speculative assets. For most holders of Bitcoin, the asset is not a medium of exchange but a bet—on scarcity, inflation hedging, or eventual systemic adoption. Likewise, the majority of Ether sits idle, not circulating within decentralised apps but parked on centralised exchanges or custodial wallets as investors wait for price appreciation. *This speculative layer has overwhelmed the functional layer, even for the most 'blue-chip' assets in the crypto ecosystem.*

This imbalance has been exacerbated by the structure of the market itself. Unlike traditional equities—where dividends, cash flows, and regulatory disclosures impose a tether between price and performance—crypto assets are frequently decoupled from any earnings model. Most tokens have no revenue, no customers, and no requirement to deliver financial statements. What moves them is sentiment, narrative, and liquidity. In this sense, they resemble penny stocks or early-stage venture plays more than mature financial instruments. The difference is that in crypto, such characteristics are not limited to obscure corners of the market—they are pervasive.

Take Dogecoin, a cryptocurrency launched as a joke in 2013. With no core development team, no roadmap, and no clear function, it nonetheless reached a market capitalisation of over $80 billion during the bull market of 2021. Its ascent was driven almost entirely by internet memes, celebrity endorsements, and speculative fervour. That Dogecoin still exists is not surprising; that it remains one of the most widely held crypto assets is. *It embodies the strange new reality of digital markets, where value is ascribed based on virality rather than utility.*

Contrast this with use-case-driven crypto assets, which seek to solve specific problems in financial infrastructure, data management, or digital ownership. Stablecoins, for example, have proven one of the clearest success stories. By pegging their value to fiat currencies, assets like USDC and USDT provide a functional medium of exchange for digital transactions, particularly in countries with capital controls or volatile local currencies. In Argentina, Nigeria, Turkey, and Lebanon, stablecoin adoption is not speculative—it is adaptive. Individuals use them to preserve purchasing power, settle contracts, and send cross-border remittances with speed and minimal friction. *Here, crypto acts as a workaround for systemic deficiencies in fiat-based systems, not as a ticket to speculative gain.*

Similarly, protocols like Chainlink or Filecoin offer infrastructural utility. Chainlink delivers decentralised oracles—feeding external data into smart contracts—without which many blockchain-based applications would fail. Filecoin provides decentralised cloud storage, enabling users to rent out excess storage capacity on a global network. Whether these services prove economically sustainable is still debated, but the ambition is undeniably functional. *They attempt to solve coordination problems in data, compute, or liquidity—not merely to attract capital for its own sake.*

The market, however, rarely rewards utility on its own. Assets with clear use cases can remain undervalued or unnoticed, while pure hype tokens skyrocket. This reveals a core structural asymmetry in crypto investing: *what works technologically is not always what performs financially—and vice versa.* The decoupling of use and price creates a minefield for investors seeking exposure to durable, long-term projects. In traditional venture capital, illiquidity acts as a filtering mechanism. One cannot day-trade early-stage startups. In crypto, that discipline is removed. Pre-product tokens can list on decentralised exchanges and generate millions in volume before a single line of code has shipped.

This speculative structure is further fuelled by tokenomics—the design of a token's issuance, allocation, and incentive structure. Many projects launch with large insider allocations, short vesting schedules, and artificially constrained supplies to simulate scarcity. They are optimised for market cap inflation, not product delivery. Retail investors, drawn by rising charts, enter liquidity pools where insiders quietly exit. This is not unique to crypto; pump-and-dump schemes have long existed in traditional finance. But the speed, scale, and opacity of such manoeuvres in decentralised markets are unprecedented. *In many cases, the economics of the token are deliberately designed to front-load hype and back-load utility—if utility ever arrives at all.*

Still, it would be a mistake to dismiss the entire space as speculative froth. Much like the early internet—where Pets.com and Amazon coexisted—crypto hosts both the absurd and the profound. Projects like Aave, Compound, or Uniswap offer decentralised lending, borrowing, and exchange mechanisms that function without intermediaries. Their tokens grant governance rights or fee-sharing to users, creating a kind of quasi-equity structure for protocol stakeholders. Whether these models can sustain themselves in the face of regulatory scrutiny and shifting incentives remains to be seen. But they do represent a coherent attempt to *embed financial services into programmable code*, offering global access without traditional gatekeepers.

Indeed, one of the most compelling arguments for crypto's real-world use lies not in any one token, but in the architecture it enables. Decentralised finance (DeFi), non-fungible tokens (NFTs), and decentralised autonomous organisations (DAOs) may or may not achieve mass adoption—but they offer novel models of ownership, identity, and coordination that traditional finance struggles to replicate. Even when the assets themselves are volatile, the underlying architectures may possess lasting value.

For the thoughtful investor, then, the question is not whether an asset has risen 300% in the past year, but *whether it does anything*. Can it be used for payment, settlement, computation, storage, or coordination? Does it solve a problem that fiat or Web2 systems have failed to address? Is there evidence of organic adoption, outside of speculative trading? These questions are neither easy nor infallible. But they orient the investor toward substance over noise.

Importantly, some assets may migrate from one category to the other. Ethereum began as a use-case-driven smart contract platform. Yet during the ICO boom of 2017 and again in the DeFi summer of 2020, it became a hotbed of speculation. Today, its status is hybrid: used by developers and dApps, but also hoarded by investors. Others, like Solana or Avalanche, have oscillated between narratives of functionality and bursts of speculative hype. *This fluidity underscores a key insight: use and speculation are not mutually exclusive, but dynamically entangled.*

Navigating this entanglement requires more than technical literacy. It demands a sober reckoning with human behaviour—our susceptibility to novelty, greed, and the illusion of control. Markets are not efficient machines but emotional theatres, and crypto is perhaps the most unconstrained stage we've yet built. In this theatre, some assets will become foundational infrastructure. Others will vanish without a trace. The difference lies not in how loudly they are promoted, but in *how persistently they are used.*

In the end, sustainable exposure in crypto does not come from guessing the next pump, but from identifying the protocols, platforms, and primitives that people will use whether or not the price is rising. Utility may not always be rewarded immediately, but over time, *use tends to leave a footprint that speculation cannot fake.* In an industry where belief is cheap and liquidity is fast, that footprint may be the only reliable compass investors have.

Is This a Product or a Ponzi?

A surprising number of intelligent people—professionals, engineers, even seasoned investors—have lost money in crypto schemes that, when scrutinised, bore little resemblance to genuine innovation. The pattern is familiar: slick marketing, vague promises of decentralised disruption, and a token economy with sky-high "yields" that seem to emerge from thin air. What follows is often a quiet collapse, with the project's website abandoned, its creators vanished or rebranded, and a once-hyped token reduced to digital dust. The question is not merely one of fraud, but of discernment: *how can one tell the difference between a functional crypto product and a financial mirage?*

At the heart of the matter lies a conceptual misalignment. Unlike traditional companies, many crypto projects do not sell goods, generate revenue, or create tangible services in the way businesses have for centuries. Instead, they operate within tokenised ecosystems—offering digital assets whose value depends not on earnings or utility, but on the belief that others will soon pay more. This dynamic makes the distinction between a product and a Ponzi less clear-cut than it first appears. Indeed, some of the most notorious collapses in crypto history—from Bitconnect to TerraUSD—were cloaked in technical language and ecosystem jargon that obfuscated their underlying circularity.

A Ponzi scheme, in its classical form, pays early participants with funds from later ones, without creating any independent source of value. This structure collapses when new inflows slow down. In crypto, the analogue isn't always direct. Projects often involve some form of staking, liquidity provision, or yield farming—mechanisms that sound sophisticated but frequently function in ways indistinguishable from a Ponzi's logic. *If a protocol's "yield" is paid primarily from new user deposits, not genuine economic activity, the risk profile shifts dramatically.*

Consider TerraUSD and its sister token, Luna. Marketed as a decentralised stablecoin pegged to the dollar, Terra relied on an algorithmic mechanism that burned or minted Luna to stabilise UST's price. The system appeared to work—until it didn't. When confidence faltered, a self-reinforcing death spiral ensued. UST lost its peg, Luna hyperinflated, and over $60 billion in paper wealth evaporated in days. What made Terra's collapse instructive wasn't merely its speed, but the fact that it had been championed by major funds, exchanges, and influencers who failed to critically assess the model's fragility. *Economic soundness was replaced with narrative momentum.*

One of the most seductive red flags in the crypto world is the promise of "risk-free yield." While traditional finance can offer modest returns on treasury bills or bank savings—backed by institutional guarantees and central bank stability—many crypto protocols offer double-digit, even triple-digit, annual percentage yields (APY) with vague disclaimers and unclear funding sources. These yields are often paid in the project's native token, whose value is entirely speculative. When demand for that token dries up, so too do the returns. This yield illusion gives the false impression of productivity while relying on token inflation to maintain momentum.

A sound crypto product should perform a verifiable function, provide some form of economic service, and rely on mechanisms that do not collapse when market sentiment turns. Ethereum's network, for example, processes smart contracts that power decentralised finance applications, NFTs, and a host of programmable transactions. Transaction fees—known as gas—are paid in ETH, reflecting actual demand for block space. That demand can fluctuate, but its basis is transparent and economic. *Utility, not merely tokenomics, is what separates infrastructure from imitation.*

Contrast this with meme tokens, which often lack purpose beyond virality. Dogecoin, Shiba Inu, and others have soared and crashed on waves of cultural momentum, sometimes generating windfalls for early holders, but rarely sustaining real use. They highlight a key behavioural trap:

speculative assets often thrive not despite their lack of fundamentals, but because of it. The absence of substance allows for narrative flexibility. A token can mean anything to anyone—a joke, a rebellion, a community symbol—until reality sets in.

Transparency is another essential filter. Legitimate projects publish detailed documentation, open-source their code, and subject their smart contracts to independent audits. They also make clear what the token does—whether it's used for governance, transaction fees, collateral, or staking—and how its value might evolve. Ponzi-like projects often obfuscate these details, offering jargon-heavy whitepapers that describe token mechanics in abstract or recursive terms. *If you can't explain how value enters and sustains a system without mentioning price appreciation, you're likely dealing with circular logic.*

Governance structure offers further clues. Sustainable protocols often empower users to influence development through decentralised mechanisms, though these systems vary widely in practice. Projects that concentrate control in a few wallets or opaque multisig arrangements—particularly when founders can mint new tokens or drain liquidity at will—introduce hidden centralisation risks. That isn't merely a philosophical problem; it can be the vector for rug pulls, sudden changes in rules, or outright exit scams.

Behavioural dynamics must also be considered. A hallmark of dubious projects is the presence of evangelism untethered to technical or economic grounding. When community discourse centres around price predictions, loyalty pledges, and conspiratorial thinking about "FUD" (fear, uncertainty, doubt), rather than code updates, security audits, or user adoption, intellectual hygiene breaks down. *A cult of belief often fills the void left by the absence of substance.* This fervour isn't accidental—it's cultivated to maintain buy-in, suppress scepticism, and sustain inflows.

To assess whether a crypto asset is a product or a Ponzi, one must adopt the posture of a forensic analyst, not a fan. Ask:

Does the project produce something valuable, or merely shift tokens between participants?

Are the returns generated by real demand or by token inflation?

Who controls the levers of issuance, liquidity, and protocol changes?

What would happen if no new users joined—does the system still function, or does it unravel?

While regulation may eventually clean up the space—through clearer definitions, mandatory disclosures, and enforcement—the responsibility today falls largely on the individual. The decentralised nature of crypto, while empowering, also removes many of the safeguards that traditional investors take for granted. There are no guarantees, no central bank backstops, and often, no recourse. This demands a higher bar for scepticism, analysis, and intellectual humility.

It also demands the ability to walk away. The most effective protection against speculative traps isn't technical expertise or regulatory clarity—it's the discipline to decline an opportunity that cannot be understood or verified. In the crypto landscape, *the things most worth investing in rarely need to shout to be heard.*

Chapter 4
Risk, Volatility, and Why Most People Lose

More people have lost money in crypto than have made it, yet the allure of extraordinary returns continues to draw participants. This is not a mere quirk of volatility—it is baked into the system. The market's architecture, shaped by both design and evolution, disproportionately rewards traders and insiders rather than passive investors. To grasp why, one must look beyond price charts. It demands confronting behavioural biases, information asymmetry, systemic fragility, and the very mechanics of the platforms themselves. Losses in crypto are rarely random; they are often a product of the incentives at play, amplified by human psychology.

Modern investors are accustomed to decades of relative stability, buffered by regulation and institutional safeguards. Stocks have halts, brokers are licensed, insurance schemes cover bank failures. None of this exists in crypto's frontier. What looks like a parallel financial universe—decentralised, boundless, full of opportunity—is often a hall of mirrors. Assets may be new, but the methods of loss are ancient: greed, haste, misinformation, poor risk management. And in crypto, these forces operate at an accelerated pace.

Advocates often describe volatility as a temporary side-effect of growth or the cost of revolutionary potential. Yet volatility is not incidental—it is foundational. Price swings power the speculative engine. Without them, the promise of rapid wealth evaporates; without narrative cycles, liquidity dries. Volatility keeps the ecosystem liquid, memeable, and perpetually on the edge of the next "cycle." It enables leverage, gamifies trading, and fuels social virality. For the average participant, however, it is what shreds portfolios.

The risks are not confined to price movements. Custody risk—where and how one stores assets—has been a persistent Achilles' heel. Billions have vanished through exchange hacks, compromised wallets, and custodial mismanagement. Mt. Gox, once the world's largest exchange, lost 850,000 bitcoins in 2014. More recently, FTX's collapse revealed billions misappropriated under the guise of institutional legitimacy. The issue was structural as much as criminal. In traditional finance, custody is mundane; in crypto, it can be fatal.

Even self-custody—the ideal of controlling one's assets—is perilous. Private keys can be lost or stolen. Recovery mechanisms are opaque, often irreversible. The very tools that confer sovereignty also strip away safety nets. For the sophisticated operator, this is a feature; for most, a minefield. Crypto's mantra, "be your own bank," sounds empowering until it translates to: "no one will save you." Freedom comes with total liability.

Crypto's 24/7 availability compounds these risks. Unlike traditional markets with hours, weekends, or circuit breakers, crypto never sleeps. Constant access is intoxicating—and exhausting. Decisions are made quickly, under pressure, in a landscape of endless stimuli. Participants chase pumps, panic on dips, and confuse activity for strategy. Markets move relentlessly, and so do mistakes.

Platform design exploits these tendencies. Exchanges profit from trading volume, not user success. Leverage is aggressively marketed. Interfaces resemble gaming apps. Reward structures push daily logins, leaderboard climbing, and short-term speculation. Long-term outcomes are secondary; churn is king. Beneath the veneer of democratized finance lies a business model built on perpetual engagement.

The mythology of crypto's early millionaires—Bitcoin windfalls, Ethereum ICO flips, Dogecoin tales—creates survivorship bias. Every viral success masks thousands of quiet failures: holders who bought too late, misjudged a rug pull, or panicked at a downturn. Platforms have no incentive to highlight losses. The narrative of widespread success persists, but reality is inverted: most participants subsidise the gains of a few.

Risk in crypto is also systemic. Crashes are rarely isolated. Bitcoin itself is volatile; when it falls, liquidity evaporates, collateralised positions unwind, and stablecoins can de-peg. DeFi protocols often use one token as collateral to mint another, forming a fragile chain. When a single link breaks, collapses can be rapid and total. Traditional portfolio theory struggles here: diversifying across multiple crypto assets offers little protection when all are correlated by liquidity, sentiment, or shared infrastructure. The illusion of diversification is one of crypto's quieter traps.

Behavioural finance is central to survival. Crypto exploits nearly every human bias: loss aversion, overconfidence, confirmation bias, FOMO, and the sunk cost fallacy. Scarcity tactics, presale deadlines, countdowns, and gated communities amplify urgency. Social channels reward loyalty, marginalise scepticism, and elevate token holding to moral identity. Entering this world without a disciplined framework is akin to walking into a casino where your instincts are the house advantage.

Navigating this requires clarity of strategy and temperament. Investors must know themselves: are you chasing narratives or investing in fundamentals? Can you assess protocol risk, token utility, governance, and market depth—or are you trusting the noise? Crypto's apparent equality masks asymmetry: retail participants do not compete on the same field as professional funds, insiders, or bots. Without self-awareness, the playing field becomes a trap.

Yet this is not a call to avoid crypto. Rather, it is a call to approach differently. The error is not participation; it is participation without filters, frameworks, or recognition that the space is a casino cloaked in revolution. Those who succeed are rarely the most zealous or idealistic—they are prepared. They understand volatility as central, not incidental. They treat exposure as calculated allocation, acting with timing and restraint.

This chapter is an invitation to prudence. Risk itself is not the enemy; misunderstood risk is. Most losses occur not because the system is inherently flawed, but because participants enter with the wrong map. What follows is an attempt to redraw that map: naming the terrain, exposing the traps, and offering guidance for navigating the space with eyes wide open.

Crypto Is Built for Traders, Not Investors

The seductive narrative of crypto as a long-term investment opportunity has obscured a more structural and sobering reality: *the ecosystem is fundamentally engineered for trading, not investing*. This is not a matter of user error, insufficient education, or poor timing. It is a matter of architecture, incentives, and the very mechanics by which most crypto platforms generate revenue and maintain engagement. Retail participants enter the market expecting a version of traditional investing—buy low, hold long, benefit from compounding—but quickly find themselves trapped in a game with different rules, different players, and no pause button.

Unlike regulated equities, where most wealth accumulation stems from dividends, fundamentals, and long-term corporate value creation, crypto's valuation logic is often circular and self-referential. Assets are valued based on liquidity, hype velocity, and anticipated future adoption rather than current cash flows or tangible use cases. This distinction is crucial. Investing is typically grounded in a logic of underlying productivity. Trading, by contrast, thrives on movement, sentiment, and *volatility as an asset class*. In crypto, the latter dominates—volatility isn't a nuisance; it is the product.

This design serves platforms more than participants. Exchanges, the central arteries of the ecosystem, earn fees per transaction. The more activity, the more profit. It makes no difference whether users gain or lose—so long as they move. This is evident in how most trading platforms are structured: real-time charts with flashing tickers, gamified interfaces, leverage options one click away, and constant alerts designed to provoke action. Users are nudged, if not shoved, into high-frequency engagement. It's not a portfolio dashboard—it's a behavioural funnel into compulsive trading. *The design is addictive by intent.*

This poses a psychological trap for traditional investors. Accustomed to thinking in years, they find themselves operating in minutes. Long-term conviction buckles under daily price whipsaws. Attention becomes fragmented. Instead of accumulating understanding, participants accumulate alerts. The constant presence of price and the infinite scroll of opinions create an environment in which even seasoned investors struggle to maintain clarity. And once a portfolio becomes something you check hourly, it stops being an investment and starts becoming a scoreboard.

This is where structural design meets cognitive vulnerability. Crypto exploits a range of behavioural biases in ways traditional markets cannot. Loss aversion, confirmation bias, and recency effect are amplified in a 24/7 environment without trading halts or regulatory guardrails. The always-on nature of the market removes the forced reflection time built into traditional exchanges. Investors are not only exposed to volatility—they are immersed in it, emotionally and informationally. The result is a loop: action prompts reaction, which triggers feedback, which encourages further action. *Investing becomes impossible when attention is always in crisis mode.*

One of the more insidious dynamics is the blurring of investing and gambling. Platforms promote staking rewards, airdrops, mystery tokens, and perpetual trading as rational strategies, when in reality they function as behavioural nudges to keep users engaged. Retail investors, seeking passive income or long-term yield, are lured into sophisticated trading products they barely understand. Leveraged tokens, futures contracts, and liquidity pool positions are pitched as tools of financial empowerment, but they carry risks that even seasoned traders approach cautiously. *What is marketed as opportunity often conceals exposure.*

This asymmetry is compounded by information inequality. Insiders, developers, and venture-backed whales typically have access to private rounds, preferential pricing, and off-chain information. They can time exits with greater precision and influence price direction through coordinated actions. Retail, by contrast, is downstream—operating on lagging data, Twitter sentiment, and half-understood whitepapers. It is not an equal market. The surface optics of decentralisation hide an *intensely hierarchical system* where timing and information determine who extracts value and who provides it.

But the deeper challenge lies not just in how the market is structured—but in how participants misread that structure. Many assume they are investing when they are, in fact, speculating. They treat early-stage tokens like mature stocks, applying models that do not fit. They confuse staking yields with dividends, token burns with buybacks, and developer updates with corporate earnings reports. This misalignment of mental models leads to miscalculated risks. *What appears to be a long-term investment thesis is often a short-term liquidity bet in disguise.*

So why do so many keep returning, despite poor outcomes? Because for a brief moment, the dream feels possible. Crypto markets are asymmetric in return potential, and early winners become folk heroes—avatars of escape, luck, and irreverent wealth. These stories dominate the culture, creating a survivorship bias that overpowers rational evaluation. The underlying message is clear: *play often enough, and you might get lucky too.* The problem isn't that everyone believes this—it's that *just enough people actually do get lucky to keep the illusion alive.*

To shift from being a participant to a rational allocator requires more than caution—it requires an entirely different orientation. The first step is to recognise crypto for what it is: *an ecosystem optimised for trading activity, not for long-term value storage.* This doesn't make it fraudulent or useless—it simply means that applying long-horizon investing strategies without adapting to the context is like bringing chess strategies to a poker table. Success depends on knowing the game you're in.

What, then, can be done differently? First, clarify intent. Is this a trade or an investment? Is the position based on thesis or hope? Is the downside acceptable? Without clarity, all exposure becomes reactive. Second, reduce information noise. The most dangerous trades often begin in group chats and influencer feeds. Curate inputs deliberately. Third, minimise activity. Time in the market is not synonymous with attention in the market. *Discipline often means boredom, and in crypto, boredom is an edge.*

Fourth, build in friction. If you can trade everything from your phone at 2 a.m., you will. Introduce delays—whether technological, procedural, or mental. Use cold wallets not just for security, but for sobriety. Treat every repositioning as a cost. Fifth, adopt asymmetric strategies consciously. Crypto's upside is real—but so are its drawdowns. Allocate accordingly. Position sizing, liquidity buffers, and psychological detachment are not optional. They are preconditions for longevity.

Finally, reject the mythology of constant participation. Just because markets never close does not mean you must always be open. Some of the best trades are the ones not taken. Some of the best positions are held without commentary. And some of the best investors are those who know when *not* to play.

Crypto does not punish ignorance immediately. It flatters first. It rewards impulsiveness just long enough to build confidence, and then it flips the script. The danger is not losing money—it's misunderstanding *why* you lost, and believing it was just bad timing. Most people in crypto aren't unlucky. They're just playing the wrong game with the wrong expectations.

To win in crypto, one must learn to think like a trader, even when choosing not to trade. The discipline is not just in execution—but in orientation. And the investors who endure will not be those who chase every pump, but those who build frameworks sturdy enough to withstand both silence and noise. *In a market built for motion, stillness can be the most radical act of all.*

Volatility Isn't Just Noise—It's the Game

Most new entrants into the world of crypto markets view volatility as an unfortunate defect—an irritating by-product of immaturity, a source of anxiety, and something to be managed or hedged away. But this framing misunderstands the architecture and logic of the entire ecosystem. *Volatility is not a flaw in crypto; it is its central feature.* It is the engine that powers returns, attracts attention, fuels narratives, and sustains the speculative energy that defines the market. To treat it as noise is to misread the game entirely.

In traditional financial theory, volatility is viewed through a risk-adjusted lens: the higher the price movement of an asset, the greater the uncertainty around its value, and thus the higher the potential cost to the investor. But crypto was never built on the premise of fundamental value discovery in the first place. The vast majority of crypto assets have no cash flows, no balance sheets, and no intrinsic models to anchor their price. Their valuation is driven almost entirely by *what people believe others will believe next.* In such a reflexive system, volatility becomes not just a by-product but a necessary function—a mechanism for price discovery, social signalling, and market differentiation.

And so, volatility is not simply tolerated; it is monetised. Exchanges, which are the infrastructural backbone of the ecosystem, profit directly from trading volume—not stability. The more the price moves, the more trades are triggered, whether by algorithms, stop-losses, leverage calls, or good old-fashioned fear and greed. This is not a bug. It is the business model. *Volatility begets activity. Activity begets fees. Fees sustain the system.*

This incentive structure creates a loop in which price movement is amplified by design. Structural leverage—available across most crypto trading platforms in forms as aggressive as 20x, 50x, even 100x—ensures that even minor shifts in price can trigger cascading liquidations. When prices fall by a few percent, overleveraged positions are forcibly closed, adding to sell pressure and creating a self-reinforcing decline. When they rise, the same mechanism works in reverse. Volatility, therefore, isn't merely organic chaos; it is a *mechanically engineered outcome* of market architecture.

Compounding this dynamic is the absence of circuit breakers, regulatory constraints, and liquidity buffers that would typically dampen extreme moves in legacy markets. Crypto operates continuously—24 hours a day, 7 days a week, 365 days a year—with no enforced pause for reflection or institutional intervention. This uninterrupted exposure means that sentiment can spiral far faster and further than in traditional systems. The absence of stabilising anchors makes sentiment *the price.* Rumours become trades. Tweets become trendlines. And emotional contagion spreads with zero latency.

But to attribute volatility solely to structure is incomplete. Crypto markets are also *psychologically volatile* because they exist at the intersection of hope, ideology, and opportunism. They are populated not by passive investors but by engaged participants—evangelists, speculators, and builders—each with high conviction and low patience. These communities are tribal by nature, defensive by necessity, and often driven more by identity than analysis. When such groups engage with a market that never sleeps and has few rules, sharp price swings are inevitable. *Volatility is the expression of collective belief adjusting in real time.*

Take Bitcoin, for instance. Its volatility is often rationalised as the growing pains of a nascent store of value. But it is also the result of conflicting narratives: Is it digital gold? Is it a hedge against inflation? Is it a payments network? Is it a libertarian escape hatch? The inability to answer these questions definitively means that price floats on shifting sands of interpretation. And each new macro event—whether a central bank announcement or a geopolitical shock—reshuffles those interpretations instantly.

Ethereum offers its own version of narrative-driven volatility. As a platform for decentralised applications, smart contracts, and financial experimentation, its valuation is inextricably linked to the perceived success or failure of its ecosystem. When gas fees spike, developer activity dips. When a decentralised exchange is hacked, trust erodes. When a protocol launches a promising upgrade, optimism floods in. Every on-chain action becomes off-chain speculation, and vice versa. Ethereum's volatility is not a deviation from its purpose—it is the price of its ambition.

Beyond these dominant players, the rest of the crypto landscape—so-called altcoins—amplify these effects to extremes. Many of these projects are low-float, thinly traded tokens whose price can be moved by a single tweet, YouTube video, or coordinated group chat. Their value propositions are often abstract, their user bases tiny, and their code untested. In such an environment, volatility is not a surprise; *stability would be.*

For those attempting to allocate capital in this environment, the traditional language of volatility management—standard deviation, Sharpe ratios, VaR models—can feel not only insufficient but misleading. These metrics presume statistical normality in a system governed by narrative jumps, liquidity gaps, and sudden structural failures. The real volatility in crypto is not captured by models; it is embedded in design, community dynamics, and sentiment velocity. *It is not just a measurement problem—it is a category error.*

This leads to a critical shift in mindset. Rather than trying to suppress or escape volatility, thoughtful participants must learn to contextualise it. Volatility is information. It tells you where attention is focused, where leverage is concentrated, and where conviction might be weakest. When properly read, it is a map of fragility and exuberance. When misunderstood, it is a trap.

The most seasoned actors in crypto do not fear volatility—they budget for it. They size positions accordingly, maintain liquidity buffers, and treat portfolio construction as a probabilistic game, not a deterministic puzzle. They expect drawdowns. They build around durability, not just upside. And most importantly, they do not interpret price movement as moral judgement. *An asset can fall 50% without being a failure. It can rise 300% without being a success.*

This detachment is rare among retail investors, who are often emotionally tethered to positions in ways that impair judgement. A sudden price drop can feel like a personal insult; a parabolic run, like moral vindication. This emotional misalignment leads to poor decisions: panic selling, revenge trading, overexposure. It turns market movement into psychological whiplash. And because crypto lacks institutional players with long-term mandates, retail sentiment often sets the tone—accelerating cycles of euphoria and despair.

This is where volatility becomes not just a structural feature or a psychological consequence, but a *social phenomenon*. Entire online cultures have formed around volatility—celebrating gains, mocking losses, and reinforcing the idea that constant price action is a virtue. Memes, influencers, and algorithmic trading bots co-create a landscape where *movement equals meaning*. In this environment, to hold a stable asset is to be invisible. And in a world that rewards visibility, invisibility is death.

Yet there is opportunity in the chaos. For those willing to understand the mechanics, map the incentives, and maintain emotional discipline, volatility can be a source of signal, not merely noise. It reveals stress points. It shows where narratives are thin. And it often precedes structural change—new regulation, better protocols, smarter design. *Volatility precedes maturity; it doesn't preclude it.*

Indeed, one could argue that the path toward crypto's eventual stability—if such a destination exists—must go through volatility, not around it. Just as emerging markets experience wild swings before institutional confidence settles in, so too must crypto undergo its convulsions before coherence emerges. The challenge is not to eliminate volatility but to survive and learn from it. And for those who mistake the noise for the game, the game for the noise, or fail to understand either, the cost will be real and repeated.

To navigate crypto effectively is to recognise that volatility is not an anomaly, not a distraction, and not a brief phase—it is the defining texture of the space. The question is not how to avoid it, but how to interpret it. *Only then can volatility become an asset rather than a liability.*

Custody, Hacks, and Counterparty Risk

Few retail participants grasp the extent to which simply *holding* crypto carries risk. Unlike traditional financial systems, where intermediaries such as banks and brokerages absorb, underwrite, and manage layers of custodial exposure on behalf of clients, crypto's decentralised ethos pushes these responsibilities directly onto the end user. This shift from delegation to self-custody has philosophical appeal—sovereignty, control, censorship-resistance—but it also creates profound operational and psychological challenges. *The risk of loss in crypto is not theoretical; it is technical, behavioural, and often permanent.*

The most visible manifestation of custodial risk is the collapse of centralised platforms—exchanges, lending desks, and broker-dealer hybrids that hold user funds in pooled wallets. Time and again, these platforms have failed spectacularly. From Mt. Gox in 2014 to FTX in 2022, the pattern is familiar: opaque governance, misused client assets, regulatory arbitrage, and flawed or non-existent auditing frameworks. Retail users, seduced by convenience, entrust assets to institutions whose balance sheets they cannot see, whose solvency they cannot verify, and whose operations they do not understand. *The result is asymmetric risk: full downside exposure with none of the protections that come with regulated custodianship.*

To understand why this persists, one must appreciate the paradox of crypto infrastructure. Centralised exchanges (CEXs) dominate crypto markets not because they reflect crypto's decentralised ideals, but because they offer frictionless access, fast execution, and liquidity aggregation that decentralised platforms have yet to match. For the average user, trading on Binance or Coinbase is significantly easier than interacting with a self-custodied wallet or a decentralised exchange (DEX). But this convenience comes at a price: users relinquish control over their private keys, becoming unsecured creditors in jurisdictions that often offer little legal recourse. *Not your keys, not your coins* is more than a slogan—it is a warning.

Even platforms that appear robust may be structurally fragile. Many lend user deposits to generate yield or deploy them in liquidity pools that are exposed to smart contract vulnerabilities. Some operate without clear jurisdictional oversight, relying on patchwork compliance strategies to attract international clients. In practice, this means that a user depositing funds into a platform may be unknowingly exposed to leverage, illiquidity, or misappropriation. *Counterparty risk in crypto is not limited to bad actors; it extends to well-intentioned but poorly governed intermediaries.*

For those seeking to mitigate these risks, self-custody is the natural response. But this too introduces complexity. A private key—essentially a long, randomly generated number—confers absolute control over a crypto wallet. Lose it, and the assets are irretrievable. Share it, and the assets can be stolen. Store it improperly, and you may fall victim to phishing attacks, SIM swaps, or physical theft. Unlike a bank account, there is no customer service line, no password reset, no legal path to restitution. *With great power comes great irreversibility.*

There are, broadly, three primary self-custody models. The first is the software wallet—a digital application, often on a mobile device or desktop, that stores private keys locally. These are convenient and widely used, but susceptible to malware, device compromise, and social engineering. The second is the hardware wallet—a physical device that stores private keys offline, such as Ledger or Trezor. These are more secure but introduce usability trade-offs and require careful handling. The third is multi-signature custody—where multiple keys are required to authorise a transaction. This model is used by sophisticated investors and institutions, but requires coordination and technical expertise.

Each model introduces its own version of operational risk: how are keys generated? Where are they stored? Who has access? What happens in the case of death, incapacitation, or team dysfunction? These questions, trivial in theory, become existential in practice. Many early crypto adopters have lost access to life-changing sums through simple user error—mistyped passphrases, lost devices, untested recovery procedures. *Self-custody is not just about security—it is about process discipline, redundancy planning, and psychological resilience.*

To address these challenges, a growing number of professional custody solutions have emerged. These include regulated trust companies, institutional-grade vaults, and insured cold storage providers. Entities like Anchorage, BitGo, and Coinbase Custody offer secure storage options for large holders, often backed by insurance and external audits. While these offerings reintroduce some of the centralisation crypto was meant to avoid, they also provide a necessary trade-off between autonomy and operational robustness. For many investors, *the question is not decentralisation versus centralisation, but which risks they are better equipped to manage.*

Beyond custody, the ecosystem is rife with counterparty exposure embedded in smart contracts, liquidity pools, and staking protocols. Users who lock tokens into DeFi platforms are often unaware of the smart contract dependencies involved. Code bugs, oracle failures, and governance attacks have drained hundreds of millions from supposedly "audited" contracts. And because most DeFi protocols are permissionless, exploits are not legally actionable—they are, by definition, permissible within the logic of the code. *In crypto, what is technically possible is often socially irreversible.*

Take the example of the Wormhole bridge hack in 2022, where an attacker exploited a vulnerability in cross-chain messaging to mint unauthorised tokens, draining over $300 million in assets. The bridge was backed by major investors and had undergone audits, but the attack vector was still missed. Such incidents highlight a core reality of decentralised finance: security is probabilistic, not guaranteed. *Audit does not mean safe; it means tested under known conditions.*

Layered on top of these technical risks are jurisdictional uncertainties. Crypto is a global asset class with fragmented regulatory treatment. In one country, a platform may be fully licensed; in another, it may be under investigation or banned entirely. Users often have no idea where their counterparties are domiciled, what legal frameworks apply, or which insolvency procedures govern disputes. This legal opacity exacerbates counterparty risk. Unlike traditional financial systems—where deposit insurance, bankruptcy courts, and enforcement agencies provide a safety net—crypto often operates in legal grey zones where *code is law* until the law arrives.

None of this is to suggest that crypto custody is unworkable. But it is to say that *custody in crypto is an active decision, not a passive default.* Investors must choose where and how to hold assets with intentionality—balancing usability against security, trustlessness against redundancy, and autonomy against support. No solution is risk-free. But each comes with trade-offs that must be understood, not assumed.

Pragmatically, there are several emerging best practices. First, use centralised exchanges only for execution—not for storage. Withdraw funds after trades settle. Second, for meaningful sums, invest in a reputable hardware wallet, learn how it works, and test recovery procedures in advance. Third, for those managing institutional or multi-party assets, implement multi-signature or key sharding strategies that distribute control across trusted individuals or devices. Fourth, for assets deployed in DeFi, limit exposure to well-audited protocols, stay current with governance developments, and cap allocations based on risk tolerance.

And finally, always assume that failure is a possibility. Not because crypto is inherently flawed, but because any system—especially a young one with asymmetric incentives—carries structural fragilities. The aim is not to eliminate risk, but to surface it, understand it, and prepare accordingly. *In crypto, custody is not a technical task; it is a fiduciary responsibility.*

Behavioural Bias in a 24/7 Market

The crypto market never sleeps. It does not close for holidays, pause for lunch, or defer action until the morning bell. This temporal structure—always on, always moving—is not incidental; it is fundamental. Unlike traditional markets that impose rhythms through trading hours, circuit breakers, and institutional cycles, crypto's infrastructure is anarchically fluid. Every tick of price, every meme, every announcement can ripple through global exchanges at 3am just as easily as at 3pm. For the individual investor, the consequence is clear: *the market is always open, and so too is your temptation.*

This round-the-clock accessibility preys not merely on convenience, but on cognition. Human decision-making is not designed for uninterrupted vigilance. The same heuristics that evolved to help us avoid predators and conserve energy are now deployed—often dysfunctionally—in the face of price charts, app notifications, and social media hysteria. *What feels like a strategic response to market movement is frequently just an emotional reaction to noise.* Understanding the behavioural traps triggered by this environment is not just academic; it is a matter of financial survival.

Start with **availability bias**—the mental shortcut that causes us to overestimate the importance of information that is recent, vivid, or widely circulated. In a crypto context, this often manifests as overreactions to headlines, tweets, or token pumps. The deluge of 24/7 updates, memes, and hype-driven narratives crowds out long-term thinking. In such an environment, *the loudest story often feels like the most important one,* regardless of its actual substance. Traders chase momentum not because they've evaluated fundamentals, but because they fear missing out on the next vertical move.

This segues directly into **FOMO**—Fear of Missing Out—a uniquely corrosive force in the psychology of speculative markets. Crypto, with its moonshots and meme coins, amplifies FOMO to pathological levels. The promise of asymmetry—of turning £500 into £500,000—encourages extreme risk-taking, especially during bull markets. Retail participants, observing the sudden wealth of early adopters, internalise a narrative of inevitability: *if I don't act now, I'll be* *left behind forever.* This mindset erodes caution, distorts time horizons, and creates the conditions for boom-bust cycles. Entire market phases—DeFi Summer, NFT Mania, Alt Season—are driven more by social contagion than by sound analysis.

Compounding this is the phenomenon of **loss aversion**, a bias wherein the psychological pain of losing is roughly twice as powerful as the pleasure of winning. In volatile markets like crypto, this bias exerts a distorting gravitational pull. Investors often hold onto losing positions, not because they believe in the asset's long-term value, but because they cannot emotionally tolerate crystallising the loss. *"I'll sell when I break even"* becomes a recurring mantra—one that often ends in deeper drawdowns. Ironically, the same traders who hesitate to exit losing positions will quickly dump winners at the first sign of profit, locking in small gains while letting large losses fester.

Then there is **recency bias**, the tendency to overweight recent experiences when forecasting future outcomes. If a token has gone up 200% in a month, traders assume it will continue to rise. If it has collapsed 90%, they may assume it is doomed. In reality, crypto assets are often cyclical, non-linear, and driven by exogenous catalysts—technological, regulatory, or macroeconomic. But the human mind prefers trend extrapolation over probabilistic reasoning. *What just happened feels like what will keep happening.*

The architecture of crypto platforms further exacerbates these psychological pressures. Most exchanges are built less like financial institutions and more like casinos. Visual dashboards display real-time P&Ls, top movers, leaderboard rankings, and countdowns to token launches. App interfaces glow with colour-coded signals and gamified rewards, nudging users towards action rather than reflection. *These design choices are not accidental—they are behavioural engineering meant to maximise engagement, not investment outcomes.*

Consider the impact of **anchoring**—the cognitive bias in which individuals fixate on arbitrary reference points. If an asset once traded at £100 and now sits at £30, investors may believe it is undervalued, regardless of whether its fundamentals have deteriorated. Conversely, if a token launched at £1 and now trades at £20, many will assume it's "expensive," even if adoption has soared. Anchoring distorts our sense of value, often leading to mispriced expectations and irrational entry points.

Adding to this is the feedback loop created by **social proof**. Traders look to others for cues on what is valuable, especially in uncertain environments. Crypto communities—Reddit threads, Telegram groups, Twitter influencers—function as collective sentiment machines. When prices rise, optimism compounds. When prices fall, panic spreads. The echo chamber effect can be intense: if everyone in your feed believes in a coin's future, dissent becomes psychologically expensive. *Many investors are not* *making independent decisions; they're outsourcing conviction to the crowd.*

Importantly, these behavioural traps are not limited to novices. Even sophisticated investors fall prey to them, especially under pressure. The 24/7 nature of crypto creates fatigue, erodes focus, and encourages short-termism. The absence of scheduled trading windows means that *every moment feels actionable.* There is always one more chart to check, one more coin to research, one more opportunity slipping away. This constant stimulation creates decision fatigue—a cognitive state in which judgement degrades over time, leading to impulsive trades and strategic drift.

So how does one resist? Not with willpower alone. Behavioural defences must be structural, not situational. One approach is **automation**—pre-committing to entry and exit rules, portfolio rebalancing schedules, and position sizing before emotional variables enter the frame. Tools like limit orders, algorithmic strategies, and rebalancing bots can act as guardrails against irrational overtrading. Another approach is **environmental design**—deliberately reducing exposure to information flows that provoke action without insight. This might mean disabling notifications, curating who you follow, or limiting logins to set times of day.

Moreover, investors must adopt **meta-cognition**—the practice of thinking about one's own thinking. This means recognising when you are acting from emotion rather than logic, when you are reacting rather than reasoning. It requires journaling decisions, reviewing mistakes, and stress-testing convictions against contrarian views. *The goal is not perfect objectivity—an illusion—but structured awareness.*

Finally, a disciplined crypto strategy must include *strategic disengagement*. Just because markets are open doesn't mean you should be. The most successful investors are those who treat crypto not as a video game, but as an allocation decision within a broader portfolio framework. They define goals, articulate theses, and accept that missing out on some gains is the price of avoiding catastrophic losses. In a market designed to trigger the worst parts of human psychology, *doing less can be a feature, not a flaw.*

The 24/7 nature of crypto is both its superpower and its psychological trap. It invites participation but penalises undisciplined presence. The investor who understands their own mind—its limits, biases, and blind spots—holds the most enduring edge. Not because they will predict the next bull run, but because they will survive what others don't. *And in crypto, survival is strategy.*

Chapter 5
A Framework for Rational Exposure

The single most pervasive error among crypto participants is rarely choosing the wrong asset; it is choosing the right asset in the wrong size. Volatility alone does not erode wealth—misjudged exposure does. The line between a manageable drawdown and a full-blown emotional crisis is rarely the coin itself; it is how much of your financial and psychological capital you commit. In a market where 70 per cent drawdowns are more common than quarterly earnings reports, sizing ceases to be an afterthought and becomes central to sustainable participation. Without a rational framework for allocation, even the clearest conviction can metastasise into recklessness.

At the heart of this framework lies a deceptively simple truth: enormous allocations are unnecessary for crypto to exert meaningful influence in a portfolio. A thoughtfully chosen 1–5 per cent position, integrated with care and actively managed, often suffices to express a view on the future while safeguarding the present. This is not timidity; it is disciplined stewardship. Unlike traditional equities, whose trajectories are anchored in earnings and dividends, crypto remains structurally experimental. Its future is negotiated not only in code, but in courts, cabinets, and collective perception. Exposure, therefore, must be guided more by balance than by enthusiasm.

Yet restraint alone is insufficient. A rational approach begins with a personalised investment thesis. This is far from an abstract exercise. Your thesis must be specific: is your allocation motivated by faith in digital gold? A belief that programmable finance is inevitable? Or a desire for exposure to decentralised infrastructure? Each rationale demands different assets, holding periods, and risk considerations. Without a coherent thesis, a crypto portfolio is indistinguishable from a gamble; coherent conviction underpins coherent allocation.

From conviction arises risk budgeting. Crypto does not fit neatly into conventional categories of growth, income, or capital preservation. It behaves like an asset but moves like an option, blending characteristics of commodities, technology stocks, and speculative instruments. Portfolio inclusion must therefore account not just for potential returns, but for risk integration. Age, income stability, liquidity needs, and loss tolerance all shape appropriate exposure. A 30-year-old with a flexible career and substantial savings will approach a 5 per cent allocation differently from a 65-year-old retiree drawing down capital.

The next question is uncomfortably candid: can I afford to lose this money? This is not rhetorical. Every pound invested should be treated—both mentally and mathematically—as potentially irrecoverable. This is not fatalism; gains are possible. Yet the path to reward is littered with gut-wrenching volatility, regulatory uncertainty, and market dislocations. If you cannot endure a halving of your investment without upheaval, your position is mis-sized. The oft-repeated phrase "only invest what you can afford to lose" may be cliché, but its core truth is existential: crypto's optionality pays only to those who survive the ride.

This chapter is neither cheerleading nor alarmist. It is about structure. Crypto attracts extremes—of returns, rhetoric, and behaviour—but intelligent exposure demands proportion. Rational sizing is not risk aversion; it is risk awareness. It requires clarity about what you own, why you own it, how much you own, and what it could realistically do to your broader financial stability. Too little exposure renders the exercise moot; too much transforms an investor into a zealot—or a casualty.

There is no universal rule, and this chapter does not pretend otherwise. Yet certain principles endure: clarity over hype, frameworks over FOMO, resilience over reaction. In a landscape that rewards boldness but punishes recklessness, the challenge is to be precise without paralysis. This is not about predicting the next breakout token; it is about defining the role crypto plays in your financial identity, and constructing a system that reflects that role rationally, consistently, and durably.

A well-calibrated crypto position is more than a trade—it is disciplined belief made tangible. It embodies your time horizon, worldview, and risk calculus. Crucially, it is structured so that you can endure—through bull markets, bear markets, and all the irrational exuberance in between. By the close of this chapter, you should not only understand the mechanics of rational exposure, but also possess the clarity and confidence to implement it. In a market designed to seduce through chaos, structure is the anchor—and this chapter is that anchor.

The 1%–5% Rule: Position Sizing for Sanity

There is no shortage of stories about early crypto investors who turned a modest allocation into life-changing wealth. But far fewer headlines are written about the millions who overallocated, panicked during a drawdown, and exited at a permanent loss. These stories don't generate clicks—but they dominate the lived experience of retail participants. *The defining difference between a volatile asset that enhances your portfolio and one that erodes it isn't price movement—it's position size.* The 1%–5% rule exists not to limit upside, but to safeguard resilience. In a domain defined by exponential returns and extreme downside, *modest exposure is not just prudent—it is strategic.*

Unlike equities or bonds, crypto assets operate without intrinsic cash flows, are subject to evolving regulation, and often trade on sentiment rather than fundamentals. These characteristics do not make them valueless, but they do make them volatile. Bitcoin's 80% drawdowns, Ethereum's high-beta swings, and the boom-bust cycles of altcoins are not bugs of the system—they are features of an emergent asset class finding its footing. Amidst this volatility, *psychological survivability becomes as important as financial viability.* Position sizing is not simply about statistical diversification—it is about ensuring you can hold through turbulence without emotion hijacking your strategy.

A 1%–5% allocation forces discipline. At 1%, your crypto holdings are allowed to compound quietly, without dominating your financial attention or distorting your risk appetite. At 5%, you still maintain a meaningful stake in one of the most asymmetric opportunities in modern finance—but one that cannot sink your financial future. This range acts as a volatility buffer, absorbing sharp drawdowns without pulling the emotional ripcord. Most importantly, *it enables you to reframe crypto not as a make-or-break bet, but as a high-conviction satellite within a larger, risk-balanced portfolio.*

Consider the practical mathematics. If a 2% crypto position falls by 70%, your overall portfolio experiences a 1.4% hit. That is painful, but manageable. It does not trigger panic. It does not require you to liquidate other assets or rethink your retirement plan. It is simply volatility contained. Conversely, if crypto rallies 10x, a 2% position becomes 20% of your portfolio—enough to rebalance, de-risk, and still materially benefit from upside. This asymmetric outcome—where potential gains dwarf capped losses—is at the heart of why a small position can still yield meaningful portfolio impact. *The 1%–5% range does not neuter opportunity; it tames risk while preserving upside.*

Critics of such modest sizing often argue that small allocations are pointless—that they lack the conviction needed to move the needle. But this misunderstands the nature of compounding and risk-reward asymmetry. The goal is not to guess correctly and go all-in. The goal is to build a position size that is large enough to matter if you're right, but small enough to survive if you're early, wrong, or simply unlucky. *The most sustainable strategy in crypto is not being right—it's staying in the game long enough to benefit when you are.*

There is also a behavioural dimension. The smaller your position, the easier it is to stay rational. Investors who overweight crypto tend to track price obsessively, anchor their self-worth to market performance, and oscillate between euphoria and despair. This erodes decision quality. It tempts short-term reactions at the expense of long-term conviction. A well-sized position, by contrast, grants psychological distance. It lets you think in years, not hours. It lets you observe market cycles with curiosity, not panic. It transforms crypto from an obsession into an allocation.

Financial advisors, family offices, and institutional allocators have converged—often independently—on the 1%–5% rule not because of groupthink, but because of empirical observation. This range consistently balances risk and relevance. It reflects crypto's current maturity level and fits coherently within broader portfolio theory. For individuals without institutional support, this heuristic is even more important—it acts as a constraint against the emotional overexposure that social media and bull markets constantly incentivise.

Still, the right size is never just about percentages. It must be anchored in personal context. A 28-year-old engineer with high income, low expenses, and a long investment horizon might reasonably allocate closer to 5%—or slightly more—without risking ruin. A 60-year-old retiree with fixed income needs and a short runway should likely lean towards 1% or less. The rule is not a rigid formula, but a principled boundary—a sanity check against the distortions of hype and herd behaviour.

Moreover, sizing should not be static. As markets mature, as your conviction deepens, and as your life circumstances evolve, your crypto allocation can evolve too. But that evolution must be grounded in process, not emotion. Rebalancing is not just a portfolio mechanic—it is a discipline that reminds you: crypto is part of your financial system, not the whole of it. *When exposure grows by accident rather than intent—usually after a bull run—it must be trimmed back to balance, not fuelled further out of greed.*

The great irony of crypto is that its largest risks are not technical or regulatory—they are behavioural. Position sizing is the most powerful behavioural tool available. It lets you participate in innovation without betting the farm. It allows you to sleep at night without ignoring opportunity. It is the difference between being a speculator chasing upside and being an investor building durable wealth. In crypto, restraint is not weakness—it is strategy.

Viewed through the right lens, the 1%–5% rule is not a limitation; it is a design principle. It acknowledges uncertainty while still expressing belief. It provides a stable bridge between conviction and caution. It makes room for risk without requiring you to surrender stability. And it frames crypto participation not as a binary decision—"in or out"—but as a calibrated spectrum of intelligent exposure.

In markets built on exponential change and unpredictable cycles, your greatest edge is not prediction—it is preparation. Position sizing is preparation. It is the quiet foundation beneath every sustainable crypto success story. And it is one of the few levers fully within your control. Whether you believe crypto is the future of finance or simply an optional hedge against monetary experimentation, your exposure must match your thesis, your tolerance, and your reality. The right size is not the one that impresses others—it is the one that lets you endure. And over the long arc of investing, *endurance is what compounds.*

Defining Your Crypto Thesis

The worst reason to invest in crypto is because someone else did. Yet this is precisely how most retail exposure begins—through osmosis, hearsay, and borrowed conviction. A friend made money on a token you've never heard of. A podcast host says it's still early. A subreddit calls it "generational wealth." Somewhere in the noise, action replaces clarity. The result is not an investment strategy, but a reactive stance—chasing narrative velocity instead of grounded belief. The antidote is building a personal crypto thesis: *a structured, evidence-informed rationale that defines what you believe, why you believe it, and how those beliefs translate into exposure.*

Unlike traditional asset classes, crypto resists easy categorisation. It is not a monolith. It is a sprawling, experimental ecosystem encompassing monetary protocols, decentralised finance platforms, non-fungible assets, infrastructure tools, and social coordination experiments. Each of these categories contains radically different risk profiles, technological designs, and market dynamics. To navigate this landscape intelligently, investors must make philosophical and practical choices. Not what *the market* believes—but what *you* believe, in a way that can withstand scrutiny.

A sound thesis begins with a use-case hypothesis. What is the fundamental utility of the asset or protocol you're considering? If you're looking at Bitcoin, your thesis might be rooted in its properties as a decentralised, non-sovereign monetary asset. That leads to further inquiry: Do you believe the world needs such an asset? Do you believe Bitcoin is the best candidate? How does this belief compare to gold, sovereign bonds, or other stores of value? This is not academic posturing—it is the scaffolding that allows conviction to be tested rather than assumed.

If Ethereum is in focus, the questions shift: Do you believe in the need for a programmable, decentralised settlement layer? Do you understand how Ethereum's base layer differs from the applications built on top of it? Are you assessing it as a tech platform, a coordination substrate, or an investment in digital infrastructure? Each framing leads to different expectations about revenue models, security trade-offs, regulatory risks, and network effects. Your thesis must be clear about what Ethereum is to you—because its ambiguity to others will be reflected in price volatility.

The most robust theses are anchored in time horizon. Crypto is a long-duration asset class masquerading as a short-term game. Daily price action obscures the fact that most serious protocols are still in their infancy. Networks like Solana, Avalanche, and Arbitrum are early-stage infrastructure projects—judging them on 30-day returns is akin to evaluating Amazon in 1997 based on quarterly web traffic. If your belief is that decentralised computing or open financial rails will gain traction over a decade, then your portfolio should be constructed to reflect that horizon—not the dopamine loops of daily candles.

This is where personal context becomes paramount. A graduate student with a five-year career runway and no dependents may rightfully approach crypto differently than a mid-career professional funding children's education or a retiree preserving wealth. There is no universal thesis—only the intersection of macro conviction and personal circumstances. Building your thesis requires honest introspection: *What am I optimising for—growth, protection, access, or experimentation? What can I afford to be wrong about? What will I regret missing out on?* These are not theoretical questions. They shape everything from allocation size to asset selection.

A mistake many investors make is importing other people's convictions wholesale. This leads to a patchwork portfolio: a little bit of Bitcoin for store-of-value, some Ethereum "just in case," a few DeFi tokens because someone tweeted about APYs, and maybe a gaming token because "it's early." What results is not strategy, but noise. Every position becomes a source of stress rather than insight. A personal thesis, by contrast, acts as a decision filter. It tells you what *not* to buy, how much to own, and when to walk away. *It replaces impulse with intention.*

To illustrate, consider two investors with different but coherent theses. One believes that Bitcoin is the only crypto asset that matters, based on its monetary properties, decentralisation guarantees, and predictable issuance. This investor allocates a fixed portion of their portfolio to BTC, ignores all altcoins, and views price volatility as noise relative to a 10-year horizon. Another investor believes that decentralised financial infrastructure will challenge traditional banks, so they build exposure to Ethereum, Uniswap, Aave, and Chainlink, viewing them as part of a future-proofed financial stack. Both are acting on defined beliefs, not speculation by proxy. *It is not their thesis that guarantees success—it is their clarity.*

Conviction must also evolve. A good thesis is not static; it is falsifiable. If a protocol fails to deliver promised upgrades, loses developer traction, or becomes structurally compromised, your thesis must be willing to adapt—or dissolve. Likewise, if real-world adoption accelerates, use-cases mature, or regulatory clarity improves, conviction can justifiably deepen. *Your thesis should be alive—a dynamic reflection of evidence, not a shrine to sunk cost.* The moment you can no longer explain your crypto positions in one paragraph without using someone else's words, it's time to reassess.

Many confuse a thesis with a prediction. But a thesis is not a forecast—it is a framework. You do not need to predict prices. You need to understand drivers. For example, if your belief is that rising sovereign debt and fiat debasement will drive demand for crypto assets, you are making a macroeconomic assertion, not a price prediction. That assertion can then be tested against data: capital flows, monetary policy trends, inflation correlations, and adoption patterns. The stronger the evidence, the stronger the thesis. If the evidence weakens, so should the conviction.

A mature thesis also accounts for the *how*, not just the *what*. How will your crypto exposure be implemented? Will you hold spot assets directly, use ETFs, participate in staking, or engage with DeFi protocols? Each path introduces different risks: custody, slippage, counterparty exposure, or tax complexity. Your thesis should not merely dictate which assets you hold—it should inform how you hold them, why, and with what contingencies.

None of this requires being a technical expert. You do not need to read whitepapers or audit smart contracts. But you do need to think clearly, sceptically, and independently. In a domain where noise is constant and credibility is often performative, *clarity is a superpower*. A coherent crypto thesis is not about pretending to know the future—it's about defining what kind of uncertainty you are willing to own, and on what terms.

Lastly, a thesis brings peace of mind. In bull markets, it keeps you from overreaching. In bear markets, it keeps you from capitulating. When friends make quick profits or sensational losses, your thesis provides an internal compass. It does not remove risk, but it contains it. *It makes investing in crypto feel less like gambling and more like stewardship—of capital, conviction, and attention.*

The chaos of the crypto landscape rewards those who move with clarity, not velocity. By defining your crypto thesis, you reframe the space from a speculative free-for-all into an investable domain, with logic, structure, and boundaries. It is not the brilliance of your thesis that will determine your success—it is its coherence, adaptability, and alignment with who you are as an investor. And that clarity—grounded, self-generated, and earned—is ultimately your greatest edge.

Risk Budgeting: Crypto vs the Rest of Your Portfolio

The most dangerous mistake in crypto is not losing money—it's misunderstanding what you risked in the first place. For most investors, losses in volatile assets aren't just numerical—they're psychological, behavioural, and often disproportionate to the size of the actual position. The difference lies in context. An investor with £5,000 in Bitcoin, whose total net worth is £100,000, is taking a very different risk than someone with the same amount but a £20,000 net worth, or someone allocating it within a leveraged portfolio. Position size is only one part of the equation; the rest is how it interacts with the total architecture of your financial life. *Risk budgeting*—the act of deliberately allocating exposure across assets based on their volatility, correlations, liquidity, and personal constraints—is the difference between informed investing and blind speculation. In crypto, it's not optional. It's foundational.

Cryptocurrencies live at the far end of the risk spectrum. They are structurally volatile, relatively illiquid, regulatory-adjacent, and operationally exposed. They are also asymmetrically promising. This combination creates an intellectual dilemma: how does one responsibly include a highly risky, highly uncertain, and highly narrative-driven asset class into a long-term portfolio designed for stability, growth, or wealth preservation? The answer is not to ignore crypto. Nor is it to "go all in." It is to *risk-budget* with discipline and clarity—embedding crypto in the portfolio with eyes wide open, not shut with hope.

Traditional portfolio construction often revolves around asset classes with defined characteristics: equities provide growth, bonds provide income and ballast, cash provides liquidity. These relationships, while occasionally unstable, are grounded in institutional memory and decades of data. Crypto lacks that history. It is not yet clear whether its long-term behaviour is closer to equity, commodity, venture capital, or something else entirely. What is clear, however, is that its volatility profile dwarfs most other assets. Bitcoin, considered the most mature crypto asset, has seen drawdowns of over 80% multiple times in its short life. Altcoins often collapse 90–99% in a single cycle. *No serious investor should allocate to such assets without a clearly capped exposure strategy.*

This is where the concept of a *risk budget* earns its place. Unlike capital budgeting, which looks at how much money to allocate, risk budgeting considers how much *volatility, stress*, or *uncertainty* an investor can absorb—emotionally, financially, and temporally. A 30-year-old with stable employment, low living costs, and no dependents might reasonably budget 3–5% of their total portfolio toward crypto—knowing that even a complete wipeout would not compromise their financial future. A 60-year-old nearing retirement, reliant on fixed income and liquidity, might rationally cap exposure at 1%—if at all—positioning it as an optional, not essential, element. *Risk is not about the number—it's about its relationship to everything else.*

Liquidity needs shape this relationship decisively. Crypto assets can, and often do, experience sudden liquidity shocks. Exchanges freeze. Protocols fail. Tokens collapse. Even well-functioning networks are prone to slippage and friction during periods of high volatility. Unlike publicly traded equities or government bonds, there is no guarantee you can exit a position efficiently, especially under stress. This makes crypto uniquely unsuitable as a liquidity reserve. No matter how bullish your thesis, crypto should never be the money you may need to access in a crisis, or the capital that bridges an unexpected expense. *Risk budgeting demands compartmentalisation—not just of capital, but of purpose.*

Income stability is another crucial dimension. Someone with variable income—freelancers, entrepreneurs, or early-stage professionals—faces greater uncertainty around future earnings. Crypto, by its nature, compounds that uncertainty. Allocating significant portions of wealth to a highly volatile, non-yielding asset while having variable cash flows elsewhere creates fragility. In contrast, a salaried professional with predictable income can more confidently absorb volatility, provided the crypto position is bounded and clearly ring-fenced. Again, the issue is not just *how much* you own—it's *how well the rest of your portfolio absorbs it.*

Correlation plays a subtler but increasingly important role. In the early days of crypto, Bitcoin was touted as uncorrelated with traditional markets—a hedge against fiat currency debasement, central bank overreach, or global uncertainty. While partially true in isolated cycles, empirical data since 2020 suggests growing correlation between Bitcoin and equities, particularly tech stocks. This weakens the diversification case and forces a rethink: if crypto behaves like a high-beta component of an equity-heavy portfolio, then its role is not hedging but amplification. *A sound risk budget must adjust exposure in light of actual, not aspirational, correlations.*

Volatility targeting provides one practical approach. Let's say your broader portfolio has an annualised volatility of 10%, and you're considering adding an asset with a volatility of 80%—not uncommon in the crypto world. To maintain risk parity, that crypto position would need to be sized significantly smaller than its notional amount might suggest. This is where the 1%–5% guideline emerges—not as dogma, but as a statistically informed principle. It is not about limitation; it is about calibration. Just as one doesn't allocate 30% of a retirement portfolio to biotech penny stocks, one doesn't allocate indiscriminately to crypto—even if the upside is tempting.

A deeper layer of risk budgeting considers portfolio convexity: how do different exposures behave under extreme conditions? Crypto may crash independently, or it may crash alongside everything else. It may soar when other assets stagnate—or fail when they do. Because the asset class is still emergent, its behaviour under global stress conditions remains under-defined. A war, regulatory crackdown, or cross-border capital control could trigger chaos in ways not yet stress-tested. Prudence suggests that crypto exposure must always be viewed as *risk additive* rather than *risk neutral*, unless clear counter-correlation data emerges.

This conservative stance is not a rejection of crypto's potential. It is a mature response to its unknowns. Investors often confuse risk with volatility, but the true risk is *uncompensated exposure to events you don't understand, can't control, and haven't prepared for.* Crypto, for all its promise, carries precisely that profile. To include it in a long-term portfolio is not foolish—but to do so without a framework is. The job of the investor is not to maximise returns at any cost, but to *align risk with capacity and conviction.* Crypto demands both.

Finally, psychological readiness deserves explicit recognition. Risk budgeting is not merely a mathematical exercise—it is a behavioural one. Ask yourself: *If my crypto holdings dropped 70% tomorrow, would I panic, double down, or do nothing?* Each response reveals whether your allocation was emotionally coherent or merely speculative. If you find yourself constantly checking prices, refreshing apps, or doubting your decisions, your exposure is likely too large. Sound risk budgeting *feels boring.* It does not hijack your attention. It gives you confidence because the downside has already been accounted for.

Risk budgeting is the bridge between personal context and market exposure. It replaces FOMO with structure. It filters narrative through logic. It converts uncertainty into defined boundaries. For investors serious about making crypto part of their portfolio—not as a hobby, not as a punt, but as a considered asset class—this is not a peripheral conversation. It is the centrepiece. It does not matter whether Bitcoin goes to £500,000 or £5,000—what matters is that your exposure made sense either way.

In the end, your crypto allocation is not a referendum on the future of money. It is a referendum on your relationship to risk. Budget accordingly.

What You Can Afford to Lose—Literally

No investment rule is more widely cited or more casually ignored than the maxim: *only invest what you can afford to lose.* It is repeated like a safety label on financial packaging—ubiquitous, vague, and quietly disregarded in moments of euphoria. Yet in the world of crypto assets, this principle is not a disclaimer. It is a requirement. And unlike in more traditional markets, where risk can often be diversified or diluted, crypto carries a uniquely binary proposition. The asset you hold might double. It might disappear. There is no middle ground of polite underperformance or mild tracking error. There is transformation or ruin. So the operative question becomes not just *how much could I afford to lose in theory?*, but *how much am I truly prepared—mathematically, emotionally, and psychologically—to see evaporate without regret?*

The first error most retail participants make is to conflate financial capacity with emotional tolerance. A high-income earner might "afford" to lose £10,000 in a spreadsheet sense—but if that same loss sparks sleepless nights, compulsive checking of price charts, or arguments at the dinner table, the exposure was not affordable in any meaningful way. *What you can afford to lose is not what you can technically survive. It's what you can endure without losing composure, clarity, or conviction.* Investing in volatile assets like crypto while secretly hoping they will never crash is not rational strategy—it's passive denial. And markets are merciless to denial.

The second layer of misjudgement arises from *mental accounting*. Investors often segment their capital into artificial categories: "this is my serious money," "this is my fun money," "this is my crypto moonshot." On paper, these labels appear responsible—they suggest awareness, boundaries, segmentation. But in practice, losses in the "fun" category rarely feel amusing. They bleed into the rest of one's financial and emotional landscape. The moment the same investor who thought they could shrug off a loss starts making reactive decisions—panic selling, revenge buying, abandoning other financial plans to "average down"—the psychological compartment has failed. *There is no such thing as firewalled capital when your identity is involved.*

And that's the deeper issue: *identity exposure*. Crypto is not just volatile—it's narrative-saturated. When you invest in a protocol, token, or NFT project, you are often buying into a belief system. You're not just a passive investor; you are now a stakeholder in a technological future, a participant in a cultural revolution, or a self-proclaimed early adopter. The social media algorithms, influencer echo chambers, and tribal dynamics of the space blur the lines between financial risk and social belonging. This is not benign. Once you have internalised a position as a reflection of your intelligence or foresight, the loss becomes personal. *You are no longer losing money. You are losing face, credibility, and perceived competence.* In that light, the "afford to lose" question becomes existential.

To move from abstraction to practice, the principle needs quantification. A useful exercise is to imagine two extreme but plausible futures for your crypto holdings: one where they drop 90% in value and stay there for years, and one where they 10x within 18 months. In both cases, what would your response be? If a 90% drawdown would lead you to sell in panic, abandon the asset class, or second-guess all your other investments, then your position size is too large. If a 10x gain would distort your broader asset mix, tempt you to quit your job, or inflate your lifestyle, then your position size is too influential. *A well-calibrated crypto exposure is one that neither breaks you in failure nor blinds you in success.*

This principle also extends beyond individual psychology to the architecture of broader financial planning. A healthy investment portfolio should be robust to shocks—both internal and external. Crypto, by its nature, introduces asymmetric shocks: a bug in a smart contract, a sudden regulatory intervention, a coordinated attack on an exchange. These are not tail risks. They are recurring events. Any capital allocated to crypto should be treated as *expended at the point of purchase*. Not because it necessarily will be lost—but because planning for it as unrecoverable forces sharper thinking. It forces margin. It forces humility. It removes the silent assumption of recovery that undermines so many risk decisions.

Institutional investors are often better at this not because they are smarter, but because their governance requires them to treat every line item as probabilistic. They use scenario analysis, stress testing, drawdown models. They assign a probability to ruin, not just a forecast of returns. Retail investors, by contrast, often anchor to best-case outcomes—"this could be the next Ethereum"—while discounting all mechanisms of failure. If individuals approached crypto with the same probabilistic lens as institutions—not just on price projections, but on *value at risk*—they would instinctively resize positions, adjust expectations, and improve survivability. *Success in crypto is not just about identifying winners. It's about avoiding ruin long enough to participate in the upside.*

The tension here is one of scale. Crypto promises the extraordinary. And extraordinary outcomes tempt disproportionate bets. The impulse is understandable: if an asset can return 50x, why would one cap exposure at 1% of the portfolio? Why not swing harder? The answer is behavioural. *It's easy to imagine a future in which you win. It's harder to imagine staying rational along the way.* A 1% position that 50x's becomes 50% of your portfolio. Can you resist trimming it too early? Can you resist doubling down when it retraces? Can you handle the envy, the pride, the fear, the spotlight? *Few people are wired to handle sudden wealth with discipline.* Even fewer are prepared to watch paper gains collapse without panic.

And then there is the question of liquidity. Unlike most traditional assets, many crypto positions cannot be exited smoothly. Low float, thin order books, token lockups, and custodial issues mean that marked-to-market wealth is often *not* accessible wealth. To treat it otherwise is to mistake illusion for optionality. *If you couldn't access your crypto for six months, would your financial life remain intact?* If not, you are not operating within your affordability zone.

Time horizon plays a final, often under-discussed, role. Investors frequently claim to be "long term" until volatility tests their resolve. Crypto is not just volatile—it is *cyclical,* with multi-year boom-and-bust patterns driven by macro liquidity, speculative appetite, and technological maturation. A "long-term" view that cannot survive a 2-year winter is not a plan. It is a wish. *Affordability is not just about surviving loss—it's about sustaining participation.* If your conviction, cash flow, or personal circumstances might change dramatically in the face of drawdowns, then the position size is wrong—regardless of your belief in the technology.

The litmus test is brutally simple: if your crypto exposure went to zero tomorrow, would your life be disrupted? Would your goals be delayed? Would your identity suffer? If the answer to any of those is yes, then you have exceeded your affordable risk. The goal is not to fear crypto—it is to place it in a container so that its volatility does not spill over into the rest of your life.

The point of investing is not to be right. It is to be resilient. Crypto, for all its excitement, demands a level of internal preparation most investors never consider. Not because the asset class is inherently evil, or doomed, or rigged—but because it operates in a domain of extremes. Extremes of return, extremes of behaviour, extremes of culture. And extremes require discipline.

Discipline begins with a number. That number is not your bullish price target. It is the amount you can truly, *literally*, afford to lose. Once you have it, you've given yourself the most valuable thing in all of investing: room to breathe.

Chapter 6
Beyond Buying: Earning, Yielding, and Using

The prevailing notion of cryptocurrency as a high-stakes speculative gamble—essentially a bet on token prices—captures only a fraction of the truth. Most participants, whether retail or institutional, engage with crypto as though it were merely an asset to hold or flip. Beneath the surface, however, lies a sprawling ecosystem of financial primitives and operational mechanisms: staking, lending, liquidity provision, payments, savings. Each offers an alternative to passively buying and waiting. The problem is not that these mechanisms are hidden; it is that they are frequently misrepresented, oversold, or presented as effortless income streams. Crypto can make yield seem effortless—but beneath the veneer are tangible risks of leverage, protocol fragility, and opaque counterparty exposure, all demanding careful scrutiny before engagement.

To grasp what it means to "earn" in crypto, one must first separate yield from safety. Traditional finance, for all its inefficiencies, maintains a recognisable relationship between risk and return. Government bonds yield less than high-yield corporates for reasons easily understood. Deposits insured by central banks earn lower interest than unsecured lending. Crypto, in contrast, often obscures these distinctions through protocol design—or through marketing narratives that deliberately mislead. A lending platform promising 12 per cent annualised returns on stablecoins may brand itself a "high-yield savings account," a phrase crafted more to soothe than to disclose. That 12 per cent is rarely a reflection of sustainable income; it may derive from circular leverage, liquidity mining incentives, or margin borrowing—making the promise seductive, not safe. Calling it income does not make it durable. It makes it enticing.

Staking complicates the picture further. At first glance, staking resembles a dividend: lock up tokens, support network security, receive rewards. Yet staking is not passive; it is bonded risk. In delegated proof-of-stake systems, rewards depend on the performance and integrity of validators. In liquid staking models, derivative tokens introduce additional smart contract risk. The apparent ease of income obscures the reality that one is being compensated not just for committing capital, but for assuming multiple layers of risk—technical, social, and systemic. In crypto, yield often monetises fragility.

The architecture behind each opportunity deserves close interrogation. Are returns genuinely earned from network activity—transaction fees, validator work, real lending demand—or do token inflation mechanisms artificially generate them? Are platforms securing assets with audited contracts, insured custody, and transparent reserves—or are they sleek black boxes? The collapses of centralised lending platforms such as Celsius, BlockFi, and Voyager offer cautionary lessons. Their failures were not lightning strikes but the slow unravelling of mismatched assets and liabilities, promised yields without transparency, and users mistaking a polished interface for genuine security. Convenience is not custody; a friendly UI is not risk mitigation.

Understanding the difference between centralised and decentralised services is equally vital, yet often misunderstood. Centralised exchanges—Binance, Coinbase, Kraken—offer liquidity, fiat onramps, and user-friendly interfaces, but custody, data, and yield are ceded to the platform. In all but name, these are financial institutions. Decentralised protocols—Uniswap, Aave, Lido—allow direct interaction with smart contracts, often without intermediaries or KYC. The trade-off is operational, not ideological: DeFi offers transparency and composability but demands technical literacy, wallet security, and situational awareness. The choice is not "trustless versus trusted"; it is "sovereign complexity versus convenient risk."

A quieter, perhaps more consequential shift is happening outside these ideological poles: pragmatic users who neither adhere to maximalist visions nor passively invest. Freelancers in Argentina receive payment in stablecoins to circumvent currency devaluation. Migrant workers in Southeast Asia leverage blockchain remittances to avoid exorbitant fees and settlement delays. Residents of inflation-prone countries park cash in decentralised dollar equivalents to preserve purchasing power. For these participants, crypto is not an abstract bet on the future—it is a functional tool in the present, used without ideology, permission, or institutional validation.

This divergence matters because it expands the definition of success beyond price appreciation. If a protocol allows a Nigerian software engineer to send $200 home for $0.20 rather than $12, it is already effective, irrespective of short-term token performance. These real-world applications, often overlooked in media narratives fixated on speculative returns, constitute the most durable foundation for crypto's legitimacy. Usage, not valuation, is the signal that endures.

Yet even in these practical applications, complexity persists. Each on-chain action can trigger a taxable event: swapping ETH for a stablecoin may incur capital gains, staking rewards may be considered income, liquidity provision may create realised gains or losses depending on impermanent loss. These obligations are rarely made clear during onboarding. Unlike traditional finance, where institutions often handle reporting, in crypto the responsibility rests entirely on the user. Ignorance is not merely risky—it can be legally consequential.

The structural immaturity of the sector amplifies these challenges. Regulatory frameworks lag behind technology, guidance is inconsistent, and tax software is frequently incomplete. While this is not malicious, it demands heightened diligence. Responsible crypto participation requires internalising operational, legal, and fiscal consequences, not just mastering technical execution.

This chapter pivots on a central tension. Crypto promises sovereignty, flexibility, and yield—but accessing these safely requires evolving from passive investor to informed participant. The old binary of "buy or sell" has expanded into a matrix: lend, stake, bridge, borrow, farm, wrap, unwrap, claim. Each verb implies agency—and risk. Engagement now demands not only capital, but comprehension; not only conviction, but caution.

The focus here is not maximising yield. It is earning with eyes open, acting with intent, and participating with structural awareness. It is about understanding the economic mechanics underpinning platforms, the social trust embedded in protocols, and the lagging legal frameworks. It is a bridge between narrative and nuance, between hype and actual usage, between speculation and practice. It begins with a simple mindset shift: crypto is no longer something you merely buy. It is something you use—or risk being used by. Understanding this distinction is not optional. It is the difference between autonomy and exploitation.

Crypto as Cashflow? Not So Fast

The seductive narrative that crypto assets can be transformed into passive income machines has become one of the industry's most widely marketed ideas—and one of its most poorly understood. Whether it's staking your tokens for yields, lending out stablecoins to decentralised platforms, or engaging in liquidity mining that promises double-digit returns, the language of crypto cashflow has grown louder, glossier, and more aggressive. Yet much of what is described as income in this space is better categorised as repackaged risk: camouflaged leverage, unsustainable incentives, or the financial equivalent of a revolving door. What's advertised as yield may be nothing more than a redistribution mechanism underpinned by inflated tokenomics or circular borrowing.

To be clear, *income* is not inherently dishonest. But its meaning must be interrogated. In traditional finance, income typically derives from underlying economic activity: dividends from business operations, bond coupons tied to credit risk, rent from physical property. In crypto, much of the yield on offer stems from mechanisms designed not to reward productive output but to attract liquidity. These incentives—often paid out in native tokens—can temporarily boost returns while masking structural fragilities. As with any system offering unusually high returns, the first question should always be: *who is paying for this, and why?*

Take staking as a starting point. In proof-of-stake blockchains such as Ethereum, Solana, and Cardano, staking serves a legitimate and necessary function. By locking up tokens, stakers help secure the network and validate transactions. In return, they earn rewards in the form of additional tokens. On paper, this mirrors the logic of a bond—capital is locked, and compensation is offered in return. But the comparison is imprecise. These rewards are often drawn from protocol-level inflation, meaning the total supply of the token increases over time. If the staking yield is 6% but the token supply expands at 7%, the real return is negative. Worse still, these inflationary dynamics can accelerate token depreciation, punishing holders who fail to stake and creating a system where "cashflow" becomes a defensive measure against dilution, rather than an actual profit.

The risks intensify in liquid staking protocols such as Lido or Rocket Pool, which offer derivative tokens in exchange for staked assets. These instruments provide flexibility—allowing users to participate in DeFi while earning staking rewards—but they also introduce new layers of smart contract risk, slashing exposure, and systemic leverage. The more widely these staking derivatives are used as collateral across lending, borrowing, and trading platforms, the more fragile the entire ecosystem becomes. *Liquidity and yield are not free; they are subsidised by risk often invisible to the user.*

The situation becomes even more precarious in the world of crypto lending and borrowing. Platforms like Aave, Compound, and formerly Celsius or BlockFi offered users the opportunity to lend assets—typically stablecoins—in return for interest. While decentralised platforms are generally more transparent, the structure is often built on recursive borrowing: users deposit collateral to borrow more assets, which are then redeployed to farm additional yield. This can create a leveraged loop where risk is multiplied and collateral quality declines. When collateral values fall or liquidity dries up, the system begins to unwind—rapidly and without the buffers seen in traditional finance.

The collapse of Terra's Anchor protocol in 2022 was a masterclass in how "yield" can be weaponised as bait. Anchor promised a 20% fixed yield on UST, a supposedly stablecoin pegged to the US dollar. But this yield was not backed by real lending demand or profitable underwriting—it was sustained by subsidies from the Luna Foundation Guard and the assumption that new capital would continue to flow in. For a time, it worked. Billions of dollars were locked in. But when confidence cracked and redemptions surged, the system collapsed in days, erasing billions in wealth. *The yield was never income. It was an illusion subsidised by unsustainable capital inflows.*

This kind of "yield theatre" remains a pervasive issue. Platforms often present returns without disclosing that rewards are paid in illiquid or volatile tokens, which may have little real market value. APYs are calculated on token prices that fluctuate wildly, distorting the actual return. Moreover, many DeFi protocols incentivise participation by offering governance tokens, which are then used to create new liquidity pools, perpetuating a cycle of farming that has little connection to real-world economic productivity. This is not to say all yield is fraudulent. But the user must discern between *real return on risked capital* and *temporary upside from token inflation*.

So where does this leave the thoughtful investor? First, with a shift in framing. The idea of crypto as "income" should not be rejected outright, but it must be approached with the same scepticism one would apply to any asset offering outsized returns. What are the mechanics of the reward? Is the income denominated in stablecoins or volatile native tokens? Is the source of the yield organic—generated through real lending demand or protocol activity—or synthetic, generated through incentives and inflation?

Second, users must consider the opportunity cost and correlation risk. During bull markets, crypto yields may appear attractive relative to traditional instruments. But during downturns, these yields often evaporate just as prices fall—creating a double drawdown. Unlike traditional bonds or dividend stocks, which may provide consistent cashflow through economic cycles, crypto yields are often procyclical, peaking during euphoria and collapsing during fear. *An investment that loses both principal and income at the same time is not providing diversification. It is compounding exposure.*

Third, and most importantly, is the psychological dimension. Many users are lured into staking or yield farming with the promise of passive income, only to find themselves trapped in active portfolio management. They must monitor token values, smart contract updates, liquidation thresholds, and governance proposals. The notion of passive income dissolves into a full-time responsibility. Moreover, platforms are often built to gamify behaviour—offering badges, multipliers, leaderboard rankings—to drive repeated engagement. The user is not simply harvesting yield. They are participating in a behavioural casino dressed as a bank.

That said, there are real, sustainable examples of crypto cashflow—but they are modest, transparent, and tethered to actual usage. Validators on proof-of-stake networks earn rewards tied to network security. Liquidity providers on stablecoin DEXs like Curve may earn fees from genuine trading volume. Some lending platforms have evolved toward overcollateralised, low-risk lending models with risk tranching and institutional oversight. These opportunities do not promise 20% APYs. But they are more defensible, more durable, and more aligned with traditional concepts of yield. *True income is earned, not promised—and never guaranteed.*

The future of crypto cashflow lies not in promising impossible returns but in building infrastructure that reflects sustainable risk-reward trade-offs. As regulators, insurers, and institutional custodians enter the space, we may see the rise of tokenised bonds, regulated DeFi, and transparent undercollateralised lending. Until then, the onus remains on the user to apply rigour. To look past APYs and ask harder questions. To stop treating cashflow as a magic trick and instead view it as a financial contract—complete with counterparty risk, legal ambiguity, and economic assumptions.

The idea that crypto can replace a paycheque or mimic a pension fund is, at best, aspirational. At worst, it is reckless. Yield should be the *output* of clear-eyed financial reasoning, not the *input* to decision-making. When a platform offers 18% on dollars, the question should not be "How do I get in?" but "Why does this exist—and what happens if it stops?" Income is a powerful financial force. But in crypto, it must be earned with caution, monitored with care, and understood not as a gift—but as a signal of underlying risk.

To treat yield as a substitute for scrutiny is to miss the fundamental truth of crypto's evolving landscape: *there are no free lunches, only misunderstood leverage.* And that misunderstanding, if left unchecked, is what turns yield into ruin.

Centralised Platforms vs Protocols

The surface of crypto may appear uniformly digital, but the terrain beneath reveals two vastly different operating philosophies: centralised platforms and decentralised protocols. While the uninitiated might conflate the two—both offer access to crypto assets, wallets, and yield-generating products—their underlying mechanics, risk profiles, and user responsibilities diverge sharply. Understanding this distinction is not simply academic. It is foundational to any informed engagement with crypto as a financial system.

Centralised exchanges (CEXs) like Coinbase, Binance, Kraken, and Gemini represent the polished, customer-facing interface that many new users first encounter. They offer an experience akin to traditional fintech: slick apps, email logins, custodial wallets, fiat onramps, and customer support desks. These platforms operate with corporate hierarchies, compliance departments, and regulatory obligations in select jurisdictions. For many, they serve as the training wheels of crypto participation—familiar, safe-feeling, and friction-minimising.

But comfort is not a proxy for sovereignty. When using a centralised platform, users are effectively delegating trust to a single institution. The private keys—the cryptographic strings that grant ownership of crypto assets—are held not by the user, but by the exchange. This introduces counterparty risk of the most existential kind. If the exchange becomes insolvent, is hacked, mismanages funds, or is targeted by state actors, users may find themselves locked out of their assets without legal recourse or technical workaround.

The collapse of FTX in 2022 remains a stark and sobering example. Once considered a paragon of institutional-grade trading infrastructure, FTX unravelled in a matter of days amid revelations of internal misuse of customer funds. Withdrawals were halted. Balances evaporated. The illusion of security provided by centralised custody proved fragile—underscoring the industry mantra: *not your keys, not your coins.*

Contrast this with decentralised finance (DeFi) protocols—open-source smart contracts that operate autonomously on public blockchains like Ethereum, Solana, or Avalanche. Instead of interfacing with a centralised database, users interact directly with contracts that execute predefined logic: swapping tokens via automated market makers (e.g., Uniswap), lending assets to liquidity pools (e.g., Aave), or staking collateral to mint stablecoins (e.g., MakerDAO). The infrastructure is peer-to-contract, not peer-to-corporation.

In theory, DeFi returns control to the individual. There are no account freezes, KYC requirements, or service desks. Transactions are settled on-chain, transparently, and—if the code is sound—deterministically. *The protocol becomes the counterparty, and its rules are publicly verifiable.* This architecture embodies the original ethos of crypto: disintermediation, censorship resistance, and self-custody.

Yet such purity comes at a cost. DeFi users must navigate a labyrinth of technical interfaces, understand gas fees, manage wallets, verify contract legitimacy, and bear full responsibility for operational security. There is no password reset for a lost seed phrase, no recourse for sending funds to the wrong address, no FDIC insurance against smart contract exploits. The freedom to transact is matched by the freedom to err—permanently.

The question, then, is not which model is superior in the abstract, but which trade-offs an individual is willing and equipped to accept. *Centralised platforms offer ease at the expense of control; decentralised protocols offer control at the expense of complexity.*

From a financial standpoint, the differences extend to fees, yield structures, and liquidity dynamics. Centralised exchanges may offer competitive trading fees and deep liquidity in major asset pairs, but they often restrict access to niche tokens, limit leverage, and impose withdrawal limits. Their yield products—such as "Earn" features or staking services—are typically wrapped in opaque terms, with the platform acting as an intermediary between the user and the underlying protocol. This can create a misleading sense of passive safety. Users may believe they are earning interest from the exchange, when in fact the platform is relaying returns from an underlying DeFi protocol—adding a layer of hidden risk and fee extraction.

Decentralised protocols, by contrast, offer direct exposure to underlying mechanisms. Users can provide liquidity to a

Uniswap pool, deposit stablecoins into Compound, or stake ETH in a native validator—all without intermediaries. The yields may be higher, but they are unbuffered by central actors and subject to volatility, impermanent loss, and code-level exploits. Moreover, protocol incentives—such as liquidity mining or governance token rewards—can introduce complex incentive dynamics that centralised platforms simplify or mask entirely.

Security is another axis of differentiation. Centralised platforms rely on traditional cybersecurity—firewalls, KYC, multisig cold storage, internal audits—while DeFi relies on smart contract integrity and public scrutiny. Though high-profile CEX hacks have been frequent (Mt. Gox, Bitfinex, FTX), DeFi has its own track record of smart contract exploits (The DAO, bZx, Wormhole bridge, Euler Finance). *Neither model is immune to failure; they simply fail differently.*

Regulatory clarity is also skewed. Centralised platforms operate within national legal frameworks. They are subject to AML/KYC regulations, licensing, and jurisdictional restrictions. This may be an advantage for users seeking legal certainty or compliant institutional engagement. DeFi, on the other hand, operates in legal grey zones. Code is law—but human law still governs many touchpoints, especially in cross-border enforcement, taxation, and liability. For users in regulated environments, this can create uncertainty about the legal standing of DeFi participation.

That said, centralisation and decentralisation are not binary. Many platforms exist along a spectrum. Coinbase, for example, offers a non-custodial wallet that interfaces with DeFi protocols. Binance operates both a centralised exchange and a blockchain (BNB Chain) on which DeFi protocols live. Even within DeFi, protocols differ in governance. Some are governed by decentralised autonomous organisations (DAOs), while others are tightly managed by founding teams. *The reality is not a clean dichotomy but a continuum of control and risk.*

For most users, the optimal strategy may not be purist. It may involve a blended approach: using centralised platforms for fiat onramps, ease of trading, and tax reporting—while selectively engaging with DeFi protocols for specific use cases where transparency, control, or composability are paramount. This hybrid model reflects the practical constraints of most investors: they want exposure, not ideology; security, not sanctimony.

Ultimately, the decision to use centralised platforms versus decentralised protocols is less about technological allegiance and more about *contextual fitness*. A corporate treasurer seeking regulatory compliance may justifiably favour Coinbase Custody. A tech-savvy individual seeking permissionless access to emerging tokens may lean toward DeFi. A remittance user in a capital-controlled economy may require decentralisation to bypass censorship. *Every user operates with different constraints—and should therefore assess tools based on alignment with their unique goals, risks, and capabilities.*

As the infrastructure evolves, the distinctions may blur. Layer-two scaling solutions, decentralised identity protocols, and regulatory sandboxes may reduce the friction of DeFi while retaining its core advantages. Meanwhile, centralised platforms may be forced to adopt more transparent and user-centric custody models under regulatory pressure. The competitive frontier will likely favour systems that combine the *trust architecture of DeFi* with the *usability and accountability of centralised services*.

Until then, one principle remains timeless: *know whom—or what—you are trusting with your assets.* Whether it's a smart contract with 10,000 GitHub commits or a corporate entity with a glossy logo and a board of directors, trust is never free. It is earned, assessed, and—when misjudged—often regretted.

In the end, the decision is not between crypto and traditional finance. It is between *agency and convenience, visibility and abstraction, sovereignty and service.* Centralised platforms and decentralised protocols offer different answers to the same underlying question: *what kind of financial system are you willing to participate in—and at what cost?*

Using Crypto Without Going Full Crypto

You don't need to believe in the end of fiat currency or the virtues of decentralised utopias to use cryptocurrency. You don't need to mine tokens, trade NFTs, or memorise whitepapers. And you certainly don't need to be part of the online cults chanting the gospel of Web3. The quiet truth is that many people use crypto *not because they believe in it, but because it works*. They are not revolutionaries. They are pragmatists. They engage with digital assets in focused, functional ways that solve real-world problems—efficiently, securely, and often with fewer middlemen.

This emerging class of users—call them crypto realists—view digital assets as tools, not ideologies. For them, crypto is neither a bet on a decentralised future nor a political statement. It is a means to an end: to move money across borders without being bled by fees, to preserve savings in inflationary economies, or to access digital financial tools when traditional ones fall short. Their behaviour is not driven by speculative hype or libertarian dreams but by *practical necessity and calculated convenience.*

Consider Ana, a Filipino nurse working in the UK who sends a portion of her earnings home to her family every month. For years, she relied on legacy remittance services, which charged her 6–8% in fees and took up to five days to deliver funds. Now, using a stablecoin like USDC on a platform like Binance or a mobile wallet such as Coins.ph, she can send the same amount to her family in hours—with fees that barely register. Her family receives funds in pesos, which they can spend almost immediately. She doesn't need to believe in blockchain to recognise a cheaper, faster, more transparent system. *She simply knows it works.*

Or take Samuel, a Nigerian freelance web developer who earns income in USD through clients abroad. With access to the local financial system constrained by capital controls, delayed banking, and unreliable infrastructure, crypto offers an elegant workaround. Through stablecoins on Ethereum or BNB Chain, he invoices in dollars and receives payment within minutes, sidestepping bureaucracy and currency volatility. His exposure to crypto is not ideological—it is infrastructural. He is not betting on the future of Bitcoin. He is trying to get paid on time.

This class of users reflects a growing tension in crypto's evolution: between its ideological roots and its practical uptake. Many of the earliest proponents imagined crypto as a comprehensive alternative to the financial system—a parallel economy with its own ethics, institutions, and incentives. But today, adoption is often *partial, selective, and context-specific*. People don't need to adopt crypto wholesale. They just need a problem that crypto solves better than the incumbent options.

Savings in unstable currencies offer another powerful use case. In countries where inflation eats away at earnings—Turkey, Argentina, Lebanon—citizens increasingly turn to crypto not to speculate, but to preserve value. They don't need volatility; they need stability. This is why dollar-denominated stablecoins such as USDT and USDC have gained traction in places where the official exchange rate is a fiction and capital controls restrict access to foreign currency. For these users, crypto is not a vehicle for wealth creation. It is a lifeboat.

There is also growing interest among young, tech-literate users in emerging markets who do not have access to traditional financial products—credit cards, brokerage accounts, or high-yield savings tools. Crypto platforms allow them to earn interest on idle assets, access decentralised lending, or even participate in peer-to-peer insurance pools. Their usage may begin with gaming, micropayments, or airdrops—but it gradually expands into personal finance. These users are not joining crypto because they distrust banks. They are joining because *they've never had banks they could trust to begin with.*

Even in developed economies, crypto is being used without dogma. College students who earn small sums through gig work may use crypto wallets to collect payment internationally. Remote workers move their income into stablecoins to reduce conversion losses. Parents exploring passive income streams may stake tokens without caring much about decentralisation. These users are not buying into grand narratives. They are solving local problems with global tools.

Yet the accessibility of crypto does not imply simplicity. Users who engage without ideological commitment still face real trade-offs. Custodial services may expose them to platform risk; non-custodial options require a baseline technical literacy. Volatility—even in assets marketed as stable—can create unexpected losses. And tax liabilities remain murky, especially for users who treat crypto like cash but fall under capital gains frameworks in their jurisdictions. *Using crypto casually doesn't exempt you from the consequences of misusing it.*

Still, one of the most underappreciated truths about crypto is that it allows for *incremental participation*. You don't need to "go full crypto" to benefit from the technology. You don't need to stake your life savings in a DAO or live off digital tokens in a metaverse economy. You can hold a stablecoin for one week to bridge a payment gap. You can try a decentralised exchange to avoid unfair fees. You can buy a small amount of ETH to test a smart contract and never touch it again. This modularity makes crypto uniquely adaptable—it *invites interaction without demanding conversion.*

Contrast this with the early internet. Accessing its benefits required full infrastructure: a desktop, a dial-up modem, and time to spare. Crypto, by contrast, is becoming increasingly modular. Mobile-first apps, wallet-as-a-service platforms, and fiat-to-crypto bridges reduce onboarding friction. A user doesn't need to understand zero-knowledge proofs or gas optimisation to benefit from crypto's utility. In fact, many don't even know they are using blockchain-based systems. That's the point.

And this modularity is not only a technical feature. It is a philosophical shift. It suggests that crypto adoption can be driven not by evangelism but by *usefulness*. It doesn't require buy-in to radical decentralisation or mistrust of governments. It simply requires a problem that existing systems fail to solve.

Policymakers and institutions often miss this nuance. They tend to treat crypto users as a monolith—speculators, tax evaders, or radical technologists. In reality, the majority of crypto usage in many parts of the world is neither criminal nor revolutionary. It is economic. It is ordinary people hedging inflation, accessing payment rails, or preserving dignity in failing financial systems. Treating all users as speculative actors distorts regulation and threatens to undermine the very people crypto most benefits.

The decentralised finance movement would also do well to take note. Instead of chasing complex tokenomics or ideological purity, developers should focus on *practicality, clarity, and reliability*. Features like on-ramp integrations, intuitive interfaces, fiat offramps, and regulatory compliance matter more than philosophical allegiance. Mass adoption will not come from maximalism. It will come from utility.

There is a growing place for those who engage with crypto on their own terms—those who want a better way to send money, save value, or access financial tools, but who have no desire to be part of a digital revolution. These users are building a bridge between the legacy system and the emerging one—not through theory, but through action.

Crypto doesn't need to be a lifestyle to be useful. It doesn't require allegiance. It requires *function*. And in a world where many financial systems are either broken, exclusionary, or exploitative, that function is becoming increasingly difficult to ignore. Crypto realists—those who use without believing—may end up being the most important drivers of adoption. Not because they proselytise, but because they *prove* that crypto can matter, even when it doesn't mean everything.

Tax Traps and Reporting Realities

A single crypto transaction can trigger a taxable event. Not just selling for fiat, but swapping one token for another, staking for yield, or even receiving an airdrop. In some jurisdictions, just moving your own coins between wallets can raise compliance questions. The world of crypto taxation is not just complicated—it's *counterintuitive*, and dangerously easy to get wrong. What makes this terrain especially hazardous is the false sense of invisibility that digital assets often inspire. Crypto feels like it operates outside the traditional financial system, but the taxman is watching—and increasingly well equipped to do so.

The disconnect between perception and regulatory reality is striking. Many users still believe that small-scale activity, decentralised protocols, or pseudonymous wallets offer a kind of exemption from reporting. This is a myth. In the eyes of tax authorities, crypto is not an exception—it is an *extension* of the financial system, and it is taxed accordingly. The longer that users ignore this fact, the greater the risk they accumulate—not just in penalties, but in compounded liabilities that may prove devastating when finally audited or investigated.

Tax rules around crypto vary significantly by country, but the broad principles are converging. Most jurisdictions treat crypto as property, not currency. That means that every time you dispose of a token—whether through sale, trade, or use—you potentially trigger a capital gain or loss. This applies even if you never cashed out to fiat. Swap ETH for SOL? That's a taxable event. Use Bitcoin to buy a coffee? Taxable. Receive tokens through staking or yield farming? That's ordinary income at fair market value on the day received, followed by capital gains or losses when you later sell.

Even more problematic is the psychological distance between users and their obligations. In the traditional finance world, tax reporting is largely automatic. Brokerages issue annual statements, banks provide interest summaries, employers withhold on your behalf. But crypto places the onus squarely on the user. There are no standardised reporting forms, few transaction summaries, and no built-in tax withholding. You are responsible for tracking every transaction, calculating every gain, and declaring every relevant detail—often retroactively, across multiple wallets, chains, and platforms.

This burden is not just technical. It is *cognitive*. The average investor does not remember what they paid for a token two years ago, or how long they held it before swapping. They may not even realise that some DeFi transactions—liquidity provision, governance rewards, wrapped assets—have tax implications at all. Yet failure to properly track and report these events is not merely an oversight. In many jurisdictions, it is legally actionable.

The risks multiply with complexity. Yield farming, staking derivatives, and lending protocols introduce forms of *synthetic exposure* that can mask real-world tax obligations. A user who deposits ETH into a lending pool and receives a yield-bearing token in return may not realise that this token is treated as a new asset with its own acquisition date and cost basis. If that token later appreciates and is swapped or redeemed, the gain is taxable. Similarly, tokens received from airdrops or forks can be considered income—even if the user never requested or interacted with them. This is not theory. It is enforced precedent in countries like the United States, the United Kingdom, Australia, and Germany.

Some of the most common traps involve stablecoins. Users often assume that swapping between dollar-pegged assets—USDC to USDT, for example—has no tax implication because the nominal value doesn't change. But tax law doesn't measure *nominal* value. It treats each token as a distinct asset with its own cost basis. If you acquired USDC at £0.82 and swap it for USDT at £0.85, you've realised a gain. The fact that both assets are pegged to the same currency is irrelevant. The tax system sees two separate transactions, each with a reportable outcome.

The complexity is further compounded by the fractured nature of crypto recordkeeping. Most users operate across multiple wallets, exchanges, and chains. They may have held assets on Coinbase, traded on Uniswap, and staked tokens via MetaMask—all within the same tax year. Reconstructing a coherent transaction history from these fragments is difficult even for technically sophisticated users. For average investors, it borders on impossible without dedicated tooling.

Fortunately, a robust ecosystem of crypto tax software has emerged—tools like Koinly, TokenTax, and CoinTracker—that integrate with major platforms and help automate the process of cost basis tracking, gain/loss calculation, and jurisdiction-specific reporting. But these tools are not perfect. They depend on proper wallet connections, accurate categorisation of complex DeFi activity, and ongoing user input to resolve ambiguities. And even with these tools, users remain responsible for verifying the final results. Tax compliance cannot be outsourced. It can only be assisted.

The psychological tendency to minimise or rationalise crypto gains is one of the most dangerous biases in this space. Users often believe that small transactions don't matter, or that as long as they reinvest profits, they haven't "really" made money. But the tax system is indifferent to intent. If you received value, it is taxable—whether or not you realised it as cash. This is why even small-scale participants must adopt a reporting mindset. *Clarity is not a luxury. It is a shield.*

There's also a growing risk on the regulatory horizon: automatic reporting mandates. Governments worldwide are now moving to force exchanges and custodians to report user activity directly to tax authorities, much like traditional banks and brokers already do. The EU's DAC8 directive and the OECD's Crypto-Asset Reporting Framework are early examples. Once these systems go live, underreporting will no longer be invisible. It will be flagged by software and pursued automatically. And because blockchain is inherently auditable, authorities can go back *years* once they decide to investigate.

Even more troubling is the false comfort some users derive from decentralised platforms. Just because a transaction took place on-chain without an intermediary does not make it exempt. The blockchain is public. Forensic tools—used by firms like Chainalysis, TRM Labs, and government agencies—can trace flows, identify patterns, and often link addresses to individuals. The era of crypto opacity is ending, and it's not ending with a bang. It's ending with a knock on the door.

Smart investors treat tax compliance not as a nuisance, but as part of their strategy. They track cost basis in real time. They understand the difference between short- and long-term capital gains. They plan their disposals to optimise tax efficiency. They hold assets long enough to qualify for preferential rates. They consider the implications of liquidity events before executing trades. Most importantly, they build portfolios that assume visibility—not invisibility—as the default.

For professionals managing larger sums, tax-efficient structuring is essential. Depending on jurisdiction, crypto may be better held in trusts, corporate entities, or tax-sheltered accounts. Some jurisdictions offer "participation exemption" rules, which can eliminate capital gains taxes under specific conditions. Others allow for offsetting gains with prior-year losses. The variance is wide, but the principle is constant: *structure matters*.

Ultimately, the cost of getting crypto taxes wrong is not just financial. It is legal, reputational, and strategic. Penalties can include fines, interest, and in serious cases, criminal charges. But even short of enforcement, tax ambiguity creates anxiety and limits flexibility. You cannot make informed investment decisions if you don't know their downstream consequences. You cannot use crypto to its full potential if you're walking blind into traps.

The irony is that many crypto users value autonomy and control—yet they relinquish both by ignoring the tax dimension. Real control comes from informed action. From knowing what you owe, why you owe it, and how to account for it properly. In a landscape where regulators are catching up fast and tools are becoming sharper, ignorance is not safety. It is a countdown.

Crypto was built to disintermediate finance, but it does not disintermediate law. Whether you're an enthusiast, a sceptic, or a pragmatic user, the burden of tax remains—and the benefits of clarity compound. You don't need to fear the taxman. But you do need to respect the rules. Because in the end, *what you keep is not what you earn—it's what you account for accurately*.

Chapter 7
Digital Self-Custody: Why It Matters (and Scares People)

When one clasps a gold coin or leafs through a stack of banknotes, ownership is immediate, almost instinctive. In the realm of cryptocurrency, however, possession is an altogether subtler affair, anchored not in tangible objects but in a string of alphanumeric characters known as a private key. Here, holding wealth demands more than comprehension; it demands responsibility. Self-custody, at its essence, is sovereignty incarnate. It entrusts the individual with absolute control over their assets, unfettered by banks, brokers, or centralised intermediaries. Yet this very freedom unnerves even the most technologically adept. Not because it is inherently perilous, but because it dismantles the familiar scaffolding of trust, replacing it with something few have confronted directly: personal accountability for digital security.

The tension between empowerment and trepidation is not theoretical. It unfolds daily across newsfeeds, forums, and social media threads, often punctuated by cautionary tales of irretrievable losses. A single forgotten passphrase, one misclicked link, or a malfunctioning hard drive can erase wealth permanently. Unlike traditional finance, the blockchain offers no customer service, no "forgot password?" option. In this arena, one is their own bank, and with that autonomy comes a weighty custodial responsibility—both psychological and technical.

The mantra "not your keys, not your coins" has achieved near-sacred status among crypto enthusiasts. Its essence is sound: without private keys, ownership is incomplete. Yet, as a practical guideline, it oversimplifies a complex landscape. It presumes that everyone possesses the technical acumen—and psychological resilience—to manage cryptographic keys, wallet software, backups, and phishing risks. It underestimates how alien and daunting these tasks may seem to those accustomed to the simplicity of online banking, and it glosses over the nuanced trade-offs between control and convenience that every investor must consider.

Self-custody, in truth, occupies a spectrum. At one extreme are users who operate entirely offline on air-gapped devices; at the other, those who rely wholly on custodians such as Coinbase or BitGo. Many reside somewhere between these poles, perhaps juggling a MetaMask wallet in a browser or a mobile app with cloud backup. These choices are never purely technical—they are reflections of trust, lifestyle, temperament, and risk philosophy.

For many, custodial services appeal precisely because they feel familiar. Dashboards, logins, and customer support replicate traditional banking's reassuring structure. And yet, history is less forgiving. Mt. Gox's loss of 850,000 bitcoins, QuadrigaCX's founder's death along with access to private keys, and FTX's spectacular collapse—each story underscores the cost of delegating control. Convenience, it turns out, can exact a bitter price.

These failures illustrate not only that custodians can falter, but that they often do so opaquely. Most operate in regulatory grey zones, with inconsistent audits, capital requirements, and client protections. There is no deposit insurance, no government safety net, no legal guarantee of restitution. Trusting a custodian is thus a calculated wager, not a default assurance.

Yet self-custody is no panacea. For every victim of a fraudulent platform, another succumbs to their own errors—misapplied firmware updates, misconfigured smart contracts, or mistaken transfers to incompatible chains. The culprit is complexity, not malice. Though the crypto ecosystem has matured swiftly, its user experience remains delicate. Wallets are improving, yet they are not infallible, and the cost of a slip is often absolute.

So, what does it take to become one's own bank in practice? It begins with mindset. Self-custody is not about mastery of technology; it is about grasping a new framework of digital risk. Security is not a product to purchase—it is a discipline to uphold. Redundancy is not optional—it is insurance. Competence alone is insufficient; one must anticipate fallibility and plan accordingly.

Hot wallets, connected to the internet, offer convenience but invite malware, phishing, and smart contract vulnerabilities. Cold wallets, kept offline, enhance security but demand strict operational discipline. There is no universally correct choice; context dictates. Active NFT traders may prioritise immediacy, while long-term Bitcoin holders might favour hardware wallets in secure storage. Intentionality is paramount: not every crypto owner must embrace maximalist cold storage, but every owner must comprehend the risks they accept.

This friction is palpable. Traditional finance encourages offloading responsibility, relying on centralised entities for security and recovery. Crypto subverts this expectation, insisting that freedom and responsibility are inseparable. The disquiet stems not from incapacity, but from unfamiliarity with full accountability.

Responsibility, however, need not mean isolation. Competent self-custody can be scaffolded: verifying wallet addresses, mastering seed phrases, maintaining redundant backups across secure locations, practising low-stakes transactions, and recognising phishing or scam vectors. It resembles cybersecurity hygiene, though now the stakes are monetary.

And the rewards are substantial. Self-custody offers censorship resistance, permissionless financial participation, and geographic portability unattainable in conventional assets. For those under authoritarian regimes or facing unstable banking systems, it is more than principle—it is lifeline.

The wider lesson is not a universal mandate for self-custody, but a call for comprehension. The aim is strategic clarity, not dogma. Using custodial services requires awareness of outsourced risks; choosing self-custody demands recognition that errors may be irrevocable. Either choice is valid, but only if deliberate.

Ultimately, this discussion is not a campaign for or against any method. It is an invitation to engage thoughtfully with custody, to move beyond slogans and convenience into informed decision-making. Whether holding £100 or £100,000 in digital assets, the question is not whether custody matters, but how well one understands the choice made. In a system designed to eliminate intermediaries, that understanding is the closest semblance of protection.

The Promise and Problem of Private Keys

Control over assets has always implied a certain degree of exposure. In traditional finance, the bank vault protects your savings, but also defines the institution's authority over them. The trust model is externalised: we assume safety not because we manage the mechanisms of custody ourselves, but because someone else—typically a licensed, regulated entity—has made that promise on our behalf. Cryptocurrency collapses this arrangement. With a private key, you don't just access your funds—you *are* the vault. The promise is radical: full ownership, full control, no middlemen. The problem is equally radical: full responsibility, full liability, no recovery hotline.

A private key, technically speaking, is a randomly generated number—long, complex, and practically impossible to guess—which, when paired with a public key, grants access to the underlying digital assets on a blockchain. Whoever holds this key can move the assets. There is no ID check. No login page. No password reset. The system is trustless in the purest sense of the word—trust is replaced by cryptographic certainty. But this design assumes something few people have ever had to do: manage digital sovereignty at the individual level.

The mental shift required to adopt self-custody is not trivial. Most people have never had to think about entropy, seed phrases, device compromise, or key sharding. They've never had to simulate disaster scenarios involving house fires, phishing links, or forgotten backups. Traditional financial infrastructure has long abstracted these risks away. Banks insure deposits. Brokerages offer fraud protection. Cloud services duplicate data across redundant servers. Crypto, in contrast, strips away the abstraction and demands direct engagement with threat modelling. What if you die unexpectedly—can your spouse or child recover your funds? What if your laptop is stolen—have you encrypted your keys? These are not corner cases; they are the core cases.

The promise of private keys lies in their neutrality. Anyone, anywhere, with an internet connection and the correct key, can transact with a blockchain. This is an astonishing achievement. It makes borderless finance possible. It enables financial inclusion for people in countries with no stable banking infrastructure. It allows a Ukrainian fleeing invasion or a Venezuelan escaping hyperinflation to carry meaningful value across borders on nothing more than a USB stick—or a memorised string of words. This is not science fiction. It is reality. And yet, the very attributes that make it powerful also make it fraught with risk.

Most crypto users today do not manage their own keys. They access assets through centralised exchanges—Coinbase, Binance, Kraken—which hold the private keys on their behalf. This arrangement resembles traditional finance more than it does the decentralised ethos crypto claims to champion. Onboarding is easy. Interfaces are familiar. Risk feels abstract. But users who take this route must internalise a blunt truth: if you don't hold your keys, you don't control your assets. What you own is not a self-custodied cryptoasset; it is a platform balance, subject to the solvency, security, and legal obligations of the exchange.

Consider the case of Celsius, the now-defunct crypto lender. Users who deposited assets into Celsius did so under the assumption they retained ownership. In practice, those assets became liabilities on the company's balance sheet. When the firm collapsed, users found themselves classified as unsecured creditors—not asset owners. Their funds were not "lost" through theft or hack; they were lost through misunderstanding of custody. Similarly, in the infamous Mt. Gox hack, users learned too late that their Bitcoin holdings were vulnerable not because they had lost their keys, but because they had never held them in the first place.

Yet self-custody is not a panacea. It replaces institutional trust with technical trust, and that comes with its own failure modes. The simplest of these is loss: a misplaced seed phrase, an accidentally erased drive, a mistaken transaction to an invalid address. But the more insidious failure is *operational fatigue*. Keeping keys secure over months or years demands not just good habits, but ongoing discipline. It's easy to be vigilant for a week. It's hard to maintain perfect security hygiene for a decade. People get complacent. Devices degrade. Threats evolve. And in crypto, *mistakes are not reversible.*

This is the paradox of the private key: it represents both freedom and fragility. The very structure that liberates you from intermediaries also leaves you exposed to your own fallibility. And unlike with a stolen credit card or compromised brokerage login, there is no recourse if you err. The blockchain will faithfully execute the command, regardless of whether it was entered by mistake, under duress, or by a malicious actor. Code does not empathise.

For this reason, many security experts advocate for a *graduated model of custody.* Not everyone needs to manage their entire crypto portfolio in cold storage. Some assets—especially those used for frequent trading or experimentation—may justifiably reside in hot wallets with limited balances. Larger, long-term holdings can be migrated to hardware wallets, paper backups, or multi-signature vaults. The point is not to pursue ideological purity but to practise appropriate risk segmentation. The level of custody should reflect the user's technical aptitude, the size of the position, and the acceptable margin of error.

There is also a growing ecosystem of custody support tools that bridge the gap between full autonomy and complete delegation. Solutions such as MPC (multi-party computation), social recovery protocols, and institutional-grade custodians offer models where access can be decentralised or shared among trusted parties. These hybrid systems aim to preserve the sovereignty of self-custody while mitigating single points of failure. Yet they are not without trade-offs—especially when it comes to transparency, cost, and technical complexity.

The philosophical tension underlying all of this is one of trust versus control. Traditional finance asks us to trust third parties. Crypto asks us to trust ourselves. Neither option is inherently superior; each has failure points. But crypto's innovation is not that it *removes* trust—it's that it *reassigns* it. From corporations to code. From compliance to computation. From institutions to individuals. And for that reassignment to be effective, users must understand the mechanics of private keys—not just what they do, but what they demand.

A private key is not a magic wand. It does not grant immunity from risk. It merely changes the locus of responsibility. To use one well is to accept that you are the final line of defence. That you cannot outsource judgment. That digital wealth, like analogue wealth, is vulnerable to human error. But also that, when handled competently, it becomes more resilient, portable, and censorship-resistant than anything traditional finance can offer.

Ultimately, the debate between custodial and non-custodial models is not binary. It is contextual. It hinges on goals, risk appetites, and life stages. A student experimenting with DeFi may accept more volatility and exposure than a retiree preserving savings. An activist journalist operating under a repressive regime may favour full autonomy, while a corporate treasurer may prefer third-party assurance. The challenge is not to dictate the right answer—but to elevate the quality of the question. What does control mean to *you*? What risks are you willing to bear—and which ones are you outsourcing without knowing it?

Answering these questions requires more than technical guides or YouTube tutorials. It demands introspection, clarity, and intellectual honesty. It requires users to move beyond marketing slogans and confront the real implications of digital self-sovereignty. And while private keys may seem like a niche detail in the broader crypto landscape, they are, in fact, the cornerstone of its promise. Understanding them deeply is not optional—it is foundational.

Hot vs Cold Wallets: Tradeoffs That Matter

The question of where and how to store digital assets is not just a matter of convenience—it's a determinant of risk posture. The distinction between hot and cold wallets is one of the most consequential choices any crypto holder will make, whether they own £500 or £5 million in digital assets. It shapes the likelihood of theft, the accessibility of funds, the level of operational overhead, and the probability of irreversible mistakes. Yet for many, the decision is made haphazardly—driven by app interfaces, market euphoria, or convenience bias rather than by thoughtful, risk-adjusted planning. The result is often either excessive exposure to security vulnerabilities or paralysing complexity that discourages proper usage altogether.

To grasp the implications, we must first strip away the jargon. A **hot wallet** is any crypto storage solution that is connected—directly or indirectly—to the internet. Think of mobile wallet apps, browser extensions like MetaMask, desktop software clients, or even custodial exchange accounts. They are called "hot" because they are online by default, and therefore continuously exposed to potential digital attack surfaces: phishing, malware, keyloggers, compromised browsers, and more. Their advantage is clear: instant access, smooth transactions, user-friendly interfaces, and integration with decentralised applications (dApps). Their drawback is equally clear: *the more connected your keys are, the more reachable they are—by you, and by everyone else.*

In contrast, a **cold wallet** is entirely offline. It might be a hardware device (like a Ledger or Trezor), an air-gapped computer, a paper backup of a seed phrase, or even a series of metal-engraved mnemonics buried in a garden shed. Cold storage removes keys from the attackable digital surface, rendering them impervious to online hacks. But that air gap introduces friction—deliberate, security-enhancing friction. Transactions require deliberate connection, confirmation, and often physical intervention. Cold storage is not about speed—it is about *reducing your operational exposure to zero until you consciously reintroduce it.*

The tradeoffs between these two categories are not binary; they operate on a spectrum. The right answer depends less on ideology than on a matrix of three key variables: *frequency of use, investment size, and technical comfort.*

For example, a user who actively trades tokens across decentralised exchanges may need quick, fluid access. Delays caused by connecting and authorising a hardware wallet could cost them price slippage, lost arbitrage opportunities, or failed bids. In such a case, keeping a capped amount of working capital in a hot wallet—say £2,000—makes sense, assuming the user accepts the elevated exposure and rotates out gains into a safer, offline location.

Conversely, a long-term investor holding £50,000 worth of Bitcoin and Ethereum with no intention of trading should not rely on a browser-based wallet or a mobile app with minimal security. Here, a cold wallet—ideally with redundant backups, secure seed storage, and well-documented recovery protocols—becomes not just advisable, but essential. *If you don't plan to move it soon, secure it as if you may never touch it again—because you might not be around to fix a mistake.*

That brings us to the often-overlooked dimension of *operational continuity*. Digital self-custody is not only about avoiding hackers; it is about making sure that your assets survive your own life events. Can your spouse, child, executor, or trusted partner access your holdings if something happens to you? Are instructions legible, comprehensive, and securely stored? Cold wallets, by their very nature, risk becoming inaccessible not because they are breached, but because no one remembers how to unlock them. Hot wallets tend to at least offer account-based recovery mechanisms (albeit with weaker security), but cold storage is far less forgiving. The absence of centralisation is both its virtue and its Achilles' heel.

There is also the matter of *key exposure during setup*. Many users mistakenly assume that once they purchase a hardware wallet, their security posture is maximised. What they miss is that the critical moment is not usage—it's generation. If you initialise a cold wallet using a compromised computer, or write your seed phrase on notepad software, you've already lost the integrity of your wallet before it ever held value. Cold wallets are secure only if the keys were created and stored under uncompromised conditions. That's a high bar for most users.

Moreover, hybrid compromises often emerge. Users who store a cold wallet's seed phrase in cloud storage, email it to themselves "just in case," or take a photo and back it up to iCloud, have nullified the coldness of their setup. The phrase is now reachable—by attackers, spyware, or third-party services. In such cases, *the illusion of security is more dangerous than the absence of it*.

The optimal model for most people is **tiered custody**. Think of it as compartmentalisation with intention. Small, everyday holdings—comparable to the cash you'd carry in your wallet—can reside in hot wallets. Medium-term holdings might be secured in a software wallet on a secure desktop, with multi-factor authentication. Long-term or generational holdings should be committed to hardware wallets with properly managed backups and redundancy.

The balance between accessibility and resilience should track your actual financial behaviour—not your imagined crypto identity.

This is where technical comfort becomes decisive. A software engineer or crypto-native user may have the confidence to manage multi-sig wallets, custom scripts, and elaborate cold storage configurations. But a doctor, academic, or entrepreneur with limited time and zero interest in key management may be better off using a third-party custody provider with strong legal indemnities, even if that feels like betraying the crypto ethos. *Security is not about purity—it's about reliability.*

Unfortunately, many wallet solutions fail to communicate these tradeoffs clearly. Marketing often exaggerates simplicity ("just plug and play") or security ("military-grade encryption") without acknowledging that *the threat vector is not just technology—it is you.* Your devices, your habits, your backup hygiene. The hard truth is this: *a sophisticated tool in untrained hands becomes a liability.* A well-maintained hot wallet used with vigilance can be safer than a misconfigured cold wallet left to gather dust, forgotten by its owner and invisible to their heirs.

Real-world failures reinforce this point. In 2021, a UK-based investor lost access to over £4 million in Bitcoin stored in a hardware wallet because the seed phrase was mistakenly memorised with one word out of order. There was no way to recover the funds. In 2022, a teenager in New York was charged with stealing $37 million from a DeFi user by exploiting a compromised seed phrase stored in an old email inbox. These are not edge cases; they are foreseeable outcomes of misaligned custody practices.

The decision between hot and cold wallets is not just about how often you plan to use your assets—it is a reflection of your ability to shoulder operational complexity. And it changes over time. A twenty-something building a portfolio may favour fluidity. A forty-something raising children may prioritise recoverability. A seventy-something preparing an estate may focus on clarity of inheritance. *Your wallet strategy should evolve as your life does.*

So how do you make the decision concretely? If you access funds daily, actively interact with dApps, and accept the risks of exposure for the sake of agility, a well-secured hot wallet—perhaps sandboxed on a dedicated device—is pragmatic. If you hold significant value, transact infrequently, and are confident in your ability to document, back up, and manage keys properly, a cold wallet is likely the correct path. If you fall somewhere in between—as most do—layer your approach. Use both, with intention.

There is no universal solution, only situational wisdom. And that wisdom begins with asking the right questions: How much can I afford to lose? How often will I transact? How much technical responsibility am I willing—and able—to assume? If I disappear tomorrow, who can unlock my vault?

The right wallet is not the one with the flashiest hardware or the most marketing hype. It is the one that aligns with your *actual life,* not your idealised crypto persona. In the end, the true risk is not using hot or cold wallets. It is not knowing why you're using one over the other.

Not Your Keys, Not Your Coins—Really?

It is a slogan that echoes through the crypto community like a mantra: *"Not your keys, not your coins."* To many, it serves as a rallying cry for personal sovereignty, a shorthand for the core ethos of decentralised finance. It encapsulates a hard lesson learned through failed exchanges, frozen withdrawals, and vanishing platforms. And yet, like most maxims, it simplifies a complex and nuanced reality into something that can easily mutate into dogma. The phrase is both directionally true and practically incomplete—empowering when understood, dangerous when blindly followed.

To understand what's at stake, we must examine what it means to "own" cryptocurrency in any meaningful sense. When you purchase crypto and store it in a custodial account—say, on a centralised exchange like Binance or Coinbase—you do not hold the private keys to those assets. You possess a claim on them, much like a bank customer has a claim on the funds in their account. The assets are listed under your account ID, but they are under the operational control of the platform. This means you are exposed to all the risks of custodial failure: insolvency, hacking, regulatory seizure, withdrawal limits, or even simple technical failures.

The history of crypto is punctuated by moments when this abstraction collapsed into crisis. Mt. Gox in 2014 remains the original cautionary tale: over 850,000 Bitcoins lost or stolen, with customers unable to access their funds. More recently, the collapse of FTX demonstrated that size and prestige offer no immunity from mismanagement and fraud. Clients who had assumed their crypto was safely parked on a reputable exchange woke up to find those balances were little more than numbers on a screen—numbers with no backing, no recourse, and no guarantee.

And yet, this is not the whole story. While it is true that control of private keys equates to control of funds, the leap from that principle to universal self-custody is neither necessary nor always rational. The world is full of people who do not want, or should not be asked, to manage their own keys. Elderly investors, technophobic professionals, or time-poor parents may not be well suited to handle the operational demands of secure self-custody. Asking everyone to become their own bank sounds noble until you realise how many people have lost access to funds due to lost passwords, corrupted backups, or miswritten seed phrases. *The road to digital sovereignty is strewn with well-meaning corpses.*

Indeed, even the most committed crypto-native users often adopt hybrid strategies. A trader may keep their daily liquidity on a trusted exchange to benefit from faster execution, margin tools, and integration with fiat on-ramps—while relegating the bulk of their portfolio to cold storage. A DAO treasurer may prefer a multi-signature wallet controlled by elected members, rather than entrusting all funds to a single seed phrase held by a volunteer. These are not failures of conviction. They are signs of maturity—an understanding that *risk management trumps purity*.

Still, it is essential to grasp the real implications of not controlling your keys. A custodial provider does not just hold your assets; they can lend them, lock them, re-hypothecate them, or restrict your access to them depending on regulatory conditions. In this context, the crypto you see in your account is not functionally different from fiat in a traditional bank. It is not censorship-resistant. It is not self-sovereign. It can be frozen or clawed back. For users in regions with political instability, currency debasement, or capital controls, these distinctions are not theoretical—they are existential.

Moreover, custody arrangements alter your exposure profile. If your assets are held on an exchange and that exchange is hacked or goes under, your recovery prospects depend on jurisdiction, insolvency law, and your place in the queue. Self-custody eliminates counterparty risk—but replaces it with *self-inflicted* risk. A stolen hardware wallet with no recovery seed is a total loss. A miswritten phrase is unrecoverable. These tradeoffs cannot be wished away.

Freedom is not free—it costs attention, discipline, and systems thinking.

The absolutist interpretation of "Not your keys, not your coins" also neglects the legitimate role that professional custodians can play. Institutional investors managing tens or hundreds of millions in crypto cannot rely on a single hardware wallet or spreadsheet. They require insured custody, audited protocols, disaster recovery frameworks, and legally binding service-level agreements. For these actors, security is a matter of infrastructure, not ideology. Their holdings are not sovereign in the crypto-anarchist sense, but they are secure in a manner appropriate to their fiduciary obligations.

There is also a moral dimension to consider. Encouraging universal self-custody without acknowledging the steep learning curve creates a false binary: you either care about freedom and hold your own keys, or you're a lazy, centralised pawn. This is unhelpful and untrue. Many people deeply value financial autonomy but lack the technical confidence to manage cryptographic secrets without support. Telling them they don't "really" own crypto unless they self-custody is akin to telling a homeowner they don't *truly* own their house unless they also pour their own foundation and wire the electricity. *Ownership is not invalidated by reliance on expert infrastructure.*

And yet, despite these caveats, the original warning retains its urgency. Platforms go under. Passwords get reset. Terms of service change. If your crypto only exists as a number on a centralised platform, you must understand that it is, legally and practically, not under your control. It may be accessible. It may be convenient. It may even be insured up to a certain limit. But it is not *yours* in the cryptographic sense. This distinction matters most in moments of crisis, not in times of calm.

So where does this leave the thoughtful investor? It begins with *intentional custody*. If you choose to keep your assets on a centralised exchange, you should know exactly why—and you should be prepared to move them off at short notice. If you embrace self-custody, you should invest in your own operational readiness: backup routines, secure storage, contingency planning, and tested recovery. If you straddle both worlds, you should map your custody architecture to your liquidity needs, legal constraints, and risk tolerance.

There is no one-size-fits-all answer, but there is a clear principle: *don't outsource custody out of convenience or ignorance—only do so out of considered tradeoff.* The crypto landscape is littered with users who failed to ask hard questions until it was too late. Some lost everything because they assumed their exchange was "too big to fail." Others lost it because they underestimated their own fallibility as key managers. Both errors stem from the same root: confusing simplicity with safety.

To say "not your keys, not your coins" is to express a warning. But to understand the phrase fully is to grasp its limits as well as its power. Crypto is not just about eliminating middlemen; it's about understanding the function they serve and choosing whether, when, and how to replace them. Ownership is not just technical—it is practical, legal, and psychological. It resides not only in code, but in capacity.

Custody, in the end, is not a status. It is a responsibility. The question is not whether you should hold your own keys. The question is: *Are you ready to be the last line of defence?* If the answer is yes, act accordingly. If the answer is no, don't lie to yourself. Find infrastructure that protects your interests—and then monitor it like your wealth depends on it. Because it does.

Case Studies in Custody Gone Wrong

It is tempting to attribute the largest losses in crypto history to fraud, malice, or extraordinary bad luck. Yet a more uncomfortable truth lurks beneath the headlines: time and again, the fatal weakness has not been criminality, but complacency. The defining failures in custody have often been rooted not in deliberate theft but in poor risk management, technical misunderstanding, and a failure to anticipate the gravity of what was being entrusted. Custody, it turns out, is not merely a matter of storage—it is an exercise in foresight, process discipline, and understanding the precise nature of control.

The collapse of Mt. Gox in 2014 remains the canonical case. At its peak, the exchange handled 70% of all Bitcoin transactions globally. It was, in effect, the heartbeat of early crypto trading. Yet behind the interface lay an infrastructure that had spiralled into chaos. The firm lacked standard reconciliation procedures, stored private keys in hot wallets for long periods, and had no coherent audit trail. For years, Bitcoin was being siphoned from the exchange without notice. By the time the breach was discovered, approximately 850,000 BTC were missing. The founder, Mark Karpelès, was not convicted of theft but of record falsification. This was not Ocean's Eleven—it was operational entropy. *Users trusted the front-end experience, while the back-end silently bled value.*

That same pattern—of trust placed in systems not designed for scale or resilience—resurfaced in the 2022 collapse of FTX. By then, the industry had matured, and FTX marketed itself as a professional-grade platform with global compliance aspirations. It was backed by high-profile venture capital, its CEO was feted in Washington, and its brand was splashed across sports arenas. Yet beneath the surface, customer deposits were being commingled with trading capital from the affiliated hedge fund Alameda Research. The exchange's balance sheet was porous, risk controls were performative, and its leadership lacked the internal checks that financial institutions take for granted.

While FTX's actions veered into criminal territory, its implosion is not simply a morality tale. Many users parked assets on the platform not because they lacked options, but because they perceived convenience as safety. They conflated brand visibility with solvency, and regulatory conversations with regulatory compliance. *The collapse was not just a betrayal—it was a misreading of what custody truly entails.*

Celsius, BlockFi, and Voyager—three centralised crypto lenders that imploded in 2022—offer further lessons. Each promised users attractive yield on deposited crypto, positioning themselves as modern alternatives to traditional banks. But their operations were built on leveraged bets, unsecured loans, and aggressive duration mismatches. These firms were not banks. They were opaque hedge funds funded by retail depositors under the guise of fintech. And when the crypto markets turned, their business models proved fatally brittle. Depositors found themselves in the position of unsecured creditors in bankruptcy courts.

In each case, the term "custody" was used liberally—but misunderstood functionally. Depositors believed they had stored assets. In practice, they had issued them. These platforms had neither the regulatory protections of insured banks nor the prudence of conservative custodians. They had no capital buffers, no lender of last resort, and no clear legal recourse for users. What users mistook for custody was in fact unsecured exposure masked by friendly UX.

Even DeFi protocols, hailed for their transparency and code-based governance, have not been immune. In 2021, the Poly Network exploit saw over $600 million drained via a vulnerability in smart contract code. The hacker later returned the funds, but the breach underscored an essential truth: custody in DeFi depends on smart contract integrity, not customer service hotlines. Users must assess not only where their assets are, but *how* they are governed—by multisigs, by DAOs, or by immutable code. Misreading that layer of logic is functionally equivalent to handing your funds to an unvetted third party.

Even smaller-scale failures illuminate the systemic problem. In 2020, the Canadian exchange QuadrigaCX collapsed after its founder died suddenly—reportedly the only person with access to the exchange's private keys. Over $190 million in user funds were lost. Post-mortem investigations revealed troubling questions about the legitimacy of the operation itself. Yet even assuming good faith, the operational fragility was staggering: one person, one laptop, no redundancy. *This is not custody; it is catastrophe waiting for a trigger.*

These incidents—diverse in mechanics but aligned in consequence—highlight the key failure point: assumptions. Users assumed platforms were solvent. They assumed "deposit" meant protection. They assumed brand names equated to governance. But assumptions are not safeguards. And in decentralised finance, where traditional regulators offer little protection and the technology itself can be unforgiving, misplaced assumptions become existential threats.

Still, the lesson is not to abandon custody solutions—but to interrogate them. The first question should not be "Is this easy to use?" but "Who controls access to my funds, and under what conditions?" If the answer is a third party, the follow-up must be: "What are their incentives, what are their liabilities, and what recourse do I have if they fail?" If the answer is code, the questions shift to: "Has it been audited? Who can upgrade it? Is there an emergency kill switch?" *Every custody choice embeds a trust model—even the ones that market themselves as trustless.*

A recurring theme across these case studies is the *absence of process maturity.* The entities that failed did not just mishandle crypto—they mishandled custody as a discipline. They failed to segment duties, to run scenario tests, to establish redundant backups or multi-tier recovery systems. Most did not fail all at once. They failed slowly, via unchallenged practices and a culture of informality. In that sense, the danger was not malevolence. It was the quiet comfort of unchecked assumptions.

What makes this risk especially dangerous is its asymmetry. Custody failures are not like market losses. They do not offer second chances. A rug pull, a mis-signed transaction, a bankrupt exchange—these are not paper losses. They are evaporations of capital. And often, they are preventable not through technical wizardry, but through *boring operational hygiene.* A proper disaster recovery plan, a tested withdrawal protocol, a clear division between customer funds and operating capital—these are dull practices that prevent devastating outcomes.

For the thoughtful investor, these examples are not reasons to disengage from crypto—they are reasons to engage more deliberately. They reinforce that risk is not just about volatility; it's about control structures. They show that custody is not a binary between centralised and decentralised, but a continuum of design decisions, each with its own implications. And they remind us that while crypto promises to disintermediate finance, it does not absolve users from understanding where, how, and by whom their assets are being held.

Ultimately, the failures chronicled here should not be viewed as anomalies. They are cautionary tales from a maturing ecosystem—proof that trust, transparency, and infrastructure are not optional luxuries but foundational requirements. *The question is not whether crypto needs better custodians. It's whether users will learn to demand them before they're needed.*

Chapter 8
Beyond Bitcoin: Stablecoins, CBDCs, and the Future of Money

If Bitcoin posed the original question—what might money be without government—then stablecoins and Central Bank Digital Currencies (CBDCs) confront us with an even more consequential one: what happens when both states and protocols vie to rewrite the very infrastructure of value itself? The crypto revolution began by challenging fiat authority, yet it has now become the stage for a subtler, higher-stakes struggle—one that is not merely decentralisation versus centralisation, but sovereignty versus interoperability, transparency versus control, and innovation versus compliance. Digital assets are no longer in doubt; the question is who dictates the rules and whose ledger ascends as the global standard.

Popular narratives around cryptocurrencies tend to fixate on volatility, speculation, and decentralised ideals. Yet the instruments wielding the most geopolitical power are often those that remain steady: stablecoins. Pegged to fiat currencies but native to digital rails, these tokens have quietly become the connective tissue between crypto and the traditional financial system. They are the liquidity layer of decentralised finance, the dollar incarnate on-chain, and the practical medium for remittances, payroll, trade settlements, and even savings in economies where local currencies falter. Their promise, however, rests on foundations ranging from institutional robustness to algorithmic experimentation. A stablecoin is only as sound as the trust underpinning its peg, and as transparent as the entities sustaining that trust.

Take USDC, administered by the Centre consortium and issued by Circle, presenting itself as the ecosystem's model citizen: fully reserved, regulated under U.S. law, and subject to external audits. Contrast that with Tether—the largest stablecoin by volume—whose opacity, variable reserves, and regulatory scrutiny have not prevented its continued dominance. And then there are algorithmic stablecoins, which forsake fiat entirely in favour of incentive-driven governance and smart contracts. In principle, they promise decentralised stability, yet disasters like Terra's UST illustrate that such decentralisation can collapse spectacularly. The fragility of these systems is not incidental; it defines the risk landscape of an emerging financial primitive.

While stablecoins digitise existing monetary frameworks, CBDCs aim to reinvent them from within. From China's digital yuan to the European Central Bank's digital euro, and exploratory pilots by the U.S. Federal Reserve, central banks are issuing state-backed digital currencies that function not as speculative instruments but as programmable cash. Unlike stablecoins, which are liabilities of private firms, CBDCs would be state liabilities, potentially granting consumers direct access to central bank money in digital form for the first time. The ramifications are profound: governments could deliver stimulus instantly, automate tax collection, or even impose negative interest rates directly. Yet such capabilities also carry the potential for unparalleled surveillance, censorship, and behavioural steering. When money is encoded, it ceases to be inert—it becomes a policy instrument at the individual level.

CBDCs are more than a modernisation of payments; they redefine the architecture of monetary authority. The state, in this vision, controls both the issuance and the channels of money itself. The geopolitical stakes are high: China frames the digital yuan as a counterweight to U.S. dollar supremacy, the ECB positions the digital euro to curtail private-sector dominance, and emerging markets explore CBDCs to reduce dependency on foreign banking corridors. This is no longer theoretical. Programmable currencies are now an arena of strategic contest.

An intriguing twist is the stablecoinisation of the U.S. dollar itself. Though the United States has been slow to deploy a CBDC, dollar-backed stablecoins have become de facto dollars across much of crypto—and in segments of the real economy. In Argentina, Turkey, Lebanon, and Nigeria, USDT and USDC shelter savings from inflation, enable global transactions, and bypass formal banking limits. In Ukraine, they have facilitated wartime humanitarian aid. In Hong Kong, traders traverse between crypto and fiat using stablecoins. This is dollarisation via protocol—a quiet extension of American monetary influence without direct Federal Reserve sanction.

The implications cut both ways. Stablecoins reinforce dollar primacy in a digital, borderless economy, yet simultaneously bypass traditional capital controls, challenging the regulatory frameworks that sustain that dominance. This friction has not gone unnoticed. U.S. regulators debate money laundering, sanctions evasion, and whether stablecoins constitute securities. The Federal

Reserve weighs the macroeconomic effects of private money operating alongside public currency. Meanwhile, emerging markets confront the threat of capital flight and currency substitution. Every participant perceives both opportunity and risk—perspective-dependent, of course.

Beneath these debates lies a deeper question: what is money for? Is it a public good, stewarded by accountable institutions, or a protocol-layer utility optimised for efficiency and programmability? Is monetary sovereignty strengthened by state-issued CBDCs, or diminished by decentralised networks settling value without permission? Will the next global reserve currency be a digitised dollar or a code-governed synthetic basket of assets? These are not speculative musings; they are the fundamental tensions shaping the monetary order of the twenty-first century.

This chapter confronts those tensions head-on. It examines stablecoins not just as instruments of peg maintenance, but as vessels carrying implications for legal rights, collateral transparency, and systemic risk. It investigates CBDCs through the lens of live pilots and emerging systems, not merely whitepapers. It maps the geopolitical chessboard of programmable currencies, considering trade, surveillance, financial inclusion, and sovereignty. And it explores the boundary between centralised issuance and decentralised liquidity, where protocols such as MakerDAO or Curve blur conventional distinctions between traditional finance and decentralised design.

In so doing, the narrative transcends simplistic binaries—"crypto good, government bad" or vice versa. It portrays a layered, evolving ecosystem where design choices carry political, economic, and ethical weight. Readers are guided to differentiate innovation that empowers users from design that entrenches control. It reveals how the logic of money is being rewritten—not in textbooks, but across GitHub repositories, legislative drafts, and the wallet interfaces of millions.

The future of money is not a predetermined destination; it is a contested process. As this process unfolds, the lines between private innovation and public authority, between programmable trust and institutional legitimacy, will continue to blur. For anyone serious about investing, building, or understanding the forces at play, it is no longer enough to watch Bitcoin's price. One must scrutinise the architecture of digital trust, asking: who designs it, who governs it, and who ultimately benefits when it becomes the new normal?

What Is a Stablecoin, Really?

The most consequential innovation in crypto may not be Bitcoin or Ethereum, but the unassuming concept of the stablecoin—a digital token that doesn't try to make anyone rich. Stablecoins are not designed for moonshots; they're designed for certainty. And yet, beneath their promise of price stability lies a lattice of economic engineering, trust assumptions, and systemic vulnerabilities that even seasoned investors routinely underestimate. To understand stablecoins is to peer into the quiet engine room of decentralised finance and global digital liquidity. It is also to confront an uncomfortable truth: *stability, in crypto, is often an illusion of optics rather than a guarantee of structure.*

At their core, stablecoins are crypto assets whose value is pegged—typically to a fiat currency like the US dollar. They are engineered to maintain a fixed price, usually 1:1, with their reference asset. That peg, however, is a design objective, not a metaphysical truth. It depends entirely on how the stablecoin is backed, how that backing is managed, and how redemptions are honoured under stress. In a world where digital markets operate 24/7 and sentiment can shift in minutes, the question is not whether a stablecoin can hold its peg in tranquil times—it is whether it can survive a storm.

Fiat-collateralised stablecoins are the most familiar category. Their model is deceptively simple: for every token issued, the issuer holds a corresponding amount of fiat currency or near-cash equivalents in reserve. USDC, issued by Circle and governed by the Centre consortium, is the archetype here. It publishes monthly attestations from a major accounting firm, adheres to US financial regulations, and claims full backing by dollar-denominated cash and short-term US Treasuries. This makes it attractive to institutions, fintechs, and policymakers looking for a compliant, transparent token. But even this well-engineered vehicle is not immune to systemic stress. In March 2023, during the Silicon Valley Bank crisis, USDC briefly lost its dollar peg when it was revealed that Circle had over $3 billion in uninsured deposits at the collapsing institution. The peg was eventually restored, but not before markets absorbed the lesson that even "fully reserved" doesn't mean "fully bulletproof".

Tether (USDT), the largest stablecoin by market cap and volume, is a more complicated story. It dominates crypto trading pairs globally and is especially prevalent in offshore markets. But Tether's reserve transparency has been murky for years. For a long time, it claimed to be fully backed by dollars, but offered little evidence. Under regulatory pressure, it later disclosed a reserve mix that included commercial paper, secured loans, corporate bonds, and other risk-weighted instruments. While Tether has since reduced its exposure to opaque assets and increased its holdings in Treasuries, it remains unregulated in most jurisdictions and avoids the rigorous disclosure regime embraced by USDC. This creates a paradox: the most widely used dollar-denominated stablecoin is also the one with the least institutional oversight. And yet, it has weathered more market chaos than its competitors—suggesting that trust in stablecoins is not just about transparency, but about perceived resilience in practice. *Tether is, for many traders, a known risk with a track record of surviving turbulence, even if its underlying structure remains imperfectly understood.*

Beyond fiat backing lies the more esoteric realm of algorithmic stablecoins—tokens that use on-chain mechanisms and incentive engineering to maintain their peg without traditional reserves. The appeal here is clear: decentralisation. By avoiding reliance on centralised entities, these coins aim to offer censorship-resistant, scalable, and trustless forms of money. But the history of algorithmic stablecoins is littered with failure. The most infamous example is TerraUSD (UST), which used a mint-and-burn mechanism tied to its sister token LUNA to maintain its peg. When confidence in the model eroded, the mechanism collapsed in a death spiral, wiping out over $40 billion in value in a matter of days. The failure was not due to a coding error—it was a structural flaw in the design logic. In stablecoin architecture, *liquidity guarantees must survive reflexivity,* and UST's model could not handle the feedback loop between falling price and rising redemptions. Other algorithmic projects have fared better—DAI, for instance, originally collateralised in ETH, now uses overcollateralisation and increasingly relies on real-world assets—but even it has migrated towards hybrid models, revealing the limits of purely algorithmic stability in practice.

The fragilities of stablecoins are not just technological or financial—they are regulatory and political. Their rapid adoption has raised alarms in Washington, Brussels, Beijing, and beyond. Policymakers worry that privately issued stablecoins could undermine monetary sovereignty, facilitate capital flight, or destabilise traditional banking. The Financial Stability Board, IMF, and central banks across G20 nations have repeatedly called for global frameworks to regulate them. Meanwhile, U.S. congressional efforts to pass comprehensive stablecoin legislation have stalled, caught between competing priorities of innovation, financial surveillance, and consumer protection. The regulatory vacuum leaves stablecoin issuers navigating uncertain terrain, where de facto standards substitute for legal clarity, and where a single enforcement action could reshape the market overnight.

Yet for all their risks and inconsistencies, stablecoins continue to thrive because they solve real problems. For the unbanked in emerging markets, they provide access to dollars without requiring a bank account. For cross-border freelancers, they offer instant settlement without FX fees or correspondent banking delays. For decentralised applications, they enable programmable money flows, escrow contracts, and automated liquidity provision. Even in institutional finance, stablecoins are being piloted for use in repo markets, settlement layers, and tokenised securities. Their utility is not theoretical. It is evidenced by trillions of dollars in on-chain volume, growing interoperability with traditional finance, and the expansion of integrations with payment processors, wallets, and merchant services. *Stablecoins are not just part of the crypto ecosystem—they are the infrastructure enabling its connection to the broader world.*

Still, every stablecoin carries trade-offs. Fiat-backed coins offer simplicity and speed, but at the cost of centralised custody and regulatory exposure. Algorithmic coins promise decentralisation but often require complex risk management and fragile incentive structures. Hybrid models attempt to blend the best of both worlds, but inherit the operational risks of both paradigms. For users, the challenge is not simply choosing a token—it is understanding *what backs it, how redemptions work, what legal protections apply, and what scenarios could cause the peg to break.* Stability, in this context, is not a binary—it is a spectrum defined by trust, structure, and governance.

The architecture of stablecoins is also reshaping the broader logic of financial inclusion and dollar dominance. In regions with unstable currencies or capital controls, stablecoins offer citizens a financial lifeline that is faster, more accessible, and harder to block than traditional options. This creates new questions: should dollar-backed stablecoins be treated as digital extensions of U.S. monetary policy? Are they a form of informal dollarisation, or a tool of soft power? If a stablecoin becomes systemically important in a developing country, what responsibilities—if any—do its issuers or regulators have toward that economy? These are not theoretical debates. In countries from Argentina to Lebanon, from Nigeria to Venezuela, citizens are already answering them in practice, wallet by wallet.

There is also the matter of systemic risk. As stablecoins become more deeply integrated into financial markets—both decentralised and traditional—they may introduce new forms of interdependence. If a major stablecoin issuer fails, or a peg collapses under redemption pressure, it could trigger cascading liquidations across exchanges, lending protocols, and derivative platforms. This is not idle speculation: the near-depeg of USDC during the SVB crisis led to momentary stress across multiple DeFi platforms. As tokenised assets proliferate, and as CBDCs remain years from mass adoption, stablecoins will continue to act as the duct tape of financial infrastructure. But *duct tape is only safe when used within its design limits.*

The most dangerous thing about stablecoins is not their volatility, but their apparent *lack* of it. When a financial product promises safety and delivers it most of the time, users tend to treat that stability as permanent. But stability in stablecoins is always conditional—on collateral quality, on counterparty behaviour, on legal clarity, and on the collective psychology of the market. A dollar-denominated token that cannot be redeemed for a dollar in stress scenarios is not a stablecoin—it is a delayed volatility instrument. Understanding that difference is not just a technical matter. It is a prerequisite for using these instruments wisely in portfolios, payment systems, and regulatory frameworks.

To ask what a stablecoin "really" is, then, is to engage with one of the most layered, consequential, and fast-evolving questions in modern finance. It is to recognise that these tokens are not simply pegged coins—they are active expressions of economic design, trust calibration, and technological governance. Their future will not be determined by slogans or ideology, but by the clarity of their architecture, the integrity of their execution, and the resilience of their peg under fire. Stability, after all, is not a feature. *It is a stress-tested outcome.*

The Central Bank Strikes Back

The most significant experiment in the history of money is now underway—not on the frontier of crypto innovation, but within the heart of central banking. Central Bank Digital Currencies (CBDCs) are no longer theoretical. They are being piloted, tested, legislated, and—in some cases—quietly rolled out to millions. China's e-CNY already reaches over 260 million wallets. The European Central Bank is advancing its digital euro. The Bank of England, Federal Reserve, and Reserve Bank of India are actively exploring their own digital currencies. What was once the domain of crypto maximalists and monetary policy wonks has now become a geopolitical contest over the architecture of digital cash. *But behind the headline developments lies a deeper question: what happens when governments, not miners or protocols, issue programmable, traceable, and potentially surveilled money?*

CBDCs promise modernised payment systems, increased financial inclusion, reduced transaction costs, and real-time settlement. Yet these technical efficiencies obscure a profound shift in how money functions—and who controls it. A CBDC is not merely a digital version of cash. It is a new kind of monetary instrument: *state-issued, software-embedded, and potentially policy-enforceable at the wallet level*. This has enormous implications not only for payment infrastructure but for privacy, autonomy, and the future of financial control.

To grasp what's at stake, one must understand what CBDCs are designed to replace—or, more precisely, absorb. Today, the dominant instruments of digital value are private: bank deposits, mobile wallets, credit card networks, and, increasingly, decentralised tokens like stablecoins. These operate within (or adjacent to) the state's regulatory perimeter but remain intermediated by private entities. CBDCs shift the model. They allow the state to issue money directly to citizens or institutions—without requiring a commercial bank as intermediary. In doing so, they collapse layers of financial intermediation, creating both efficiencies and risks.

A retail CBDC is, in essence, a digital bearer asset backed by the central bank. Unlike traditional bank deposits, it carries no credit risk: it cannot default. That makes it attractive in times of financial stress. But it also reshapes the role of commercial banks. If citizens can hold money directly with the central bank, why trust a private bank at all? In systemic crises, CBDCs could accelerate bank runs, as users move funds from fragile banks into the perceived safety of the central ledger. To mitigate this, most proposed designs include tiered interest rates, holding limits, or non-remunerative balances. But even these safeguards acknowledge the core tension: *CBDCs alter the basic contract between savers, banks, and the state.*

Monetary policy, too, could evolve dramatically. Today, central banks influence money supply indirectly—by setting interest rates, conducting open market operations, or altering reserve requirements. CBDCs enable direct transmission. In theory, central banks could distribute stimulus payments with programmable conditions: spend within 30 days, or it expires. They could impose negative interest rates, enforce transaction restrictions, or target specific demographics with surgical precision. This is not speculative—these capabilities exist today in programmable wallets and smart contract infrastructure. The question is not whether CBDCs *can* enable such features, but whether they *should*. What begins as a tool for efficiency may become a vehicle for coercion.

The debate over privacy lies at the heart of the CBDC dilemma. Physical cash is anonymous, permissionless, and resilient. A CBDC—by default—is none of those things. Unless specifically engineered to protect user privacy, digital currencies offer granular visibility into who spends what, where, and when. Governments assert that such visibility is essential for anti-money laundering, counter-terrorism, and tax compliance. But civil liberties advocates warn of creeping financial surveillance. Once every transaction is traceable, dissenting speech, controversial donations, or even politically inconvenient purchases could be monitored—or blocked. China's e-CNY, for instance, allows authorities to freeze funds or limit spending by location and category. Western central banks have pledged to protect privacy in their designs, but technical architectures often prioritise compliance over confidentiality. *The architecture of a CBDC reflects its political values—and those values vary starkly across regimes.*

This raises an uncomfortable truth for liberal democracies: if CBDCs are designed with privacy at their core, they may be less useful for enforcement. If they are designed with enforcement at their core, they may become incompatible with liberal norms. The compromise might lie in tiered privacy, where small-value transactions remain anonymous, but larger flows require identification. Yet even here, the boundary between necessary oversight and intrusive monitoring remains contested. Once surveillance infrastructure is embedded in a monetary system, rolling it back becomes politically and technically difficult. *The erosion of cash may thus be the erosion of transactional freedom*—and that trade-off deserves public debate, not just technical review.

Beyond domestic policy, CBDCs introduce new vectors in geopolitics and financial infrastructure. If digital currencies become programmable, sovereign-controlled assets, they can be embedded into foreign policy and trade strategy. China's Belt and Road Initiative has already incorporated the e-CNY in cross-border settlements. Russia and Iran have explored CBDCs to bypass SWIFT and US sanctions. Meanwhile, stablecoins like USDC and USDT serve as dollar surrogates in countries with weak currencies. In this context, CBDCs are not merely monetary tools—they are instruments of economic influence. *The global competition over digital currency standards mirrors the Cold War contest over communication protocols, only this time, the stakes include monetary sovereignty.*

CBDCs also represent a centralising response to the decentralisation thesis of crypto. Bitcoin, Ethereum, and other permissionless networks offer an alternative: money governed by code, not central banks. Their promise is freedom, openness, and resilience. CBDCs reclaim the state's role as sole monetary authority. To some, this is a necessary reassertion of public trust. To others, it is a retrenchment of centralised power. In practice, both models may coexist—but not without friction. If CBDCs are interoperable with decentralised finance (DeFi), they could offer liquidity and regulatory clarity. If they are walled off, they risk stifling innovation and fragmenting digital markets.

This tension is already visible in regulatory approaches. The EU's MiCA legislation carves out space for regulated stablecoins, but signals caution toward decentralised protocols. The US has yet to enact comprehensive digital asset legislation, but individual agencies have cracked down on crypto firms while exploring CBDC pilots. The irony is acute: while governments develop digital currencies to modernise their economies, they often do so by stifling the very innovations that made CBDCs feasible. The future of money is being shaped not just by technical merit, but by regulatory posture—and the balance between caution and ambition remains unsettled.

At a more philosophical level, CBDCs force societies to reconsider what money *is*. Is it a bearer instrument, like cash—owned outright by the holder and free to be spent without oversight? Or is it a conditional instrument—subject to rules, permissions, and policy levers? Is it a neutral medium of exchange, or a vector for social engineering? These questions are not rhetorical. In a programmable money system, rules can be encoded, not merely enforced. Subsidies can be made spendable only at approved vendors. Payments can be geo-fenced, time-restricted, or reversed by central command. The nature of money shifts from passive store to active agent.

The rollout of CBDCs is not inevitable, nor is its trajectory uniform. Some countries may delay, others may leap ahead. Some will favour privacy-preserving designs, others will emphasise control. But the underlying momentum is clear: *a decade from now, most advanced economies will have some form of digital sovereign currency*. The question is what values and constraints will govern its use.

If stablecoins were the private sector's attempt to modernise money, CBDCs are the state's counter-offer. They bring legitimacy, legal clarity, and infrastructure investment. But they also bring new risks—of surveillance, control, and dependency. The tension between these models—permissionless versus state-sanctioned, anonymous versus traceable, decentralised versus centralised—is not merely technical. It is civilisational. It reflects competing visions of how economic value should be created, transmitted, and governed.

CBDCs may indeed offer safer, faster, cheaper payments. But *the terms of that convenience will define the future of financial liberty*. To ignore those terms—or to delegate their definition to technocrats alone—is to forfeit agency in one of the most consequential shifts of our time. If money is power, then the digitisation of money is the reconfiguration of power itself. And that makes the rise of CBDCs not just a monetary event, but a civic one.

Dollarization 2.0?

The United States dollar dominates international finance not because it was imposed but because it solved problems other currencies could not. In times of crisis, when trust erodes and capital flees, the dollar becomes a refuge. It underpins global trade, anchors reserves, and lubricates credit flows across borders. Yet today, a new form of dollarisation is quietly proliferating—not through governments, but through crypto rails. *Dollar-backed stablecoins—privately issued, publicly used—are becoming the functional dollars of a fragmented financial system.*

Tether (USDT) and USD Coin (USDC), once obscure instruments favoured by crypto traders, are now integral to how dollars flow across borders, circumvent capital controls, and reach populations far from traditional banking infrastructure. In countries with high inflation or currency instability—Argentina, Lebanon, Nigeria—dollar-backed stablecoins are not speculative tools; they are *survival mechanisms*. They offer a store of value, medium of exchange, and pathway to global markets, often without the permission of banks or states. This quiet monetary revolution isn't theoretical. It is happening—transaction by transaction, app by app, far from the headlines but visible in the data.

To understand this shift, one must examine what these stablecoins are and how they function. A dollar-backed stablecoin like USDC or USDT is a digital token issued on a blockchain, purportedly backed 1:1 by actual dollars or equivalent assets held in reserve. These reserves are managed by centralised entities—Circle in the case of USDC, Tether Holdings for USDT—which act as de facto private central banks, issuing and redeeming tokens based on demand. The token itself can be sent peer-to-peer on public blockchains, settled in seconds, with no banking intermediary. That's the breakthrough. Traditional dollarisation depends on access to US dollars through official or grey market channels. *Stablecoin dollarisation bypasses those channels entirely.*

The numbers are telling. As of mid-2025, over $130 billion worth of stablecoins circulate globally, with the vast majority denominated in US dollars. In many decentralised applications (DeFi), dollar-backed tokens have become the primary unit of account. In emerging markets, dollar stablecoins often trade at premiums to local currency due to demand for stability and dollar exposure. In some cases, they are more liquid and accessible than physical dollars or bank-issued equivalents. The stablecoin, once a crypto-native curiosity, is now *a parallel dollar system,* one that operates outside SWIFT, skirts correspondent banking, and thrives in jurisdictions where trust in local money is low.

This creates a powerful incentive alignment. For individuals, stablecoins offer inflation protection and remittance efficiency. For businesses, they streamline cross-border payments and hedge currency risk. For developers, they enable programmable financial services without waiting for legacy institutions. But the implications go deeper: *they entrench the dollar as the default digital currency of the internet*. Not by force, but by utility.

This is dollarisation by architecture. In the analogue world, the dollar spreads through central banks holding reserves and trade being invoiced in dollars. In the digital world, it spreads through smart contracts, mobile wallets, and liquidity pools. And unlike traditional dollarisation, which requires coordination with US authorities or financial institutions, stablecoin dollarisation can happen independently—even against the wishes of local governments.

Consider Venezuela. Amid hyperinflation and currency controls, residents turned to physical dollars and later to crypto as alternatives. Today, dollar-backed stablecoins have become an essential tool for freelancers, importers, and families receiving remittances. In Nigeria, the government's ban on crypto exchanges has done little to slow the rise of peer-to-peer dollar stablecoin use. In Ukraine, USDT has functioned as a quasi-currency in wartime conditions, providing reliable value transfer where banks have failed. These are not edge cases—they are blueprints for how *the future of monetary resilience may no longer depend on formal state channels.*

Yet this new form of dollarisation is not without friction. It raises complex questions about regulation, sovereignty, and monetary control. If stablecoins become de facto currencies in weak economies, do they undermine central banks? Do they facilitate capital flight? Are they instruments of US influence, even if privately issued? Paradoxically, dollar-backed stablecoins may extend the dollar's global reach while also accelerating regulatory backlash from countries that perceive this as an erosion of their monetary autonomy.

Regulators in emerging markets have begun to respond. Some have cracked down on stablecoin usage, citing concerns about financial stability and capital leakage. Others, like Brazil, have taken a more pragmatic route—integrating digital assets into formal payment systems and licensing local providers. Meanwhile, the IMF has warned of "cryptoisation" risks in vulnerable economies, arguing that reliance on dollar stablecoins could exacerbate boom-bust cycles and reduce fiscal room for manoeuvre. *The real challenge is not whether stablecoins work, but whether the jurisdictions in which they thrive are equipped to govern their consequences.*

On the other side, US policymakers face their own strategic dilemmas. Stablecoins, though privately managed, are overwhelmingly dollar-based. Their adoption in foreign economies effectively extends dollar influence—but also exposes US monetary reach to new risks. What happens if a stablecoin issuer collapses, triggering a liquidity crisis in countries dependent on it? What if dollar stablecoins are used to finance illicit activity, inviting geopolitical blowback? Or worse, what if competitors issue synthetic stablecoins—backed by yuan or euro—and erode dollar supremacy in the digital realm?

These questions are not speculative. China's DCEP (e-CNY) already offers an alternative model: a sovereign-issued, tightly controlled digital currency designed for global trade, not ideological purity. Its export to partner nations through Belt and Road initiatives sets the stage for a currency sphere that bypasses the dollar altogether. Meanwhile, Europe's push for a digital euro and coordination with international partners signals a desire to retain relevance in a dollar-centric digital system. *In a multipolar currency world, stablecoins are no longer a niche technical tool; they are strategic infrastructure.*

That makes governance design critical. USDC, for example, has positioned itself as the regulated, transparent alternative to Tether—publishing audits, integrating with banking networks, and courting policymakers. Tether, by contrast, remains opaque but dominant in global volume, especially in less regulated markets. The bifurcation reflects a deeper divide: *stablecoins that play by institutional rules versus those that exist precisely because institutions have failed.* Both models will coexist, but their risks and political implications diverge sharply.

At a technical level, stablecoins are still evolving. Collateral models range from fiat reserves to crypto-backed assets and algorithmic structures. Most of the market has rejected algorithmic models after high-profile collapses like Terra-LUNA, reinforcing the importance of transparency and redemption guarantees. Yet even fiat-backed stablecoins are not without fragility. They rely on banking relationships, legal clarity, and reserve integrity—all of which can be challenged under stress. The banking failures of early 2023, which saw Circle temporarily lose access to USDC reserves, underscored how even the most compliant stablecoins remain tethered—both literally and figuratively—to traditional finance.

But perhaps the most transformative implication of dollar-backed stablecoins is their potential to reshape how money is used. Unlike physical cash or bank deposits, stablecoins are *natively programmable.* This means they can embed conditions, interact with smart contracts, and settle instantly across chains and platforms. The dollar becomes not just a store of value, but a medium of composability. In this model, the unit of account doesn't merely represent purchasing power—it becomes an instrument of automation, coordination, and digital sovereignty.

Whether this strengthens or weakens the dollar's position depends on who builds and governs the infrastructure. If stablecoin issuance becomes centralised in a few corporate actors, vulnerabilities abound. If it fragments across open-source protocols and decentralised liquidity pools, scalability and oversight become challenges. Either way, *the next wave of dollarisation will not be negotiated in Bretton Woods—it will be coded into ledgers, APIs, and governance protocols.*

As the global monetary system shifts from analogue to programmable, from state-led to network-driven, the lines between public money and private innovation will blur. In that blur, stablecoins offer a glimpse of both possibility and peril. They can democratise access to stable value, enable new forms of commerce, and extend the reach of trusted currencies. But they also raise uncomfortable questions about sovereignty, inequality, and dependence. The future of money may still speak in dollars—but *how, by whom,* and *under what conditions* that future unfolds remains a live contest. Dollarisation 2.0 is not a rerun of history. It is a remapping of the monetary frontier.

Where Sovereigns and Protocols Collide

Few technological innovations have unsettled governments as swiftly and thoroughly as public blockchains. Not because they threaten to replace states outright, but because they dare to *route around them.* In traditional finance, state power is embedded in the structure: currencies are sovereign, banks are licensed, and cross-border flows are monitored, intermediated, and—when necessary—interrupted. Crypto protocols do none of these things by default. They allow capital to move at the speed of software, indifferent to national borders or regulatory frameworks. *What happens when the architecture of finance no longer requires the architecture of the state?*

This is not merely a theoretical provocation—it's a geopolitical fault line. Crypto networks like Ethereum, Bitcoin, and Solana are not controlled by any state, yet they operate financial infrastructure that rivals global banks in speed, liquidity, and accessibility. Smart contracts automate trust. Tokens price risk. Stablecoins circulate with dollar exposure but without dollar oversight. To a user in Lagos or Lahore, these protocols offer a lifeline; to regulators in Washington, Brussels, or Beijing, they represent *ungoverned zones in a world built on governance.*

The result is a mounting tension between sovereign control and protocol logic. Governments prize traceability, tax compliance, and anti-money laundering enforcement. Protocols prize permissionless access, censorship resistance, and borderless design. Both value stability, security, and system integrity—but they define and enforce those principles through radically different means. The political implications are profound. As crypto adoption deepens, the real battle is not over technology—it's over who gets to write the rules of economic coordination.

This tension comes into sharp focus at key flashpoints. Consider the United States' approach to decentralised finance (DeFi). While agencies like the SEC and Treasury Department recognise that protocols are not corporations in the traditional sense, they have nonetheless pursued developers, founders, and front-end operators for alleged violations of securities laws and sanctions evasion. The case against Tornado Cash—a privacy tool built on Ethereum—illustrates the stakes. In August 2022, the U.S. Treasury sanctioned the protocol's smart contract addresses, triggering global outcry. Critics argued that code itself was being sanctioned, a move akin to banning mathematics. Yet from the government's perspective, Tornado Cash facilitated billions in obfuscated transactions, some linked to North Korean hackers. *This is the new battlefield: where digital code is interpreted as geopolitical conduct.*

Other nations are navigating these tensions differently. China, for instance, banned cryptocurrency trading outright while simultaneously launching the digital yuan (e-CNY), a state-controlled Central Bank Digital Currency (CBDC) designed to preserve monetary sovereignty in the face of crypto's rise. In China's view, decentralised finance is not innovation—it is disorder. But even in jurisdictions that embrace blockchain innovation, such as Singapore or the UAE, permissionless protocols are treated with caution. Regulators seek assurances that these systems can be made *legible*—that they can interface with Know-Your-Customer (KYC) protocols, respond to court orders, and enforce finality. But the fundamental architecture of DeFi does not accommodate such design without compromising its core principles.

This creates an uncomfortable truth: *many of the features that make crypto networks valuable are the same ones that make them politically unpalatable*. When a protocol can custody assets, issue tokens, and orchestrate trades without human intermediaries, it disrupts not just financial incumbents but the regulatory scaffolding that governs them. In some circles, this is celebrated as a triumph of technological inevitability. In others, it's viewed as a form of digital insurrection. The challenge is that both interpretations contain elements of truth.

Moreover, this clash is not evenly distributed. Protocols may be global, but their users are local. When Uniswap or Aave is used by individuals in sanctioned or capital-controlled jurisdictions, the consequences vary widely depending on who those users are. A Venezuelan fleeing hyperinflation may be seen as a legitimate user of decentralised finance; a sanctioned oligarch attempting to hide assets is not. But the protocol makes no such distinction. Its logic is uniform. Its access is indiscriminate. *And therein lies the geopolitical paradox: a tool of financial empowerment can become a tool of geopolitical defiance.*

Regulators face a dilemma. Overregulation risks driving innovation offshore or underground, as seen in the exodus of crypto firms from the United States to friendlier jurisdictions. Underregulation creates vectors for abuse, undermining trust in both protocols and public institutions.

The path forward is not to wish the conflict away but to acknowledge that we are entering a period of monetary pluralism—where state and non-state systems must coexist, often uneasily, across overlapping networks of influence and authority.

At the heart of this tension is the question of legitimacy. Sovereigns derive legitimacy from law, electoral process, and institutional history. Protocols derive legitimacy from open-source code, consensus algorithms, and network effects. The former governs through mandates; the latter through incentives. Yet both claim to serve the public good. When these systems collide—as they increasingly do—the question becomes not just who is in charge, but *what kind of governance the future of finance demands*.

One possible resolution is the rise of hybrid architectures—protocols that build in compliance mechanisms, or governments that adopt cryptographic tools to modernise public infrastructure. Examples of this are emerging. Circle's USDC works closely with regulators and publishes reserve attestations. Fireblocks, a custody infrastructure provider, offers institutional clients DeFi access with compliance tooling baked in. On the public side, Brazil's Pix system has integrated with blockchain payment rails to enable near-instant transfers. These developments suggest that *coexistence is possible—but only if both sides accept partial compromises*.

Yet even as these bridges are built, the fundamental asymmetry remains: *sovereigns can enforce laws; protocols can enforce logic*. One governs people, the other governs machines. This divergence will shape the coming decade—not just of crypto policy, but of financial architecture writ large. It will affect how trade is settled, how sanctions are enforced, how capital flows are tracked, and how citizens interact with their own money.

Some states will embrace this evolution. Others will resist it. But none will be able to ignore it. In the same way that the internet forced states to rethink information control, crypto will force them to rethink financial control. And just as the internet gave rise to new power centres—platforms, protocols, influencers—so too will crypto produce new economic actors whose influence transcends borders and laws.

In the final analysis, the clash between sovereigns and protocols is not merely about regulation or compliance. It is about *designing a shared space between institutional authority and decentralised innovation*. The stakes are not abstract. They concern who gets to move value, under what terms, with whose permission. They concern the future of financial freedom, surveillance, stability, and trust.

The sovereign is not dead. Nor is the protocol unstoppable. But the negotiation between them—messy, high-stakes, and unresolved—*will define the monetary order that follows*.

Chapter 9
Regulation, Crackdowns, and What You Need to Know

Crypto did not arrive seeking permission; it arrived rewriting the rules. In the aftermath of the 2008 financial crisis, Bitcoin appeared as a system intentionally designed to operate beyond the reach of central banks and state-backed institutions. Yet as this sector has evolved from a marginal experiment into a multi-trillion-dollar industry, the question is no longer whether regulation will arrive—it is how, where, and by whom. For investors, developers, and users alike, navigating this legal fog has become less an option than an existential necessity.

Unlike centuries-old financial systems, which grew alongside legal frameworks, crypto erupted onto the scene far faster than legislators could keep pace. One week a token might be hailed as digital gold; the next, it is reclassified as a security, a commodity, or something "entirely novel." Regulators have responded in disparate ways, from enthusiastic sandbox programmes to outright prohibitions. The result is a patchwork of rules in which the same protocol can be legal in one jurisdiction and criminalised in another. Legal clarity is no longer a luxury—it is a strategic asset.

This incoherence is more than bureaucratic inconvenience. It can determine whether a developer faces prosecution, whether an exchange may operate, or whether an investor inadvertently assumes unknowable legal risk. Consider Ripple Labs, entangled in a protracted legal battle with the

U.S. Securities and Exchange Commission over whether XRP constitutes an unregistered security. The implications stretch far beyond a single token; they strike at the legal foundations of hundreds of projects built on tokenised frameworks. Ambiguity, in this context, becomes weaponised.

At the root lies a deceptively simple question: what is a crypto asset, legally speaking? The SEC has leaned heavily on the Howey Test, a framework derived from a 1946 Supreme Court case concerning orange groves. By its terms, an asset may be deemed a security if it involves an investment of money in a common enterprise with profits expected primarily from the efforts of others. On paper, this might seem straightforward. Yet when one probes decentralised protocols or community-governed DAOs, the boundaries blur. Does a token with no central issuer qualify? What of governance tokens, or programmable money intended mainly for transactions?

The broader crypto community has been slow to absorb these legal realities. Many early adherents remain committed to the ideal of stateless finance, viewing engagement with regulators as betrayal. Yet as crypto increasingly interfaces with traditional finance, this posture grows untenable. Investors demand protections, banks require compliance, and governments insist on transparency. Distrust of the state offers no exemption. Neglecting this reality has precipitated high-profile collapses, sometimes driven not by malfeasance but by regulatory neglect.

This brings us to one of crypto's most sensitive regulatory frontiers: privacy versus compliance. Early advocates lauded crypto as a shielded alternative to traceable fiat. In truth, most blockchains are public by default, and genuine privacy-enhancing tools—mixers, privacy coins, zero-knowledge proofs—face intense scrutiny. Regulators are keen to trace flows for anti-money laundering, anti-terrorism financing, and sanctions enforcement. Consequently, Know Your Customer and Anti-Money Laundering protocols have become standard. Compliance, however, often comes at the expense of privacy, posing real operational dilemmas: what happens when users expect confidentiality but platforms are legally obliged to monitor activity?

The tension is intensifying, especially as innovations blur the line between identity, ownership, and access. Zero-knowledge proofs promise a way to verify compliance without revealing sensitive data, yet they remain complex and difficult to scale. Until these technologies mature, users face a stark choice: embrace full transparency in the name of legality, or sacrifice access in the name of principle.

For developers and investors, staying on the right side of the law requires more than ticking boxes; it demands a living awareness of a rapidly shifting frontier. Jurisdictions such as Switzerland, the UAE, and Singapore have established regulatory clarity designed to attract innovation while retaining oversight. Others, including the United States, continue to regulate through enforcement, keeping participants guessing. Global bodies like the Financial Action Task Force press for harmonised standards affecting decentralised exchanges, wallet providers, and even software developers. The era of building in legal limbo is drawing to a close.

The stakes are not only legal—they are reputational and existential. When Terra/LUNA imploded, obliterating $40 billion in value, regulatory absence left retail investors dangerously exposed. FTX, with its commingled funds and internal malfeasance, similarly benefited from gaps between jurisdictions. Grey zones enable bad actors; and when trust collapses, so too does market confidence.

This chapter does not take sides in the ideological battle between cypherpunks and state institutions. Its aim is to equip readers to navigate legal terrain with clarity and confidence. Whether a casual investor, DeFi participant, or founder issuing tokens, understanding the legal categories in which one operates is vital. Ignorance is perilous.

Yet paranoia is no strategy either. The regulatory landscape is evolving; policymakers, scholars, and enforcers themselves are still in discovery mode. This is as much a moment of opportunity as it is of risk. It is a chance to shape frameworks, engage in reasoned debate, and build systems that respect both freedom and responsibility. The goal is not to evade regulation, but to ensure it is fit for a world where code enforces rules, custody is digital, and finance is programmable.

As crypto matures, its entanglement with law will deepen. Projects will face compliance expectations; investors will need comprehension; governments will act on principle as well as precedent. Navigating this environment demands strategic literacy in the politics of innovation. Those who cultivate it will gain more than protection from missteps—they will be poised to shape the next chapter of financial freedom.

The Legal Grey Zone

A blockchain protocol may be immutable, but the laws that attempt to govern it are anything but. Across borders, crypto regulation is a study in contradiction: praised as innovation in Switzerland, banned outright in China, taxed into irrelevance in India, and scrutinised into paralysis in the United States. For an investor, this is not an abstract geopolitical curiosity. It is a live variable—one that can determine whether a project you hold is a legitimate asset, a prohibited security, or an unlicensed product subject to fines or confiscation. *The legality of your crypto portfolio is not written in code—it's written in jurisdiction.*

Crypto's borderless architecture runs headlong into the reality of sovereign legal systems. Blockchains don't care where you live, but governments do. And so, the same asset—a stablecoin, a staking product, a decentralised exchange token—can be regulated, tolerated, ignored, or criminalised depending on where the user is located. This variance doesn't merely create compliance challenges; it creates uncertainty at the structural level. A DeFi protocol may be legal in Dubai and illegal in New York. An airdrop may be taxed as income in Canada and as capital gains in Germany. *The user's geographic coordinates have become regulatory coordinates.*

The friction begins with definitions. What is a "crypto asset"? Is it property, a currency, a security, or a commodity? Depending on the country, it may be one or several—or none of the above. In Japan, crypto is legally recognised as a form of private money and is regulated by the Financial Services Agency under clear licensing requirements. In contrast, India has alternated between threats of criminalisation and vague tax policies that leave investors with more confusion than clarity. Meanwhile, the United States remains one of the most complex and consequential battlegrounds. There, regulatory fragmentation reigns. The SEC calls certain tokens securities; the CFTC calls others commodities; the IRS treats all of them as property; and FinCEN treats wallet providers as financial institutions. *One asset, four regulators, zero consensus.*

This jurisdictional discord carries tangible risks. Consider the case of Kik Interactive, a Canadian messaging company that issued the Kin token to fund its platform. In 2019, the SEC filed a lawsuit arguing that the Kin token was an unregistered security offering. Kik ultimately paid a $5 million penalty and shut down its crypto subsidiary. Whether one agrees with the ruling or not, the point is stark: a token launched by a company operating legally in one country can still face devastating enforcement actions from regulators abroad. *Geography does not shield you from regulatory reach if your users cross borders.*

More than once, the crypto industry has mistaken decentralisation for immunity. While the architecture may be decentralised, the access points—exchanges, wallet providers, payment gateways—are anything but. These entities serve as choke points through which regulators assert control. This explains why decentralised finance (DeFi), despite being architecturally borderless, often finds itself navigating the same legal terrain as centralised platforms. When OFAC sanctioned Tornado Cash, an Ethereum-based privacy tool, it didn't just block a website. It marked the protocol's smart contract addresses as off-limits for U.S. citizens, effectively criminalising interaction. This marked the first time code itself, not just people or corporations, was placed on a sanctions list. *The state's reach now extends to on-chain logic.*

For individual investors, the implications are sobering. Participating in a liquidity pool or earning yield from staking is not simply a matter of smart contract risk—it may also carry tax obligations, reporting requirements, or legal exposure. This becomes especially complicated for expatriates, remote workers, and digital nomads who may live in one country, pay taxes in another, and interact with protocols deployed on servers in a third. In a traditional investment world, jurisdiction is stable and defined by institutional presence. In crypto, jurisdiction is fluid and defined by user interaction. *Where the transaction happens is no longer obvious—but the law insists on an answer.*

Even the concept of "compliance" becomes murky in a decentralised environment. How does a protocol with no central administrator perform KYC? Who bears responsibility for consumer protection when there's no issuer? Can a DAO be sued or fined? These questions are not theoretical. They are already surfacing in courtrooms. In

2022, the CFTC filed charges against the Ooki DAO, arguing that a decentralised entity could be held accountable for offering leveraged trading services without registering as a futures commission merchant. The lawsuit treated DAO token holders as collectively liable—a precedent that, if upheld, would render token-based governance not only participatory but legally accountable. *Decentralisation does not dissolve liability—it redistributes it.*

Some jurisdictions are choosing clarity over chaos. The European Union's Markets in Crypto-Assets Regulation (MiCA) offers a comprehensive legal framework covering token issuance, stablecoins, and crypto service providers. While not perfect, it marks an attempt to regulate coherently rather than by enforcement. Similarly, countries like Switzerland and Singapore have emerged as regulatory havens—not because they are lenient, but because they are clear. They treat crypto as a serious financial instrument, not as a novelty or threat. The result is an influx of talent and capital from regions where policy remains paralysed. *Regulatory clarity has become a competitive advantage.*

This competition is not just economic—it is geopolitical. As traditional powers hesitate, emerging markets are seizing the opportunity to establish themselves as crypto hubs. El Salvador's adoption of Bitcoin as legal tender was dismissed by many as a political stunt, but it signalled a deeper trend: smaller nations leveraging crypto to sidestep dependence on dominant currencies and institutions. Likewise, Nigeria and Kenya are experimenting with crypto payments and blockchain-based ID systems, not just for efficiency, but for sovereignty. For these countries, crypto isn't about speculation—it's about *strategic optionality* in a global system stacked against them.

At the same time, regulatory overreach carries its own dangers. When the threat of enforcement is vague, the effect is chilling. Innovators leave. Capital flees. Open-source developers retreat from public contributions. Regulatory ambiguity does not merely protect consumers—it often undermines them by pushing activity into unregulated shadows. A cautious investor might ask: is a given project legally risky, or simply suffering from the absence of legal definition? Without answers, fear—not fraud—becomes the primary barrier to participation.

So where does this leave the individual investor? The answer is unsatisfyingly complex. There is no single legal regime to trust, no universally accepted definitions to lean on, no global crypto passport that guarantees compliance. Investors must *think jurisdictionally*, not just strategically. That means knowing where the protocol is headquartered—if at all. It means understanding the residency-based tax rules that apply to staking rewards, airdrops, or capital gains. And it means recognising that participating in crypto is not an off-grid activity—it is a legally interpretable one. *Even the most permissionless systems are constrained by the permissions of law.*

This is the paradox of crypto's global ambition: a borderless network constrained by territorial governance. Yet in that paradox lies a unique opportunity—for smarter investors, for better regulation, and for protocols that actively design with compliance in mind. The legal grey zone is not a void; it is a frontier. And as with all frontiers, those who map it early shape what comes after. The task is not to wait for perfect clarity, but to navigate uncertainty with informed precision. That's the new definition of due diligence.

Security or Not? The SEC Question

When the Securities and Exchange Commission (SEC) filed a complaint against Ripple Labs in December 2020, accusing the company of conducting an unregistered securities offering through the sale of its XRP tokens, it didn't merely rattle one blockchain firm—it sent shockwaves through an entire industry. Billions were wiped off XRP's market cap in days. Exchanges delisted or froze the token in the United States. Investors were left guessing. The deeper impact, however, was conceptual: the case threw a harsh spotlight on a deceptively simple but foundational question—*when is a token a security?*

It is a question with no universally agreed-upon answer, and yet it underpins much of the regulatory anxiety surrounding crypto. For traditional assets, categories are relatively clear. Stocks represent equity. Bonds represent debt. Derivatives are contractual claims. But digital tokens? They often do not fit neatly into any existing legal framework. Some grant governance rights, others offer utility access, and many do a confusing mix of both. This ambiguity creates a breeding ground for inconsistent application of securities laws—especially in jurisdictions like the United States, where decades-old legal tests are being stretched to accommodate 21st-century code.

The Howey Test, developed from a 1946 Supreme Court case (SEC v. W.J. Howey Co.), is the primary lens through which the SEC evaluates whether an asset qualifies as a security. The test is not statute but precedent, and its four-prong framework determines whether a transaction involves (1) an investment of money, (2) in a common enterprise, (3) with a reasonable expectation of profits, (4) derived from the efforts of others. It was crafted to address a Florida citrus grove scheme. Yet nearly 80 years later, this same logic is being applied to decentralised digital networks with thousands of global participants and no central management. *The law, in effect, is attempting to fit a network into a tree farm.*

The trouble is not the Howey Test itself—it remains a flexible, functional tool for evaluating economic realities over technical form. The problem is how unevenly and opaquely it is being applied to tokens. When does a "reasonable expectation of profits" exist? Does staking a token for yield qualify? Does token price appreciation count, even if not explicitly promised? And how decentralised must a network be before it no longer relies on the "efforts of others"? These are not hypothetical debates. They are the crux of ongoing enforcement actions. The SEC has argued in court that even tokens traded on secondary markets—long after initial issuance—may still qualify as securities, because their value continues to be driven by the work of core development teams. Critics argue this interpretation stretches the test beyond recognition. *If everything is a security, then the word ceases to mean anything useful.*

Some precedents do exist. In 2018, SEC Director William Hinman suggested in a widely cited speech that Ether, despite being arguably launched as a security, had evolved into something else—a sufficiently decentralised asset no longer under the purview of securities regulation. This nuanced position offered a potential path for projects to begin in legal ambiguity but graduate to regulatory clarity through decentralisation. But that speech was later disavowed as non-binding. And the SEC's subsequent lawsuits have made clear that *regulatory grace is not a policy—it is a discretionary act.*

The lack of formal rulemaking compounds the uncertainty. Instead of issuing clear guidelines tailored for crypto assets, the SEC has pursued a strategy of "regulation by enforcement." This approach creates a chilling effect. Projects often cannot know whether they are compliant until they are sued. The result is a paradox: those who want to follow the law cannot clearly understand what the law requires. Many innovators now avoid launching in the United States altogether, citing legal unpredictability as a top risk factor. *Crypto is not fleeing regulation—it is fleeing regulatory ambiguity.*

This ambiguity doesn't just affect developers—it matters enormously to investors. If a token is deemed a security, exchanges may be forced to delist it, wallets may block access, and users may be required to pass intrusive KYC checks. Furthermore, U.S. investors may be retroactively held liable for participating in unregistered offerings, even if they acted in good faith. Tax reporting requirements change. Custody rules tighten. Entire categories of financial service—staking, lending, airdrops—can become legally fraught. The difference between a utility token and a security is not philosophical. *It is the difference between owning an asset and owning a liability.*

And yet, the legal status of a token is not static—it can evolve. Many projects now argue for a dynamic regulatory framework, one that recognises the transition from centralised launch to decentralised operation. The analogy is a startup that becomes a cooperative: it begins as a coordinated enterprise but, over time, distributes governance, upgrades its protocols, and reduces dependency on any core team. This trajectory should arguably lower regulatory burdens as the token becomes more like a public good and less like a financial instrument. But the current U.S. regime lacks such a mechanism. *There is no formal process for decentralisation certification—only the fear of being labelled retroactively non-compliant.*

Other jurisdictions are taking more proactive approaches. Switzerland's Financial Market Supervisory Authority (FINMA) distinguishes between payment tokens, utility tokens, and asset tokens, each with distinct regulatory obligations. Singapore's Monetary Authority offers a licensing regime with clear thresholds. The EU's MiCA framework, though still evolving, provides a comprehensive blueprint for how crypto assets should be classified, marketed, and supervised. By contrast, the United States remains mired in litigation and turf wars between agencies, where regulatory clarity often arrives only after legal defeat. *The law here does not guide—it reacts.*

Not all tokens aim to escape securities classification. Some embrace it. Security Token Offerings (STOs), built deliberately to comply with securities law, offer digitised equity or debt instruments that benefit from blockchain's transparency and efficiency. These projects follow know-your-customer (KYC) rules, restrict trading to accredited investors, and register with appropriate agencies. But STOs represent a tiny fraction of the crypto market. Most tokens continue to operate in legal ambiguity, not because they are fraudulent, but because *there is no clear compliance pathway to follow.*

The tension reaches a head in the case of decentralised autonomous organisations (DAOs). DAOs issue governance tokens designed to coordinate community decision-making. These tokens often have no claim on profits, no central issuer, and no guaranteed price appreciation. Yet the SEC has signalled that even governance tokens could qualify as securities if they resemble investment contracts. This raises difficult questions: If thousands of users vote on a proposal, are they "relying on the efforts of others"? If a DAO funds development with token sales, is that a securities offering? What if a subset of core contributors receives tokens as compensation? *Regulatory logic becomes circular when applied to fluid, distributed systems.*

Investors should not wait for final clarity. The prudent approach is to evaluate tokens as if they *could* be securities—and assess what that means for their liquidity, risk profile, and reporting obligations. This includes understanding the issuer's legal jurisdiction, disclosure practices, and degree of centralisation. When a token has a whitepaper but no legal entity, a roadmap but no financial statements, or a foundation but no board oversight, those are not just operational gaps—they are regulatory risk signals. *Compliance risk is investment risk by another name.*

Ultimately, the question—security or not?—will not be answered once and for all. It will be answered continuously, in courtrooms, in rulebooks, in guidance letters, and through the actions of developers, exchanges, and policymakers. For now, the legal regime around tokens resembles the early days of internet law: reactive, fragmented, and full of false analogies. But history suggests this phase will not last. Regulatory frameworks eventually catch up—not always elegantly, but inevitably. The key is not to avoid law but to *engage with it early and intelligently.*

Until then, investors and entrepreneurs must operate with both legal vigilance and conceptual nuance. Every token is not a security. But every token *could* be treated as one. That is the paradox—and the prudence—of investing in a world where law and code have not yet agreed on their definitions.

Privacy vs Compliance

At the core of cryptocurrency's origin story lies an unambiguous premise: the right to transact without precondition. Bitcoin's early advocates did not just see it as a technological breakthrough, but as a philosophical correction—an unmediated financial system that placed individuals, not institutions, in control. Embedded within this was a deep commitment to privacy. Not secrecy, but sovereignty—the ability to act without needing permission, scrutiny, or exposure. Yet as digital assets have matured into a trillion-dollar asset class attracting governments, institutions, and millions of mainstream users, this commitment to privacy now stands in stark tension with another imperative: compliance.

No regulatory conversation about cryptocurrency survives long without mention of KYC (Know Your Customer) and AML (Anti-Money Laundering) frameworks. These mechanisms, long embedded in traditional finance, are designed to prevent illicit activity—terrorism financing, drug trafficking, tax evasion, and fraud. In theory, their logic is unassailable: traceability ensures accountability. But in practice, especially in the decentralised context of crypto, their application can become blunt, overreaching, and sometimes counterproductive. *The very tools designed to increase trust may erode the freedoms that made crypto viable in the first place.*

Take, for example, the global rise of Travel Rule compliance. Originally part of the Financial Action Task Force (FATF) guidelines for wire transfers, the Travel Rule requires Virtual Asset Service Providers (VASPs)—like exchanges, custodians, and wallet providers—to share identifying information about both sender and receiver in crypto transactions exceeding a certain threshold. This effectively extends the compliance perimeter beyond on-ramps and into wallet-to-wallet interactions. It also assumes that all parties involved are operating through intermediaries that can collect and share such data—a notion that breaks down entirely in peer-to-peer, wallet-based ecosystems. *A decentralised system cannot enforce centralised reporting without violating its own architecture.*

Privacy coins present an even more direct challenge. Monero, Zcash, and Dash offer varying degrees of transactional anonymity, utilising zero-knowledge proofs, ring signatures, and stealth addresses to obscure sender, receiver, and amount. While these tools offer legitimate protection against surveillance and financial discrimination—particularly in authoritarian regimes—they have also attracted regulatory scrutiny. In several jurisdictions, including South Korea and Japan, exchanges have been instructed to delist privacy coins entirely. The implication is stark: *privacy is not a feature—it is a liability.*

This regulatory hostility is not merely about preventing crime. It also reflects a worldview in which transparency is equated with safety. But this worldview deserves interrogation. Traditional banking systems are not transparent to the public—they are opaque, closed systems governed by selective disclosure. In contrast, public blockchains are radically open: every transaction is permanently recorded and visible, traceable by anyone with access to a block explorer. *Ironically, the most transparent financial system ever built is being criticised for lacking transparency.*

The emergence of blockchain analytics firms like Chainalysis, Elliptic, and TRM Labs further complicates the picture. These companies specialise in de-anonymising blockchain activity, identifying wallet addresses, tracing stolen funds, and providing law enforcement with actionable intelligence. Their tools are increasingly sophisticated, often surpassing the investigative capabilities of traditional forensic accounting. But their rise also raises ethical and legal questions. Who gets access to these tools? What are the safeguards against misuse? What happens when a wallet is wrongly flagged? *A decentralised system becomes de facto centralised when surveillance becomes a prerequisite for legitimacy.*

This is the heart of the tension. Most users do not object to regulations that prevent crime. They object to regimes that demand identification in the absence of wrongdoing. The presumption of innocence is a foundational principle of liberal democracy, yet financial regulation often inverts it—requiring individuals to prove they are not criminals before being allowed to transact. In the analogue world, such presumptions would be rejected as authoritarian. But in finance, they are standard operating procedure. *The burden of proof has shifted from state to citizen, and crypto is where the pushback is most visible.*

The challenge is particularly acute in developing markets. In countries with weak institutions, corrupt officials, or high levels of financial exclusion, the right to transact privately is not theoretical—it is survival. Activists, journalists, and dissidents often rely on crypto not as a speculative asset, but as a lifeline. For them, KYC is not a checkbox—it is a vector for surveillance, coercion, or worse. By enforcing global compliance norms without accounting for local political realities, regulators may inadvertently punish the very people most in need of financial autonomy. *A universal rulebook cannot accommodate a fragmented geopolitical world.*

Nevertheless, full anonymity is not a sustainable position either. Without some form of traceability, fraud and abuse proliferate. Rug pulls, Ponzi schemes, and cross-chain laundering operations often operate with impunity, exploiting decentralised infrastructure and disappearing into mixers, bridges, or jurisdictional loopholes. Anonymity, like any freedom, can be weaponised. The task is not to abolish it, but to regulate its abuses without erasing its legitimate uses.

Hybrid models are emerging. Zero-knowledge proofs—used in privacy-preserving blockchains like zkSync and Aztec—offer a potential solution. They allow a party to prove compliance (for example, having sufficient funds or being part of an authorised group) *without revealing the underlying data*. This shifts the paradigm from disclosure to verification. In theory, a user could demonstrate they are not on a sanctions list without revealing their identity. *Privacy and compliance need not be opposites—they can be reconciled through cryptographic design.*

Meanwhile, self-sovereign identity (SSI) protocols are gaining traction. These systems allow users to hold and control their own identity credentials, issuing selective disclosures to third parties as needed. Projects like Sovrin, Veres One, and Microsoft's ION aim to create interoperable, privacy-preserving identity layers for the internet. In a crypto context, this means a wallet address could be associated with a verified human without permanently linking that address to personally identifiable information. *This is compliance with consent, not coercion.*

Still, no amount of technological finesse can resolve the deeper philosophical divide: *who controls the right to transact?* If every interaction must be permissioned, monitored, and logged, then the internet of value begins to resemble the internet of surveillance. But if there are no safeguards, then the system risks becoming a haven for exploitation. This tension is not new—it echoes the age-old trade-off between liberty and security. What makes crypto different is that it *forces* the trade-off into sharp relief. Every design decision—centralised exchange vs DEX, custodial vs non-custodial wallet, permissioned vs permissionless protocol—carries regulatory, ethical, and philosophical implications.

Investors must internalise this complexity. It is not enough to ask whether a platform is compliant. One must ask: compliant with *what*? With whose laws? Enforced by whom? And at what cost to individual autonomy? These are not abstract questions. When Canada froze the bank accounts and crypto wallets of protestors in early 2022, ostensibly in the name of public order, it revealed the brittleness of financial freedom in even the most stable democracies. When Tornado Cash developers were arrested, it raised alarms about whether writing open-source privacy code could be construed as a criminal act. *The line between compliance and control is not always where we assume it to be.*

In the years ahead, this tension will only sharpen. As central bank digital currencies (CBDCs) roll out, programmable money will give governments even more granular control over spending behaviour. As surveillance expands, the demand for privacy-preserving alternatives will rise. And as regulation tightens, projects will have to choose: build for compliance and risk alienating the core principles of crypto, or resist and face existential legal threats. There is no stable equilibrium—only continuous negotiation.

What is clear is that privacy cannot be treated as an afterthought. Nor can compliance be dismissed as optional. The future of digital finance depends on reconciling these imperatives—not through slogans or absolutism, but through careful, deliberate design. The crypto community must resist the temptation to pick sides and instead do the harder work of building systems that *honour both freedom and accountability*. Anything less is not innovation. It is abdication.

How to Stay Legal, Safe, and Informed

The promise of financial sovereignty that drew many investors into the crypto space does not come without responsibility. Unlike traditional markets where custodians, regulators, and central banks provide a structured—albeit often restrictive—framework, crypto offers a spectrum of freedom that also entails a spectrum of exposure. In this decentralised financial frontier, *compliance is not merely a legal obligation—it is a strategic competence.* Those who treat legality as an afterthought will find themselves unprepared, not only for enforcement action, but for the practical consequences of operating in a misunderstood and rapidly evolving space.

Regulatory frameworks in crypto are not static—they are a mosaic of interpretations, precedents, and jurisdictional flux. What is permitted in Switzerland may be criminalised in China. A token freely tradable in the United States today could be declared an unregistered security tomorrow. Smart contracts deployed on Ethereum may be immutable, but the legal treatment of interacting with them is anything but. *Investors operating across this patchwork must abandon the hope for one-size-fits-all clarity and instead build habits of situational awareness.*

The first and most essential step is understanding the operational perimeter of one's activity. Are you simply buying and holding tokens on a regulated exchange? Are you participating in decentralised lending platforms or yield farming protocols? Are you issuing, promoting, or developing tokens yourself? Each of these activities carries vastly different legal implications. For example, using a platform like Coinbase may subject you to standard KYC/AML procedures, while trading on an anonymous DEX could, in certain jurisdictions, expose you to accusations of operating outside regulated markets. *Legal risk is not just about what you hold—it's about how, where, and through whom you interact with the ecosystem.*

Second, jurisdiction matters more in crypto than in perhaps any other financial arena. The borderless nature of decentralised assets lulls participants into a false sense of regulatory neutrality. But the truth is harsher: *you are always in someone's jurisdiction, even if you don't realise it.* Many legal systems claim extraterritorial reach when it comes to financial crime, sanctions violations, or securities law. The United States, in particular, has a long-standing precedent of applying its rules globally, especially when USD is involved or when platforms solicit users from within its borders. An American retail investor using a Singaporean

DeFi protocol may still fall under SEC scrutiny. Conversely, a European developer building privacy infrastructure might be liable under GDPR or local financial surveillance rules. Ignorance of these overlapping regimes is not a shield—it's a liability.

Investors must therefore become proficient in regulatory triage: understanding what laws apply, how aggressively they are enforced, and what constitutes good-faith compliance versus willful negligence. This does not require a law degree, but it does require discipline. Monitoring regulatory advisories from securities commissions, tax authorities, and anti-money laundering agencies should be a routine part of one's research process. Many countries now issue periodic guidance documents—such as the UK's FCA cryptoasset task force reports, the SEC's statements on digital assets, or the Monetary Authority of Singapore's licensing updates—that offer crucial insights into evolving expectations. *The rulebook may be fluid, but its signals are visible to those who care to look.*

Security is inseparable from legality. Poor custody decisions are not only financially risky—they are legally consequential. Losing access to crypto due to phishing, SIM-swap attacks, or compromised seed phrases may leave you with no recourse, particularly if your holdings were off-exchange and non-custodial. But beyond the loss itself, questions may arise: where were the funds sourced from? Could they be tied to a flagged wallet? Have you retained sufficient documentation to prove provenance in the event of a tax audit or fraud inquiry? *The safest wallets in the world mean little if the investor cannot demonstrate lawful acquisition.*

Maintaining auditable records is therefore vital. This includes transaction histories, receipts of purchase, staking rewards, airdrops, and especially any instances of crypto-to-fiat conversions. Several jurisdictions, including the UK and Australia, expect investors to maintain detailed logs for five or more years. Tools like CoinTracking, Koinly, or TaxBit can assist, but they require disciplined data input. *The burden of proof lies with the individual—and regulators are increasingly adept at tracing blockchain activity to hold individuals accountable.*

Staying informed is not passive—it is an active mode of engagement. The most legally resilient investors are those who understand that regulation is not a binary "allowed/not allowed" proposition. It is a conversation—between policy, technology, economics, and precedent. Attending virtual briefings from regulatory bodies, subscribing to updates from reputable law firms focused on digital assets, and following crypto-legal analysts on professional platforms like LinkedIn or legal research newsletters is no longer optional. It is strategic self-preservation.

It is also important to distinguish between *regulatory volatility* and *regulatory direction*. While jurisdictions may shift on the specifics, broader patterns are emerging. Crypto taxation is tightening globally. Stablecoins are coming under scrutiny for reserve transparency. DeFi is moving from unregulated grey zone to selectively targeted enforcement. Privacy tools are facing indirect bans through infrastructure chokepoints—exchanges, DNS providers, hosting services. *The investor who watches headlines but ignores directional movement risks focusing on the symptom rather than the cause.*

Compliance, however, must not give way to paralysis. A healthy respect for legal boundaries does not require abandoning innovation or opportunity. It requires approaching them through the lens of prudence and proportionality. Participating in a new protocol should prompt a checklist: is the team doxxed or anonymous? Is there a formal legal entity? Has the token been promoted with promises of profit tied to the work of others—raising Howey Test concerns? Does the interface collect user data, and if so, how is it protected? Is there a clear terms-of-service policy? *These are not just questions for developers or lawyers—they are due diligence for any serious investor.*

It is also prudent to use licensed or registered platforms where possible. Many countries now offer regulatory sandboxes, fintech licences, or limited-purpose registration schemes for crypto entities. Engaging through these intermediaries provides a layer of consumer protection—legal recourse in case of fraud, structured dispute resolution, and sometimes even deposit insurance for fiat balances. These trade-offs come with compliance requirements—KYC, withdrawal limits, tax reporting—but they also reduce the risk of being blindsided by enforcement actions. *Convenience may tempt users toward the least regulated option, but longevity is often found at the intersection of safety and accountability.*

Finally, cultivating a mindset of resilient flexibility is essential. Laws will change. Platforms will shut down. Tokens will be delisted. Jurisdictions will revise definitions and redraw boundaries. Investors who approach the space with rigid assumptions—whether maximalist or dismissive—will struggle. The most successful actors are those who build adaptive literacy: not just understanding what the rules *are,* but why they exist, how they are evolving, and what new behaviours they necessitate. *Legal awareness in crypto is not a static checklist—it is a dynamic competency.*

Remaining legal, safe, and informed in the digital asset space is not about avoiding risk. It is about understanding *which risks are worth taking*—and how to navigate them with intelligence and integrity. A well-calibrated crypto strategy is one that treats regulatory foresight not as a bureaucratic hurdle, but as an edge. It enables movement while others hesitate, clarity while others speculate, and protection while others suffer preventable consequences. In a landscape as unpredictable as crypto, *legal literacy is not an accessory—it is armour.*

Chapter 10
Smart Questions, Not Hot Takes

In the frenetic theatre of cryptocurrency markets, few pause to consider whether the questions they ask are worth asking at all. Speed is lauded, reflex dominates, and narratives—compressed into memes, headlines, or viral clips—often masquerade as reasoned inquiry. Yet, as history shows, investment bubbles are rarely inflated by insight; momentum and emotion carry the day. In crypto, opinions frequently outpace understanding. This chapter does not call for slowness per se; it calls for precision. For digital assets to occupy a lasting role in portfolios—personal or institutional—the foundation must be judgement, not hype. And judgement begins not with answers, but with the right questions.

"What problem is this solving?" is no mere philosophical indulgence. It is an investor's most effective filter before delving into whitepapers, Discord threads, or price charts. Many tokens and protocols are engineering feats in search of a customer. Others replicate functionality already available through simpler, cheaper, or more established systems in traditional finance. Yet investors routinely flock to projects motivated not by utility but by anticipated appreciation or fear of missing out. Asking this question early forces engagement with first principles: what is broken, who suffers, and why crypto might offer a superior solution.

The power of the crypto movement lies less in novelty than in its ability to reconfigure trust, coordination, and value exchange. These are not abstract ideals; they demand tangible traction. Remittance corridors burdened by fees and delays, for instance, present a natural space for stablecoins and decentralised exchanges. But imposing blockchain solutions indiscriminately—on supply chains, gaming, ticketing—without interrogating whether decentralisation is truly required leads to bloated ecosystems and stalled projects. Crypto is not magic; it is a tool. Tools only matter when they match the contours of the problem they are designed to fix.

"Is the model sustainable?" is the next layer of scrutiny, moving from surface-level function to structural endurance. Many protocols succeed early by flooding ecosystems with incentives: token rewards, yield farming, referral bonuses. Yet history warns that rapid growth can mask fragility. Unsustainable tokenomics act as Trojan horses: alluring on the surface, concealing emission schedules, dilution, or demand assumptions that cannot endure. High total value locked may impress, but without organic adoption—users who remain once incentives vanish—the project is unlikely to survive. True sustainability aligns user behaviour with long-term economic logic, not fleeting arbitrage.

Evaluating tokenomics goes beyond glancing at circulating supply. It demands an investor mindset attuned to incentive design, governance control, and game-theoretic principles. How are validators compensated? Who dictates governance? What are emission schedules, and how do they shape price and retention over time? Are demand assumptions grounded in empirical evidence or speculation? How do insiders interact with the protocol—aligned for the long term or poised for extraction? These are not mere technicalities; they are economic questions that require rigorous, repeated attention.

"Would this exist without crypto?" introduces a philosophical vector that slices through the noise. It is uncomfortable because it challenges redundancy. Many decentralised applications replicate centralised platforms with poorer UX, higher friction, and diminished accountability. Decentralisation carries cost and only delivers benefit where trust, censorship resistance, or composability are essential. When crypto becomes decorative rather than functional, innovation gives way to cargo-cult design.

This question also guards against the techno-optimism that colours bull markets. Not every sector needs a token; not every transaction merits a blockchain; not every digital interaction demands immutability. The decentralised web is visionary, yes, but visions unmoored from pragmatic utility are fragile. Asking whether a project would exist absent crypto clarifies whether it creates new capabilities or merely repackages the old with jargon and complexity.

Critical questions must extend to personal decision-making. Too often, investors consume narratives passively, influenced by Telegram groups, influencers, or platform hype. Chapter 10 advocates a different posture: the investor as interrogator. Constructing a personal crypto checklist is not paranoia—it is precision. It transforms scattered curiosity into coherent strategy.

Such a checklist must evolve with markets, regulation, technology, and individual risk appetite. Core questions should include: what utility does this token provide and to whom? How is value captured, and by whom? Is the roadmap credible? Who are the backers, and what is their exit path? What are inflation dynamics, and how are they governed? How will the project withstand regulatory scrutiny, security breaches, or market shocks? Answering these questions is no guarantee of success—but failing to ask them virtually guarantees vulnerability.

As the crypto industry matures, the edge shifts from access to intellectual discipline. Early adopters profited from novelty alone; today, with thousands of tokens, hundreds of blockchains, and ever-tightening regulation, the alpha lies in discernment. Those who distinguish substantive innovation from fashionable branding will outperform—not only financially, but in clarity, confidence, and resilience.

The temptation in crypto is the hot take. Yet progress stems not from reflex but reflection. This chapter invites readers to slow down—not to delay, but to refine; to replace reaction with rigour; to ask smarter questions—not to sound clever, but to cultivate competence. Ultimately, survival in crypto seldom hinges on timing; it hinges on thinking. And thinking begins with the courage to ask what others ignore.

"What Problem Is This Solving?"

The most revealing question in crypto isn't about market cap, technical architecture, or token supply—it's about purpose. Yet, amidst the thousands of whitepapers, roadmaps, and Discord announcements, this fundamental question is often the least asked. *What is the problem?* Not just any problem, but one that is *urgent, widespread,* and *uniquely solvable* through cryptographic and decentralised tools. Without this anchor, projects become exercises in technical curiosity or speculative marketing—interesting perhaps, but irrelevant to real users and investors seeking durable value.

The intellectual discipline of problem-first thinking strips away the glamour of token launches and the inertia of price action. It forces clarity. In traditional startup evaluation, product-market fit reigns supreme. But in crypto, where tokens can be monetised before the product exists—and sometimes before the team even writes code—the temptation is to reverse the sequence: build a token, then search for justification. This inversion breeds fragility. It fosters ecosystems where capital flows before comprehension and where momentum disguises meaninglessness.

Take Filecoin, a protocol designed to decentralise file storage by using a blockchain to coordinate independent storage providers. Its underlying problem—reliance on centralised cloud storage giants like Amazon and Google—is real and structurally significant. Filecoin proposes a credible cryptoeconomic model to incentivise distributed data storage with transparent pricing and verifiable redundancy. Whether or not it succeeds is secondary here. *The point is that the problem exists and the mechanism addresses it in a logically coherent way.* Compare this to many meme-based tokens or "utility" coins whose core value proposition amounts to little more than loyalty points attached to vapour.

The distinction isn't philosophical—it's practical. For investors, purpose clarity serves as a cognitive filter.

Projects solving real problems—especially ones underserved by existing financial, institutional, or technological systems—are more likely to attract genuine users, iterate through real-world feedback loops, and endure market cycles. Purpose also functions as a north star for project teams. It guides trade-offs between speed and security, decentralisation and usability, tokenomics and governance. *Without an articulated problem, decision-making becomes arbitrary, reactive, and opaque.*

But what makes a problem "worthy" of decentralisation? Not all inefficiencies demand blockchains. In fact, decentralisation introduces trade-offs: slower transaction speeds, more complex governance, and heightened coordination costs. For a project to justify its existence on a blockchain, the problem must hinge on issues that decentralisation uniquely resolves—*trust asymmetries, single points of failure, censorship risks, or opaque value extraction*. A decentralised lending protocol like Aave, for instance, provides transparent, non-custodial alternatives to traditional banks. Its core use case—peer-to-peer lending and borrowing without intermediaries—is strengthened, not weakened, by blockchain architecture. Contrast this with a tokenised dating app or ride-sharing network whose "blockchain layer" adds cost and complexity without addressing any structural weakness in current models.

Asking "What problem is this solving?" also surfaces hidden assumptions. Many crypto projects implicitly assume that tokenisation itself adds value—turning actions into financial incentives, community members into investors, or governance into market dynamics. But *incentives without scarcity or necessity decay into noise.* A problem worthy of a token must demand coordination, accountability, or liquidity that only a token can unlock. Otherwise, tokenisation becomes a distraction—an economic veneer on a product that might function better without it.

Consider Helium, which aimed to build a decentralised wireless network by incentivising individuals to run hotspot hardware using its native token. The original problem—providing low-power, wide-range connectivity for IoT devices—was valid, and the idea of crowdsourcing infrastructure was compelling. But the mechanism misaligned incentives. Most participants focused on mining tokens rather than improving network utility or coverage. The infrastructure existed, but not the value delivery. *This disconnect between problem framing and mechanism design collapsed user trust, despite impressive capital inflows.*

The elegance of the "problem-first" question is its versatility. It applies at every level—from protocol architecture to individual tokens, from DeFi platforms to NFT marketplaces. In decentralised finance, for example, the original rationale was simple: expand access to financial tools without permission or gatekeeping. But today, a significant share of DeFi activity is recursive—users borrowing against tokens to farm more tokens, rather than funding real-world economic activity. This is not to dismiss

DeFi, but to underscore that *without an anchor in actual use cases, even brilliant code becomes circular theatre.*

NFTs offer another lens. The underlying technology—provable digital ownership—is groundbreaking in contexts like art provenance, digital collectibles, or credential verification. But a large portion of the market has chased speculative gains without clarifying the underlying value proposition. What problem does a $200,000 pixelated ape solve? For some, it signals identity or affiliation. For others, it's simply a trading vehicle. Without a core utility beyond price appreciation, these assets risk collapse when sentiment shifts.

This question also guards against mission drift. In crypto, where narratives evolve faster than code, projects often mutate to chase hype. A payments platform becomes a DAO becomes an AI protocol. The original problem is forgotten or retrofitted to suit a new narrative. *When clarity erodes, coherence follows.* Purpose-first thinking enforces continuity. It keeps teams, investors, and communities grounded in what matters.

Yet the hardest problems to evaluate are not those lacking technical merit, but those solving problems that are real but marginal. A protocol may automate insurance for smart contracts, or offer decentralised identity verification—but how many users face these problems daily? Is the pain acute, or just theoretically interesting? The problem may be real, but *is it large enough, urgent enough, or painful enough to matter?* Purpose isn't merely about existence—it's about relevance.

Investors often substitute due diligence with correlation. "Big investors are backing it." "The founder worked at a FAANG company." "It's on all the major exchanges." But none of these validate that a problem is being solved. *They reflect confidence, not clarity.* To navigate crypto markets with intelligence, one must ask harder, lonelier questions. What problem is this solving—for whom, how, and why now?

Projects that endure—Ethereum, Chainlink, Uniswap—didn't merely launch tokens. They launched tools that addressed persistent challenges in decentralisation: computation, data integrity, and exchange. Their growth, despite volatility and criticism, is grounded in functionality. They're not without flaws. But their foundations are anchored in need, not narrative.

This kind of thinking is not only for developers or venture capitalists. It's for anyone putting time, money, or attention into a project. Whether you're staking tokens, contributing to a DAO, minting an NFT, or just learning about a protocol, the "problem-first" lens distils noise into signal. It reveals the distinction between vision and vapour.

In markets defined by speed, it is tempting to optimise for novelty, narrative, or network effects. But enduring value still rests on first principles. Asking "What problem is this solving?" does not make you cynical—it makes you careful. It reframes crypto from a guessing game to a discovery process. Because if the problem is not real, then the token is not a solution. It is just a speculation wearing a whitepaper.

"Is the Model Sustainable?"

The most critical threat to the longevity of most crypto projects is not regulation, security breaches, or even market volatility—it is unsustainable economic design. A protocol may have a slick interface, impressive backers, or even substantial community momentum, but *without a sound, self-reinforcing model for value creation and distribution, it will eventually implode under its own weight*. The question of sustainability forces us to move past surface metrics and speculative hype. It demands a close reading of tokenomics, incentive architecture, revenue logic, and behavioural alignment. This is where the difference between a fleeting experiment and a lasting innovation reveals itself.

Sustainability, in crypto, is less about ideological purity and more about operational coherence. Can the project sustain user interest without continuous token giveaways? Can it reward contributors in a way that doesn't cannibalise future value? Is there a built-in mechanism for economic feedback, such that growth drives utility—not just price? These are not academic hypotheticals. They are existential tests, and most projects fail them because they are engineered for growth, not for durability.

Consider Axie Infinity, once hailed as a proof-of-concept for play-to-earn models. During its meteoric rise, players in emerging markets could earn more through gaming than through local wages. But its economy was built on two tokens: AXS, a governance token with limited utility, and SLP, the reward token used for breeding new in-game characters. As user numbers grew exponentially, so too did SLP emissions. With no structural demand or burn mechanism to offset supply, the token collapsed. The game became less rewarding to play, users left, and what had been a vibrant economic microcosm dissolved into a cautionary tale. *The model was legible and enticing—but not sustainable.*

Contrast this with Ethereum. Its transition to proof-of-stake, paired with fee-burning introduced in EIP-1559, demonstrates a long-term orientation. It aligns usage with value accrual by making ETH more scarce as network activity grows. Validators are rewarded for securing the network, but not excessively. There is no infinite emissions schedule diluting stakeholders over time. *Ethereum's model acknowledges trade-offs and embeds discipline into its architecture.* This is a hallmark of sustainability: balancing user growth with fiscal responsibility and resisting the temptation to inflate away the future.

Tokenomics, while often treated as a marketing document for launch, is in fact the foundation of economic legitimacy. It determines how a protocol distributes power, rewards behaviour, and monetises its infrastructure. If the only mechanism to attract users is through issuing more tokens, then that protocol is subsidising usage rather than earning it. This works—briefly—until the cost of growth exceeds its benefits. What distinguishes a robust model is the presence of *internal demand drivers*. Uniswap, for instance, charges fees on token swaps, which accrue indirectly to liquidity providers and, potentially, to the protocol itself. There is a closed loop: usage generates fees, which sustain the system, without requiring new token emissions to pay participants.

Another essential concept is *incentive alignment*. Sustainability demands that short-term actions by individual users support long-term goals of the protocol. This is rarely automatic. Systems must be *designed* to reward behaviours that preserve rather than erode shared value. Compound, a DeFi lending platform, launched with COMP tokens to bootstrap usage. But it also introduced governance stakes—users who earned tokens could vote on protocol changes. The idea was to turn users into stewards. But over time, the low barriers to COMP farming allowed whales to accumulate governance power without necessarily caring about the protocol's health. *A model is not sustainable if it allows misaligned actors to dominate its decision-making.*

Inflation, in crypto, is often a sign of desperation. When protocols can't fund development or growth through organic means, they mint more tokens. This dilutes holders and shifts the cost of usage to the future. In a fiat system, central banks at least have policy levers to manage inflation. In crypto, many projects bake in inflation without a strategy for exit or tapering. Token supply rises perpetually, but utility and demand do not. Projects that rely on perpetual inflation to maintain basic functionality are not decentralised economies—they are *unfunded liabilities* waiting to crystallise.

This is where business model evaluation becomes vital. Many crypto projects eschew traditional revenue generation under the banner of decentralisation. But decentralisation is not an excuse for economic incoherence. A protocol that generates no revenue but consumes capital to operate is not sustainable—it is a non-profit without governance or accountability. The best projects build modular, monetisable infrastructure: data oracles that charge for accuracy (Chainlink), layer-2 solutions that charge for settlement compression (Arbitrum), or decentralised exchanges that monetise liquidity (Curve). *Revenue alone does not ensure sustainability, but it creates the economic gravity required for persistence.*

Another axis of sustainability is *token utility*. What can the token actually do, beyond being traded? If the only purpose of holding a token is to speculate, it becomes a proxy for sentiment rather than productivity. But if the token is used to pay for services, vote on proposals, or collateralise assets, it embeds itself into economic flows. This utility creates *stickiness*. The more a token is required to access valuable services, the more its demand becomes intrinsic. Projects like Lido, which facilitate liquid staking, are examples of embedding utility into core infrastructure. Users hold LDO tokens not just to speculate, but to shape governance and share in fees.

Still, even with sound tokenomics and credible business logic, sustainability requires *resilience*. Can the model adapt to shocks? Is it robust under changing market conditions? Can it survive a regulatory clampdown, a liquidity crunch, or a loss of user confidence? Many protocols are engineered for expansion but brittle under contraction. They assume a world of uninterrupted growth. True sustainability involves designing not just for upside, but for entropy. Protocols need kill switches, throttling mechanisms, and governance pathways to reform in crisis.

This brings us to governance itself. A protocol's model is only as durable as its ability to adapt. Fixed rules work in closed systems, but crypto ecosystems operate in open chaos. A project with no capacity to evolve is unsustainable by design. Conversely, projects with plutocratic governance—where power accrues to the wealthy—may find that decisions benefit insiders at the expense of users. The sustainability of a model includes *who governs it*, how decisions are made, and whether those decisions reinforce the protocol's mission.

Sustainability also requires discipline in distribution. Many token projects allocate excessive shares to insiders, venture backers, or early adopters—creating future sell pressure and resentment. A front-loaded distribution may maximise short-term price action but undermines the perception of fairness. Fairness, in turn, affects legitimacy, which affects participation. If new users feel like they are entering a rigged game, they will not stay. *Sustainable projects allocate power and reward in a way that fosters trust over time.*

Finally, sustainability is a function of narrative integrity. Does the story the project tells about itself match its economic reality? Many tokens speak of decentralisation while relying on centralised infrastructure. Others promise community governance while locking key parameters behind opaque multisigs. *If the narrative requires suspension of disbelief, the model is already compromised.* Sustainability is not just a balance sheet question—it is a matter of coherence between stated purpose, operational behaviour, and financial logic.

In traditional finance, investors analyse income statements, balance sheets, and cash flows. In crypto, the analogues exist, but are encoded differently: protocol revenues, token supply schedules, governance proposals, smart contract audits. The tools are there. What is required is the discipline to use them—not just to assess whether a project can succeed, but whether it *should*.

A sustainable model in crypto is not merely one that survives—it is one that justifies its survival by solving real problems, rewarding real contribution, and evolving with integrity. These models are rare, but they are the future. Everything else is architecture built on sand.

Would This Exist Without Crypto?

One of the most under-asked, yet most revealing, questions in the evaluation of any crypto project is deceptively simple:

Would this exist without blockchain? It is the intellectual pressure test that cuts through jargon, marketing spin, and speculative exuberance. While much of the digital asset landscape is buoyed by a kind of techno-optimism—one that presumes blockchain to be not only novel, but inherently valuable—this chapter begins with a more sobering premise: novelty alone is not utility. Nor is decentralisation automatically an advantage. The true measure of value lies in whether blockchain technology is *necessary* to solve a clearly defined problem—and whether that problem, when solved, yields real, sustainable impact.

This is not an academic exercise. It is a practical and strategic lens that distinguishes durable innovation from hype-wrapped mimicry. Many projects in the crypto space function as decentralised replicas of existing centralised services—lending platforms, exchanges, identity systems, or marketplaces—without making a compelling case for why decentralisation meaningfully improves the outcome. Worse still, a number of projects use tokens not as economic utilities, but as marketing accessories: tradable abstractions whose only function is to monetise attention and fuel speculative growth.

Not all innovation is improvement. And not all disruption is progress. There is a profound difference between building on blockchain because you can and building on it because you must. The former results in tokenised gimmicks; the latter, in systems that are otherwise impossible or vastly more efficient. Consider the classic examples of Bitcoin and

Ethereum. The former exists precisely because no central authority could credibly administer a non-sovereign monetary system. Its raison d'être is the trustless transfer of value in the absence of intermediaries. Ethereum, similarly, introduced programmable contracts that operate autonomously without needing centralised enforcement—enabling a host of use cases from decentralised finance (DeFi) to decentralised autonomous organisations (DAOs).

Yet beyond these foundational layers, the crypto ecosystem has seen an explosion of projects whose dependence on blockchain is tenuous at best. Take, for instance, decentralised social networks. Advocates claim they resist censorship and empower user ownership. But in practice, they often suffer from poor user experience, limited adoption, and unclear business models. Is censorship resistance truly the core problem of most social media users? Or is it a niche concern projected as a universal value? If the product does not solve a real problem more effectively than existing platforms—and if the use of blockchain introduces latency, cost, or complexity—it is fair to question its necessity.

This diagnostic framing becomes even more critical in enterprise and public-sector deployments. Across healthcare, supply chains, voting systems, and real estate registries, blockchain has been proposed as a panacea for inefficiencies. But again, scrutiny reveals that in many cases, traditional databases with audit logs could serve equally well—or better—without the overhead of consensus protocols and token incentives. The test, then, is not whether blockchain *can* be used, but whether its attributes—immutability, decentralisation, transparency—are the *only* or *best* way to resolve the problem. Where there is a central actor already trusted by all parties, blockchain may be superfluous. But in cross-jurisdictional contexts, or where trust is fragile or fractured, decentralised solutions can play a transformative role.

It is also worth examining the psychological and economic incentives that distort project design. The allure of token launches and liquidity events often pushes teams to embed blockchain into products prematurely or unnecessarily, simply to access funding or community hype. In this environment, the focus shifts from product-market fit to tokenomics theatrics. But economic speculation without technical or social utility is a house of cards. It may attract short-term attention, but it rarely survives scrutiny or market cycles. Investors and users are left holding the remnants of promises that were never grounded in functional necessity.

To sharpen this evaluative lens, consider the following examples. First, Helium, a decentralised wireless network, aimed to provide decentralised infrastructure for IoT connectivity. On paper, it solved a real problem: reducing central dependency on telecom monopolies. However, post-launch revelations showed that token incentives were disproportionately captured by insiders, and actual network usage remained low. The issue wasn't with the concept—it was the mismatch between token distribution mechanics and real user demand. The blockchain component wasn't irrelevant, but it didn't guarantee sustainability or effectiveness.

Contrast this with Filecoin, a decentralised storage network. Cloud storage is dominated by centralised giants, raising questions about data ownership, censorship risk, and pricing power. Filecoin's architecture, which incentivises storage providers through cryptoeconomic mechanisms, offers a meaningful alternative—*but only if it achieves sufficient reliability, cost competitiveness, and adoption.* The blockchain is not just ornamental here; it is integral. But even in such cases, the bar is high. Decentralised systems must not only be philosophically appealing; they must also be *technically superior or economically compelling* for their users.

The critical distinction, then, is not whether a project is "on-chain," but whether being on-chain is *essential*. This is where many investors, policymakers, and builders err. They conflate decentralisation with value creation. But decentralisation is not free—it imposes trade-offs in latency, scalability, usability, and governance. A blockchain-based solution should earn its keep. It must justify its cost by delivering outcomes that are otherwise unreachable, or demonstrably better in terms of security, integrity, or inclusion.

In some cases, blockchain serves not as a technological imperative, but as a political instrument. Consider decentralised finance protocols operating outside traditional banking jurisdictions. For users in countries with capital controls, unreliable banking, or financial repression, the ability to transact freely and hold assets in stablecoins is not a luxury—it's a lifeline. Here, blockchain enables economic agency where none existed. But that use case is rooted in context. For the average user in a well-regulated, stable economy, the advantages of DeFi may be marginal or even inferior when weighed against the risks and complexities.

The question *Would this exist without crypto?* therefore doubles as a reality check. It forces designers and investors alike to confront the counterfactual: If blockchain disappeared tomorrow, what would be lost—and what would remain? Projects that answer with clarity—pointing to problems uniquely solvable through decentralisation, immutability, or token-based coordination—deserve attention. Those that cannot articulate this value risk becoming artefacts of a speculative era rather than the foundations of a digital future.

This is not to dismiss experimentation. Innovation often begins with exploratory excess. But the maturity of a field is marked by discernment: the ability to separate artefacts from architecture, fads from frameworks. As the crypto space seeks legitimacy and longevity, it must move beyond novelty for its own sake and towards a culture of design grounded in problem-solving. The most enduring technologies in history—from the printing press to the internet—were not merely innovative. They solved foundational problems better, faster, or more inclusively than their predecessors.

Blockchain, if it is to have a similar legacy, must meet the same standard. It must be more than a toolkit for speculation. It must be a substrate for better systems. The first step to building or backing such systems is to ask, without apology or euphemism: *Would this exist without crypto? And if not, why not?* The strength of that answer reveals more than a white paper ever will.

A Personal Crypto Checklist

The difference between speculation and investing often hinges on the quality of questions asked before capital is committed. Nowhere is this more essential than in the crypto markets, where dazzling narratives, charismatic founders, and complex technical jargon can obscure critical flaws or outright fabrications. A well-designed checklist disciplines the mind to pause before buying into hype, enabling thoughtful investors to distinguish signal from noise. But this is not about creating an inflexible scoring system or reducing judgment to formulas; it's about consistently applying sound reasoning under conditions of ambiguity and asymmetric information. *In crypto, clarity is not given—it must be earned.*

A useful checklist is not a gatekeeper that says "yes" or "no" to every project. Rather, it is a cognitive scaffold—a way to interrogate the claims, structures, and incentives of any token, platform, or protocol. By asking the right questions in the right order, investors develop pattern recognition, sharpen scepticism where needed, and ultimately make more grounded decisions. Importantly, such a checklist should not just help spot good opportunities; it should actively help *avoid* disasters. Prevention, not just prediction, is the priority.

1. Purpose and Value Proposition

Begin with the most neglected question in crypto: *What problem does this solve?* Far too many projects present technical complexity as a substitute for purpose. Is the platform addressing a clearly defined need with real users and measurable friction points? Can that need be more effectively or cheaply addressed with existing infrastructure? If the token is the product, rather than a mechanism within a product, the red flags are immediate.

Furthermore, ask: *Why does this need a blockchain?* If decentralisation is invoked, probe what that actually delivers—resilience? censorship resistance? interoperability?—and whether the architecture delivers it in practice or merely in theory. If tokenisation is central, evaluate whether the token serves a functional role (e.g., governance, staking, fees) or merely serves as speculative bait. *Tokens without purpose are liabilities, not assets.*

2. Tokenomics and Incentive Design

Token supply mechanics are not just a technicality—they are the economic DNA of the project. Look closely at issuance schedules, supply caps (or lack thereof), allocation to insiders, and mechanisms for token sinks or burn. *A token with perpetual inflation and no demand sinks is a slow-motion dilution engine.*

Incentive design must align short-term participation with long-term sustainability. Does the system reward early users in a way that can endure once external subsidies are removed? Is there a risk of mercenary liquidity—capital chasing rewards, then vanishing when incentives dry up? Yield farming, staking APYs, and play-to-earn dynamics must be examined through the lens of sustainability. If the tokenomics require ever-increasing user growth to maintain value, the system may be functionally a pyramid, regardless of legal classification.

3. Team, Governance, and Development Activity

In a market built on code, community, and trust, who is behind the project matters. Is the founding team public and verifiably experienced in relevant domains? Is there transparent governance that allows stakeholders to participate meaningfully? Centralised control can be a short-term strength and a long-term risk. Conversely, decentralisation theatre—where power still rests with the core team despite the presence of token votes—erodes trust once discovered.

Development activity is a leading indicator of seriousness. Is the GitHub repository active with real contributors and version updates? Are there independent audits of smart contracts? Is there an engaged developer community beyond the core team? *A dormant codebase with a live token is a speculative time bomb.*

4. Regulatory Posture and Legal Risk

Given the evolving and fragmented state of global crypto regulation, investors must assess *where* the project is headquartered, *who* it serves, and *how* it engages with regulators. Is the token likely to be classified as a security in major jurisdictions? Is the project operating with appropriate licences where needed? If founders are evasive on legal questions, or if the project is deliberately domiciled in obscure jurisdictions with no meaningful oversight, consider what that implies about risk tolerance and accountability.

Privacy coins, DeFi mixers, and offshore exchanges often promise freedom from overreach—but they also pose material legal risks to users, not just operators. The balance between privacy and compliance is not just philosophical; it's regulatory realpolitik. *If the project's survival depends on remaining below the radar, it may not survive regulation's inevitable spotlight.*

5. Technology and Execution Risk

Not all code is created equal. Some projects launch with elegant whitepapers and fail to deliver working products years later. Others iterate quickly, shipping reliable infrastructure that developers and users rely on. Evaluate what has been delivered to date—not promised in roadmap slides. Is there a testnet, mainnet, mobile app, SDK, or API integration? Have bugs been resolved quickly, or have critical exploits gone unaddressed?

Understand the technical dependencies. If the platform runs on a Layer 2 solution, what risks are inherited from the Layer 1? If using an oracle or bridge, how robust is the architecture against manipulation or downtime? *Every dependency introduces a new failure mode—good investors track the risk stack, not just the surface app.*

6. Network Effects and Community Traction

Crypto assets are ultimately social organisms. Their value often depends on adoption, liquidity, and developer interest—not just technical merit. Assess whether the project is building a real community of users, contributors, and advocates. Is the Telegram or Discord channel alive with constructive discussion, or is it a hype echo chamber? Are developers building complementary tools or simply shilling token pumps?

Liquidity is another form of traction. Is the token listed on reputable exchanges with sufficient volume to support entry and exit without significant slippage? Is there on-chain usage of the token beyond speculation? *An empty protocol with a liquid token is still an empty protocol.*

7. Exit Mechanisms and Capital Pathways

Even good projects can become illiquid or irrelevant. Assess how and when you could exit a position. Are there lockups or vesting cliffs that might create sell pressure at predictable times? Is the treasury managed with transparency? Are revenues being generated and distributed, or are tokens being sold to fund development?

Tokens that rely entirely on appreciation for returns are speculation by design. Projects that produce cash flows—fees, royalties, or service revenues—allow valuation to be grounded in economics, not expectations. If the only way to benefit from participation is "number go up," the system may lack robustness. *Always ask: where does the money come from—and where does it go?*

8. Macro Fit and Market Relevance

Not every project needs to be a world-changer, but every investment should fit within a broader view of the market's trajectory. Is this protocol riding a durable tailwind—e.g., decentralised storage, global remittances, privacy tech? Or is it a derivative play on yesterday's trend? Assess how the project fits into geopolitical, regulatory, and infrastructure arcs.

Understand correlations: if the asset's fate is tightly coupled to Ethereum gas fees, Bitcoin volatility, or U.S. regulatory decisions, that correlation becomes part of your investment thesis. Projects that thrive only in bull markets but vanish in corrections offer little resilience. *Macro fragility is a hidden risk—unless you surface it with rigour.*

Synthesis: From Checklist to Discipline

A checklist is only useful if it leads to better decision-making. That means cultivating habits: delaying decisions until answers are clear, documenting reasoning before investing, and revisiting assumptions as conditions evolve. Investing in crypto is not just about recognising opportunity—it is about managing complexity and staying honest in the face of uncertainty.

There is no such thing as a perfect project. Trade-offs are everywhere. But a disciplined framework for evaluation transforms the speculative chaos of crypto into a landscape of discernible risks and potential rewards. *Clarity does not guarantee success—but it helps you fail less expensively, and learn more durably, than those who rely on instinct alone.* The investor who consistently asks the right questions will, over time, make fewer avoidable mistakes—and in crypto, that edge compounds fast.

Chapter 11
Crypto as a Mirror: What This Space Teaches Us About Ourselves

Crypto has never been solely about money. Beneath the decentralised ledgers, algorithmic governance, and ambitious reinventions of economic infrastructure, its most profound lessons concern people rather than code. For all its promises of disintermediation, permissionless access, and trustless execution, the crypto ecosystem operates as a strikingly human theatre—one that lays bare the motivations, anxieties, and mental frameworks that shape behaviour under uncertainty. In this high-stakes arena, where fortunes can shift in minutes, crypto functions as a mirror: reflecting not only what we desire, but how we pursue it—and what we are willing to believe along the way.

There is perhaps no better laboratory for the psychology of speculation. Traditional markets are buffered by regulation, institutional due diligence, and risk models that temper extremes. Crypto, by contrast, strips away many stabilisers. Price discovery unfolds publicly, around the clock, on decentralised platforms where trading, staking, farming, or minting can occur in seconds. This immediacy, coupled with the intensity of potential returns, amplifies behavioural biases: confirmation bias, herd mentality, overconfidence, and the sunk cost fallacy all operate in overdrive in a system that rewards rapid conviction and punishes hesitation.

Yet what truly distinguishes crypto is the way it entwines identity with investment. Holding a token is rarely a neutral financial position; it is a statement, a signal, sometimes a declaration of allegiance. This is especially true within tribalised subcultures such as Bitcoin maximalists or Ethereum evangelists, where financial thesis and ideological commitment merge. "HODLing" is valorised, "paper hands" derided, and volatility becomes a test of personal fortitude. Projects are debated not only for their fundamentals, but for the narratives they embody—freedom, rebellion, and utopian aspiration. Rationality contends not merely with greed, but with meaning itself.

The allure of outsider systems is central to this dynamic. For many advocates, crypto represents more than a financial innovation; it is an escape from institutions perceived as inefficient, corrupt, or exclusionary. Central banks, commercial banks, governments, and regulators are recast as untrustworthy gatekeepers, while smart contracts and DAOs emerge as symbols of empowerment. This story resonates with those who feel disenfranchised, both financially and philosophically. Beneath the code lies a revolutionary impulse: the desire to rewrite rules, to build systems that are fairer, more transparent, more accountable. Yet the emotional pull of this narrative can easily outrun functional reality. Commitment to decentralisation, like commitment to democracy, does not guarantee effective outcomes unless the mechanisms and incentives are sound.

Crypto's boom-and-bust cycles provide a vivid study of narrative inflation and hype. In each bull run, waves of believers arrive, drawn by charismatic founders, perceived breakthroughs, and media-fuelled excitement. Valuations often soar not because projects function, but because the story is irresistible. At the peak, prices reflect aspiration rather than reality. Then the inevitable contraction follows: frauds are revealed, code falters, liquidity disappears. Yet even amid collapse, infrastructure is built, lessons absorbed, and a foundation laid for the next cycle. These oscillations do not invalidate the technology, but they underscore the costs of unexamined optimism.

Rational engagement with crypto requires discipline without cynicism, scepticism without paralysis. It entails resisting the pull of popularity in favour of discerning truth, recognising that while the future may favour distributed systems, not all distributed systems merit a future. The prudent investor learns to disentangle price from value, narrative from utility, activity from traction. They pose difficult questions when others cheer and maintain curiosity when others withdraw. In crypto, speed, access, or leverage are secondary; the true advantage is clarity amid noise.

More than most asset classes, crypto demands personal calibration. It tests not only risk tolerance, but tolerance for illusion. It challenges emotional reflexes, time horizons, and the capacity to stay grounded amid euphoria or panic. Decisions are constantly interrogated: are they guided by principle or impulse, research or reputation, curiosity or fear? In this way, crypto reveals something deeper—not simply who will profit, but who possesses the discernment to endure.

This chapter treats crypto less as a strategy and more as a behavioural lens. It examines the forces motivating participation, the pitfalls that distort judgment, and the traits that underpin resilience. From FOMO to financial nationalism, from Reddit-driven rallies to regulatory clampdowns, we explore how the ecosystem mirrors the spectrum of human nature. Not with derision, but with inquiry, it illuminates what this remarkable experiment in open finance teaches about the choices we make, the systems we trust, and the selves we become when the usual guardrails are removed.

The Psychology of Speculation

If you want to understand the crypto markets, don't start with the code—start with the crowd. Crypto does not behave like traditional financial systems because it was not designed primarily by financiers or governed by regulators. It was created and adopted, often fervently, by a global swarm of technologists, idealists, opportunists, and speculators. That blend of ideology and incentive has produced a financial landscape where behaviour matters more than balance sheets, and where psychological reflexes—not just spreadsheets—drive price, participation, and volatility. *Crypto markets are behavioural laboratories in real time.*

Speculation, in its purest form, is a bet on the future value of something that has uncertain or undeveloped intrinsic worth. In the crypto space, this uncertainty is the norm. Most tokens are not valued based on traditional measures of earnings, assets, or dividends. Instead, they trade on perceived potential, virality, and narrative coherence. In such an environment, the dominant psychological forces are not caution or calculation, but *greed, fear, and the desperate avoidance of regret.* It's no accident that the term "FOMO" (fear of missing out) has become an operating principle in the space rather than a warning.

The influence of FOMO in crypto is especially acute because of the market's unique structure. The decentralised, always-on nature of crypto means that news, rumours, and price swings can spread globally without friction. There is no "open" or "close" of market hours, no pause for reflection. A new token can double in value overnight—or collapse by 90% before breakfast. In that kind of environment, hesitation feels like self-sabotage. The reflex to "get in before it's too late" is not just emotional; it begins to seem rational. *Opportunity costs are magnified by social exposure.*

This is further fuelled by identity attachment. Crypto is not simply a matter of financial preference—it often becomes an extension of personal belief and social belonging. In online communities like Twitter, Telegram, and Reddit, participants don't just discuss assets; they *evangelise* them. "Holding the line" is a test of conviction. Memes reinforce tribal allegiance. And price dips are explained away as unjust, manipulated, or irrelevant. When your investment becomes your identity, disconfirmation becomes a threat to self-concept. The result is a feedback loop of collective reinforcement: echo chambers where optimism is prized over realism and doubt is dismissed as betrayal.

But this emotional entanglement is not new. Similar psychological patterns have long defined other speculative episodes—from Dutch tulips in the 1630s to dotcom startups in the late 1990s. What's different about crypto is the level of transparency. In traditional markets, investor sentiment is often inferred indirectly—through trading volumes, fund flows, or survey data. In crypto, it is visible, visceral, and vocal. The conversations are public. The market sentiment is memefied. Wallet activity is on-chain. In essence, *the psychology of the market is not just a shadow; it's centre stage.*

Take, for example, the GameStop saga of 2021. While technically a stock market event, it shared all the behavioural DNA of crypto: community-driven coordination, narrative over fundamentals, and a suspicion of institutional actors. The emotional stakes were more than financial; they were ideological. That event was a mirror for crypto investors too—a validation of outsider power and a warning about how quickly speculative fever can turn irrational.

The prevalence of "pump and dump" schemes in altcoins further illustrates this tension. Retail investors are often lured into projects with slick marketing and sky-high promises, only to find that insiders are exiting while they're entering. These events are rarely about deception alone; they exploit basic human vulnerabilities—greed, urgency, the desire to be part of something early. Speculators convince themselves that *this time is different,* that *they're smarter than the last cohort,* that *they'll get out in time.* Most don't.

But it's important not to frame this behaviour as mere foolishness. In many ways, crypto is functioning exactly as designed: a system with low barriers to entry, high reward variance, and an open-source culture that invites experimentation. The speculative cycles may be irrational in the short term, but they are often necessary mechanisms of price discovery, capital allocation, and cultural attention. *Booms attract resources, which fund innovation, which eventually produces something real.* The problem is not speculation per se—it's the inability to distinguish speculation from investment.

One of the more subtle but powerful psychological biases in crypto is what behavioural economists call "narrative coherence." Human beings are wired to prefer stories that explain why things happen. In crypto, narratives abound: decentralisation as moral progress, tokenisation as financial inclusion, blockchain as inevitability. When prices rise, these stories are validated. When prices fall, the faithful reinterpret the decline as a setup for future vindication. This elasticity of belief is powerful—and dangerous. *When conviction hardens into ideology, investors lose the ability to adapt to changing reality.*

Another dimension is the role of social proof. In a decentralised space with little formal vetting, investors often substitute community excitement for due diligence. If enough smart people are talking about a project—on Twitter, in newsletters, on podcasts—it begins to feel legitimate. This is particularly true when big names are attached: venture capital firms, tech influencers, or founders with reputational capital. But the presence of elite endorsement does not guarantee project viability. In fact, many VC-backed tokens have underperformed dramatically after launch, especially when retail investors are left holding illiquid bags.

Yet for all these distortions, speculation has a certain clarifying power. It exposes what people value, what they fear, what they hope to gain. It forces questions that other financial domains often suppress: *What is this really worth? Who benefits if this succeeds? What am I believing that others might be missing?* These are not just questions for traders—they're foundational inquiries into how belief is priced into systems. The most thoughtful crypto investors are not those who avoid speculation, but those who understand the role it plays and the temptations it creates.

What can broader financial behaviour learn from crypto speculation? Quite a bit. Traditional markets are increasingly influenced by retail participation, online sentiment, and alternative narratives. ESG investing, meme stocks, and fintech apps have all blurred the lines between conviction, trend, and portfolio allocation. Crypto simply accelerates this reality. It shows how emotional, social, and ideological drivers are not noise in the system—they *are* the system. Price is not just a function of discounted cash flow; it's a reflection of attention, belief, and mood.

Ultimately, the challenge is not to suppress these psychological forces, but to make them conscious. Greed is not shameful, but it must be tempered. FOMO is not irrational, but it must be contextualised. Identity is not irrelevant, but it must not substitute for research. A rational investor is not one who pretends to be emotionless, but one who can recognise when emotion is distorting judgement. In the long run, clarity—about yourself, about your motivations, about the limits of what you know—is the most valuable asset in your portfolio.

Crypto has made that lesson unavoidable. It has stripped away many of the illusions of control and complexity that shroud other markets. What's left is a raw encounter with risk, belief, and human nature. Speculation, in this light, is not just a financial activity—it is a psychological practice. One that rewards self-awareness as much as strategy. And one that reveals, often more than we'd like to admit, who we are when no one's regulating our impulses but ourselves.

The Allure of Outsider Systems

Trust is rarely lost in a single moment. It erodes slowly, almost invisibly, until one day what once felt like bedrock becomes negotiable. Across the world, faith in established institutions—governments, banks, media, central banks—has thinned to a worrying transparency. In that thinning, crypto has found its most potent fuel. Not because it offers better performance or user experience—although it sometimes does—but because it offers *an alternative.* For those who feel alienated, surveilled, overcharged, or left behind, crypto doesn't just represent a new asset class. *It represents an exit.*

To understand crypto's psychological gravity, you must begin not with its technical design, but with the context into which it emerged. Bitcoin's white paper was published in October 2008, in the shadow of a financial crisis that exposed grotesque institutional failure. Banks that had long been seen as guardians of the economy revealed themselves as engines of unchecked leverage and misaligned incentives. Central banks responded with unprecedented money creation. Political systems offered little accountability. Amid this backdrop, Bitcoin's founding promise—*a peer-to-peer electronic cash system that required no trust in third parties*—was not a fringe idea. It was a plausible response to a system that had forfeited its moral authority.

This foundational moment shaped crypto's DNA. It is not just a technology of decentralisation; it is a philosophy of disintermediation. Its most vocal proponents are not merely investors—they are *refugees of broken systems.* For them, crypto isn't primarily about profit, but about autonomy. And while that may seem exaggerated to those in stable economies with functioning institutions, it resonates powerfully in regions with currency collapse, authoritarian surveillance, or unbanked populations. In Nigeria, Argentina, Lebanon, and Venezuela, crypto is not a speculative play—it's a workaround. A lifeline. A way of asserting financial agency in systems that routinely deny it.

But outsider energy doesn't always emerge from hardship. Sometimes, it comes from *ideological estrangement.* Libertarians, privacy advocates, cypherpunks, and system critics have long argued that centralised control—of money, identity, and data—poses inherent risks. To them, crypto represents not just a hedge against inflation or banks, but against coercion. They see in decentralised ledgers a means of removing trust as a single point of failure. In their view, blockchain isn't valuable because it's faster or cheaper (it often isn't). It's valuable because it's *non-sovereign. Non-permissioned.* Immutable by design. That, to them, is the breakthrough.

These emotional undercurrents—rooted in resentment, autonomy, or ideological rejection—are what give crypto its cultish vitality and its volatility. When your money is also your protest, objectivity becomes elusive. Evaluating utility becomes secondary to declaring allegiance. Projects are not simply startups; they are symbols. Technologies are not judged by outcomes, but by alignment. "Decentralised" becomes a moral claim, even when the governance is opaque. "Open-source" becomes a badge of virtue, even if the protocol is unusable. *Outsider systems breed purity tests, and purity often trumps pragmatism.*

This makes it difficult for outsiders to see crypto clearly. From the inside, institutions are presumed guilty until proven innocent. From the outside, crypto is presumed guilty by association—with frauds, hacks, and hype cycles. But neither view captures the complexity. The allure of outsider systems is not reducible to cynicism or rebellion. It reflects a broader philosophical tension: *Should power be concentrated for efficiency, or distributed for resilience? Should trust be engineered top-down, or emerge bottom-up through protocol and consensus?*

Crypto wagers—often implicitly—that the latter is more durable in a digitally interconnected world. Yet this wager comes with trade-offs. Decentralisation is not free. It often sacrifices performance, usability, and coordination. Building systems that resist capture also means making them resistant to change. Public blockchains, for all their virtues, are slow to upgrade, contentious to govern, and difficult to fix once deployed. For the rational investor, the question becomes: *When is the cost of decentralisation worth paying? When is the emotional appeal of autonomy masking a lack of functionality or economic logic?*

This is not an idle concern. Many crypto projects lean heavily on "outsider branding" while quietly operating with centralised controls. Token distributions often favour early insiders. Governance is delegated to opaque multisig wallets. Treasury decisions are dominated by a handful of actors. The rhetoric is decentralised; the execution is not. For the discerning investor, it's critical to distinguish between *the marketing of outsider status* and the *actual implementation of distributed systems.* Just because something is on-chain doesn't make it trustless. Just because it uses cryptography doesn't make it just.

Yet even when crypto fails to live up to its ideals, the appetite for alternatives persists. The failures of traditional institutions are not theoretical; they are felt. Surveillance capitalism. Bailouts for the powerful. Technocratic opacity.

Political gridlock. In many sectors—finance, data ownership, identity, media—the centralised incumbents have failed to adapt to digital realities in ways that serve citizens well. Crypto, for all its messiness, has surfaced legitimate questions: *Why does it take three days to settle a wire transfer? Why do I need a bank account to send money? Why does my credit score decide if I can rent a flat? Who owns my digital footprint?*

These are not fringe inquiries. They are modern necessities. Crypto's outsider energy gives voice to frustrations that have long gone unheard. It opens conceptual space for imagining different architectures of trust and value. That doesn't mean every experiment is wise—or even honest. But it does mean the experiments matter.

Still, emotional appeal must not be mistaken for economic viability. The fact that something challenges the status quo does not make it investable. Nor does opposition to institutional power translate into functional products. The history of outsider movements—in politics, technology, finance—is full of charismatic narratives and catastrophic execution. The crypto investor who conflates rebellion with return is not resisting power; they are surrendering to sentiment.

So what does it mean to take crypto's outsider appeal seriously *without becoming seduced by it*? It means engaging with projects that can demonstrate technical coherence, sound tokenomics, clear user value, and credible governance. It means demanding more than decentralisation as a slogan. It means evaluating whether a platform would still be compelling if it were run by a cooperative, a public agency, or a private firm—*because if blockchain is the only reason it exists, it may not need to exist at all.*

Crypto's power is not that it has solved every institutional problem. It hasn't. Its power lies in making certain problems visible. It reminds us how fragile trust can be, and how expensive centralisation sometimes becomes. It invites us to imagine—and build—alternatives. But imagination alone is not an investment thesis. Emotional resonance is not a business model. The mature crypto investor does not reject institutions blindly, nor embrace outsiders uncritically. They ask: *What is this for? Who benefits? What proof exists—not of concept, but of adoption?*

The future of crypto will not be decided by those who shout the loudest, but by those who can build systems that work under pressure, over time, and at scale. Systems that don't just appeal to our desire to exit—but that offer new ways to participate meaningfully, fairly, and securely. That's the difference between an outsider movement and an enduring one. Between disruption for its own sake, and transformation with purpose.

Lessons from the Boom-Bust Cycle

In November 2021, the total market capitalisation of cryptocurrencies reached over $3 trillion. Just thirteen months later, more than two-thirds of that value had vanished. Tens of thousands of investors who once boasted of life-changing gains were now silent, liquidated, or bitterly wiser. This pattern wasn't new. Since Bitcoin's inception in 2009, crypto has gone through at least four major speculative bubbles, each larger and louder than the last. Yet despite the volatility, a core of developers, entrepreneurs, and investors has persisted. The question is not merely why the prices collapse—asset bubbles always burst—but why they recur with such ferocity. And more importantly: *What can we learn from their aftermath?*

Every technological revolution begins with a surge of idealism. The early adopters are not in it for money—they are driven by vision, frustration, or both. In crypto's case, it was a desire to reimagine money, finance, and digital ownership without relying on centralised institutions. These are not trivial goals. They speak to longstanding issues with the legacy financial system: inefficiency, exclusion, opacity, and overreach. Yet as these ideas spread beyond their originators, they begin to attract capital. Where capital flows, speculation follows. And with speculation comes narrative inflation.

In crypto's case, narrative has always outpaced infrastructure. The promise of decentralised finance (DeFi), non-fungible tokens (NFTs), or Web3 often runs ahead of what the technology can stably deliver at scale. But that hasn't deterred investors. Because in the heat of a bull market, *the story is the product*. Projects are funded not because they have cash flow, but because they have momentum. Teams raise millions with barely a prototype. Tokens rally on announcements rather than execution. Incentives are built on self-reinforcing loops: if everyone believes it's valuable, it becomes valuable—until it doesn't.

These cycles are not unique to crypto. They echo the railway boom of the 1840s, the dot-com bubble of the late 1990s, and the SPAC frenzy of 2020. In each case, innovation sparked justified excitement. But investors extrapolated too quickly, mistook early growth for inevitable dominance, and ignored fragility underneath. The bust came not because the underlying idea was wrong, but because it had been overcapitalised too soon. *Crypto, too, suffers from premature scalability.* Projects raise before they've proven demand, tokenise before they've built trust, and market before they've secured product-market fit.

The bust, then, is not a bug of the crypto ecosystem—it is a feature of how innovation meets capital in a hyper-networked age. The velocity of digital storytelling, financial engineering, and community-building means that bubbles inflate faster than ever. Telegram groups, YouTube influencers, Discord servers, and Twitter threads become accelerants. Scarcity is designed into tokens; urgency is hardcoded into launches. Add leverage—through derivatives, staking, or "yield farming"—and a 20% pullback becomes a 70% crash. And yet, in each crash, the cycle resets. Developers retrench. Infrastructure improves. Skepticism hardens. But enthusiasm never quite dies.

Why? Because behind the boom-bust noise is something sticky: *a genuine technological frontier*. Blockchain technology *does* enable new modes of coordination, ownership, and finance. Smart contracts, decentralised identity, censorship-resistant storage—these are not marketing terms, but novel primitives. But they require time, iteration, and regulatory clarity to mature. They cannot be rushed by token incentives alone. Investors who fail to differentiate between the real and the rhetorical get swept up in hype. Those who learn to pause, question, and evaluate—even at the height of a bull run—are the ones who survive long enough to benefit from the next real wave of innovation.

What's more revealing, perhaps, is what these cycles expose about *investor psychology*. Boom-bust cycles are not just financial phenomena; they are emotional dramas. They reveal our hunger for easy gains, our herd instincts, and our susceptibility to charismatic founders. In crypto, where traditional valuation tools are limited or inapplicable, narrative fills the vacuum. Investors attach identity to tokens. They anchor belief to price action. And they internalise volatility as vindication or persecution—when prices rise, they are geniuses; when they fall, victims. This dynamic is intensified by the performative nature of crypto communities. Forums reward conviction, not doubt. Social media penalises nuance. Memes outperform whitepapers.

This creates an environment where feedback loops are turbocharged. A token doesn't merely reflect sentiment—it shapes it. As more people buy in, early holders profit, which encourages more people to buy in, until the mechanism reverses. The sell-off is not gradual; it is a cascade. Liquidity dries up, lending platforms implode, and "stablecoins" de-peg. Panic replaces euphoria, and what was once a movement becomes a cautionary tale. But for those paying attention, each cycle offers *data*—not just on market mechanics, but on human nature.

Take the ICO mania of 2017. At its peak, projects were raising hundreds of millions on little more than promises. Many failed. Some were outright scams. But others—like Ethereum—emerged stronger, having survived scrutiny and turbulence. The DeFi boom of 2020–21 followed a similar arc. It showcased the power of composable financial protocols, but also the fragility of untested smart contracts and unsustainable yield models. NFTs exploded into the mainstream in 2021, opening new avenues for digital ownership, art, and identity—but also revealing how speculative fervour can detach completely from use case or aesthetics. Each boom brought innovation and froth in equal measure.

What matters for the investor, then, is *pattern recognition*. Not in the technical-analysis sense, but in understanding *the rhythm of hype and consolidation*. There's a moment in every cycle where fundamentals decouple from price, where scepticism is dismissed as FUD (fear, uncertainty, doubt), and where "community" becomes code for cult. These are signals. They don't predict exact tops or bottoms, but they indicate that emotional excess is taking over from strategic clarity. To survive the bust, one must learn to *exit the mania before the narrative turns*—not out of fear, but out of discipline.

The corollary is also true: *the best opportunities often emerge in the wreckage*. It's after the crash—when prices are flat, enthusiasm is low, and headlines have turned mocking—that the most resilient builders quietly make progress. When capital is scarce, only the committed remain. When speculation fades, product quality matters. For long-term investors, this is the time to pay attention. Not because prices are low, but because *clarity is high*. Noise has receded. Substance reasserts itself.

This dynamic—of boom, bust, and rebirth—is not unique to crypto. It is part of a larger cycle in innovation. Carlota Perez, in her landmark study of technological revolutions, describes this pattern as the shift from "installation" to "deployment." In the early phase, capital floods into emerging technologies, often ahead of their readiness. This leads to speculative bubbles. The crash is not an end, but a transition point. It clears out excess, enforces discipline, and paves the way for sustainable growth. Crypto, by this reading, is not broken—it is *early*. The question is not whether it will recover, but which parts of it will prove enduring.

That's where the thoughtful investor must focus—not on chasing momentum, but on interrogating *resilience*. Which teams keep building when no one is watching? Which protocols quietly accrue users, integrations, or developer mindshare? Which platforms operate transparently, with robust governance and thoughtful risk management? These are not flashy questions, but they are the ones that matter when the music stops.

Ultimately, the lesson of crypto's boom-bust cycles is not to avoid risk, but to respect it. Speculation is not inherently bad; it drives attention, funding, and experimentation. But unchecked, it becomes distortion. The mature investor doesn't shun narrative—but they anchor it to facts. They remain curious, but not credulous. And they recognise that *surviving the downturn is a form of alpha*—because most don't.

So as crypto continues its uneven ascent—through more bubbles, more busts, and more attempts at legitimacy—the real edge will belong not to those who predict prices, but to those who understand *patterns of behaviour*. Because while the assets may change, the human impulses behind them do not. And in the long run, it's not technology alone that determines value—it's the judgment of those who deploy it wisely, despite the noise.

What a Rational Investor Actually Looks Like

At the height of the 2021 bull market, someone bought a picture of a cartoon rock—part of the EtherRock NFT collection—for $1.3 million. The rock didn't do anything, represent anything, or change in any functional sense. Its price spiked not because of fundamental value, but because of narrative momentum, social proof, and the contagious logic of scarcity. For some, it was performance art; for others, an act of pure speculation. But for many newcomers, watching from the sidelines as meme coins, profile pictures, and gaming tokens soared, the message was clear: if you weren't playing the game, you were losing. What passed for "strategy" in much of the crypto world was simply *not missing out.*

To operate rationally in this environment—to say "no" more than "yes," to admit uncertainty, or to question inflated valuations—was often framed as cowardice or cynicism. Yet beneath the hype, *it is precisely these traits—discipline, clarity, and scepticism—that define the rational investor*. Not the one who perfectly times every top and bottom, but the one who stays solvent, alert, and informed long enough to benefit from durable trends while avoiding fatal errors.

In a market that rewards boldness and punishes hesitation in the short term, it takes unusual psychological fortitude to stand apart. But the rational investor does not confuse *volatility with opportunity*. They understand that price movement is not always a signal, and that noise can often masquerade as urgency. Their first question is not "what could this become?" but "what is this today?" They seek *ground truth before extrapolation*, and they understand that hype, like leverage, amplifies both gains and delusions.

Importantly, rationality in investing is not about being emotionless. It is about having a *framework that disciplines emotion*. Emotional investing is not just about panic-selling during downturns—it also includes euphoric overconfidence during rallies, or anchoring to past prices and chasing sunk costs. The rational investor recognises these instincts and builds guardrails to resist them: predetermined position sizes, exit strategies, checklists of due diligence, and timelines that reflect their own needs—not Twitter sentiment or trending Discord posts.

Scepticism, often misunderstood as negativity, is another cornerstone of rational investing. It is not a posture of permanent doubt, but a method of inquiry. When a new protocol promises 100% annual yields, or a token triples overnight on no clear news, the rational investor does not rush in—they pause. They ask: *Where is the yield coming from? Who is subsidising these returns? What assumptions are being made about adoption, user retention, or token demand?* In crypto, where mechanisms can be opaque, decentralised, or novel, scepticism is not optional—it is essential.

Clarity, too, is a hallmark of rational decision-making. This means clarity of objective—am I investing, trading, experimenting, or gambling? Each mode is legitimate if consciously chosen, but disaster strikes when the boundaries blur. The person who claims to be a long-term investor but checks price charts every hour is not investing—they are absorbing noise. The rational investor aligns their actions with their time horizon, their risk appetite, and their informational edge—or the lack thereof. *They are clear about what they know, and honest about what they don't.*

Consider the contrast between two approaches to a new DeFi project. One investor reads a Medium post, sees a few trusted influencers involved, and decides to allocate 10% of their portfolio. The other reads the smart contract audit (or pays someone to), examines the token distribution schedule, compares it to competitors, and allocates a small test amount to observe protocol behaviour over time. The first may outperform in a roaring bull market—but the second is *more likely to preserve capital over the long term.* Crypto does not reward only speed; it rewards understanding—especially in the face of uncertainty.

Being rational also means being *adaptive*. The investor who locks themselves into a rigid thesis and refuses to revise when new data emerges is not disciplined—they are dogmatic. Crypto evolves rapidly. What was true six months ago may no longer hold. The rational investor maintains mental flexibility without succumbing to trend-chasing. They ask: *Has the thesis changed? Have the incentives shifted? Has the regulatory landscape introduced new risks or opportunities?* Their confidence is proportional to the quality of their information, not the volume of community excitement.

Contrary to the loudest voices in crypto, it is possible to be deeply optimistic about blockchain's potential *and* deeply critical of many of its implementations. The rational investor distinguishes between technology and token, between innovation and speculation, between aspiration and execution. They are not swayed by maximalist rhetoric or tribal identities. They do not need every trade to be a win. What they need is *a process that compounds good decisions*, even if it means forgoing moonshots in favour of more measured returns.

In practice, this often means accepting boredom. Rational investing is not thrilling. It does not deliver dopamine hits every hour. It means sitting out frothy trends. It means holding cash when nothing makes sense. It means researching things you don't immediately understand. And it means accepting that the best moves are sometimes invisible—not buying the pump, not tweeting your gains, not engaging in flame wars over layer-one supremacy.

There is also a humility in rational investing that is often missing from the crypto zeitgeist. Rather than claiming to know where the market is heading, the rational investor defines *how much not knowing they can afford*. This might mean setting maximum drawdowns, diversifying across themes, or refusing to invest in things they cannot explain in plain language. It is not about being right—it is about staying in the game.

The irony is that rational investors often *appear late* to outsiders. They do not FOMO into new coins on launch day. They wait for documentation, traction, or better valuation. They are dismissed as "missing out" until they're not. Then, when the market turns and others are trapped in illiquid positions or collapsed protocols, they are simply...quietly solvent. That is their edge. It's not flashy, but it's *repeatable*.

None of this means that rational investing is foolproof. Mistakes will happen. Markets are inherently uncertain, and crypto especially so. But rational investors *learn from mistakes*. They conduct post-mortems, not blame games. They ask whether their decision process failed, or if the outcome was simply the result of randomness. Over time, this builds not just a better portfolio, but *a better investor*—more resilient, more independent, more capable of thriving in environments where clarity is scarce and confusion is costly.

If the crypto markets are, as some argue, a stress test for investor psychology, then rationality is not just a tactic—it is a survival skill. And in a domain where narratives can be engineered, communities weaponised, and code exploited, it is also a form of *ethics*. To stay rational is to resist manipulation, to prioritise truth over trend, and to invest not just in assets, but in *integrity of process*. That is what a rational investor looks like. And in the digital economy ahead, it may be the rarest and most valuable asset of all.

Chapter 12
Designing Your Crypto Plan

Crypto has always been an arena of extremes—early adopters pitted against sceptics, maximalists confronting pragmatists, rampant speculation set against cautious experimentation. Yet, when the dust settles after each cycle, those who emerge with both clarity and intact capital are rarely the loudest voices or the boldest traders. They are the ones who arrive with a plan. A plan that does not hinge on the adrenaline of a bull market or the euphoria of headlines, but on understanding why they are participating, what role crypto occupies in their wider financial life, and how they will adjust when that role inevitably shifts.

Most people, naturally, do not construct this plan beforehand. They enter first—prompted by curiosity, peer influence, or sheer momentum—and only later confront questions of structure, risk, purpose, and commitment. That sequence is understandable. Crypto seduces through motion: stories of overnight gains, the anxiety of missing out, the allure of constant engagement. Yet movement without intention quickly becomes noise. The challenge, then, is not simply how to invest, but how to think: how to translate curiosity into intention, scattered participation into strategic engagement.

This chapter begins at that pivot point—the moment when crypto stops being a collection of anecdotes and headlines, and starts to demand serious attention. It addresses readers not with one-size-fits-all prescriptions, but with an honest spectrum of postures. The sceptic, wary of inflated claims yet unwilling to dismiss the sector entirely; the explorer, curious and risk-tolerant, yet uncertain how far to commit; the allocator, treating crypto as one piece of a broader portfolio, seeking disciplined exposure without distraction. Each archetype can engage productively, but each requires a distinct plan—not only in portfolio terms, but in mindset, boundaries, expectations, and time horizon.

There is no single "correct" approach to crypto. But there are certainly wrong ones—strategies grounded in borrowed conviction, emotional contagion, or the blind mimicry of others' actions. A plan is not something to be copied from a Twitter thread or an influencer's spreadsheet. It is something constructed through reflection, experimentation, and selective trust. A personal crypto plan is not merely the assets you acquire; it is a set of internal rules guiding your behaviour under pressure. What will you do when prices fall 70 per cent? When the media proclaims the market dead? When a friend multiplies their capital tenfold on a project you bypassed? Without a plan, those moments dictate your actions; with a plan, they test you—but do not derail you.

One of the most overlooked aspects of sound planning is knowing when not to invest. In crypto culture, abstention is often misinterpreted as ignorance or fear. Yet declining participation can itself be strategic. For some, the risks outweigh the rewards. For others, the opportunity cost—time, attention, or capital better spent elsewhere—is prohibitive. A well-articulated personal thesis validates such decisions without apology. Conviction is not measured by volume of opinion, but by depth of understanding.

Many wait for the "perfect time" to craft a plan—often after a crash, when froth has settled. Yet planning is not reactive damage control; it is forward-looking scaffolding. A robust plan does not assume markets will rise; it assumes you will encounter conflicting incentives, psychological stress, and unforeseen information, and that you will need a stable framework to respond judiciously. That is the purpose of this chapter: not to provide answers, but to offer architecture.

We will explore several model approaches—not as templates to be slavishly followed, but as mirrors to clarify your own orientation. We will examine how different investor types conceptualise allocation, security, time commitment, and metrics of success. We will guide you through formalising a crypto thesis—not in abstract jargon, but in practical terms: boundaries, objectives, and trade-offs. We will identify principles durable enough to withstand changing narratives, and distinguish between what can be planned for and what must be endured with resilience.

The goal is not prediction, but preparation. Markets will shift. Protocols will rise and fall. Technologies will evolve. Narratives will surge and collapse. Your task is not to anticipate every turn, but to cultivate a relationship with crypto that endures, rather than becomes a liability. A framework, not a forecast.

What separates durable investors from those who falter is not superior intelligence or hidden insight. It is the quiet, deliberate labour of defining a role for crypto within their financial life—and adhering to it. This chapter is designed to help you do precisely that. Not by dictating thought, but by guiding you to think through what truly matters. By its conclusion, you will not merely understand the approaches of others—you will be equipped to design your own, with clarity, flexibility, and integrity. That is the plan worth having.

Three Profiles, Three Approaches

The greatest misconception about investing in crypto is that everyone must approach it the same way. That it's either a brave leap of conviction or a timid step into irrelevance. But the reality is more nuanced—and more honest. People bring different levels of scepticism, experience, time, capital, and emotional bandwidth to the table. Pretending otherwise leads to poor decision-making and misplaced expectations. *Sound strategy begins not with "What coin should I buy?" but with "Who am I as an investor, and what role—if any—should crypto play in that identity?"*

In this light, three profiles emerge as representative archetypes: the sceptic, the explorer, and the allocator. These are not rigid categories, but practical frameworks. Each captures a mindset, a risk posture, and a set of priorities that shape how one might engage with the crypto space thoughtfully. The point is not to convert sceptics into evangelists or explorers into maximalists. The point is to offer *intellectually honest models* that help investors map their thinking to action—without guilt, hype, or dogma.

The sceptic is not ignorant, nor anti-technology. They may even be technically literate or financially sophisticated. What defines them is a cautious realism: a reluctance to embrace crypto until it proves genuine utility, regulatory soundness, or long-term economic value. Sceptics often see through the marketing fog. They notice how many blockchain pitches are dressed-up versions of old ideas or solutions in search of problems. They question unsustainable tokenomics, questionable governance structures, and the cultish rhetoric that surrounds many projects. *Their strength lies in restraint.* In a market designed to provoke FOMO, the sceptic's ability to pause, question, and wait can be their competitive edge.

A good strategy for the sceptic is built around informed abstention. They may choose not to hold crypto at all, or to do so minimally—perhaps a small exposure via a regulated ETF, a custody-backed instrument, or a well-capitalised exchange-traded product. Their primary interest lies in *monitoring the space,* not participating in it. They might follow a few credible newsletters, observe regulatory developments, or track major ecosystem shifts. For the sceptic, the goal is *to understand enough to make a defensible choice—not to validate hype or deny innovation wholesale.* Should compelling use cases emerge, they want to be ready—not reactive.

Then there is the explorer. This profile is marked by curiosity, risk tolerance, and a willingness to experiment—within limits. Explorers are not reckless, but they are willing to *learn by doing*. They want to understand crypto by engaging with it: buying small amounts of tokens, trying out decentralised applications, experimenting with wallets and staking. What distinguishes the explorer from the gambler is intent. The explorer has questions they want answered—about decentralisation, ownership, digital identity, financial inclusion—and they're using hands-on interaction to test the narratives. *They seek insight, not just returns.*

A sustainable strategy for the explorer involves boundaries. Set a fixed amount—financial or temporal—that defines the scope of experimentation. Avoid letting curiosity metastasise into distraction. Document what you're trying, why, and what you're observing. Think of this like a personal R&D budget: it's not about making money, it's about understanding. The explorer may buy into a few Layer 1 tokens, hold a stablecoin, participate in a DAO, or mint an NFT—not because these are guaranteed to succeed, but because they reveal the mechanics of how this ecosystem behaves. Explorers must also build emotional discipline. When prices spike or collapse, the temptation to pivot from learner to speculator can be strong. *The goal is not to win the game—but to understand the rules.*

Finally, there's the allocator. This is someone with a defined investment philosophy who views crypto not as a culture or ideology, but as a potential asset class. The allocator is likely already diversified across equities, bonds, property, and perhaps alternatives. They see crypto as a high-risk, high-variance domain that might offer asymmetric upside or portfolio diversification. But they approach it with sober expectations. *The allocator is not here for revolution. They are here for risk-managed exposure.*

The allocator's strategy is shaped by clear boundaries, rebalancing policies, and thoughtful position sizing. They may allocate 1–5% of their portfolio to crypto, usually through instruments that offer custody safeguards or regulatory clarity. They focus on liquidity, custody, and counterparty risk more than community drama or Twitter sentiment. They prefer simplicity—major coins, index-style products, blue-chip protocols—over speculative bets. But they don't ignore what's happening under the surface. Allocators study macro shifts in institutional adoption, infrastructure maturation, and technological development—not because they need to act on them today, but because they understand that *any exposure requires ongoing stewardship.*

What unites all three profiles is the rejection of passive participation. Each has a strategy defined not by market noise but by internal coherence. The sceptic protects against risk by waiting. The explorer absorbs risk in order to learn. The allocator manages risk through structure. Each has a plan that *fits their temperament, goals, and constraints.*

Problems arise when people mismatch their profile and their strategy. A sceptic who mimics an explorer without conviction risks cognitive dissonance and regret. An explorer who over-allocates without boundaries can be swept up in volatility and lose perspective. An allocator who buys without understanding the underlying protocols may mistake short-term gains for long-term viability. These are not merely tactical errors—they are errors of identity.

That's why this framework matters. Not to label people, but to *help them align their behaviour with their beliefs*. When someone says, "I feel like I'm missing out," the deeper question is: "What type of engagement would actually make sense for me?" This chapter doesn't prescribe a best way. It invites readers to examine themselves honestly—to calibrate ambition with caution, enthusiasm with realism, and participation with principle.

Crypto rewards the fast, but it punishes the impulsive. It rewards conviction, but it punishes delusion. It rewards adaptability, but it punishes attention fragmentation. Knowing *who you are* in this space is not a soft skill. It's the foundation of resilience.

If there's one shared principle across all three approaches, it is intentionality. Whether you choose to abstain, experiment, or allocate—do so with clarity. Let your strategy reflect your values, not your fears. Let your portfolio reflect your plan, not the market's mood. Let your actions reflect your judgement, not the crowd's enthusiasm.

In a domain that often celebrates extremes, these three profiles offer something rare: *the legitimacy of moderation.* The right crypto plan is not the one that performs best in the next bull market. It is the one you can live with, stick to, and grow through—without regret. That's not just a model. That's maturity.

From Curiosity to Conviction

One of the most underexamined facts about crypto investing is that opting out is just as much a thesis as opting in. Not investing, when done from a place of clarity rather than avoidance, is not indecision—it is decision, expressed through discipline. And yet, many people approach the crypto space with a kind of ambient curiosity: they want to learn, but not commit; they hover, but never clarify. This in-between state may feel responsible—safeguarding against error—but over time, it becomes intellectually and financially incoherent. *To engage or not to engage is not the most important question. The real challenge is articulating why you believe one or the other makes sense for you, and under what conditions that belief might change.*

The path from curiosity to conviction doesn't require becoming a crypto true believer. What it requires is a willingness to think rigorously, ask difficult questions, and reach an outcome that reflects your values, risk tolerance, and worldview—not the noise of the moment. Curiosity is a worthy starting point, but it is not a destination. It invites exploration, but without direction it quickly devolves into procrastination dressed as research. Conviction, by contrast, is a state of informed readiness. Whether that readiness leads to allocation or abstention, the through-line is the same: *you know what you're doing, and you know why you're doing it.*

Conviction is not synonymous with enthusiasm. One can have conviction that crypto is overvalued, misaligned with long-term financial goals, or too immature to merit capital—*and still be correct.* What separates conviction from complacency is the presence of a framework. It's the difference between saying "I'm staying out because I'm scared" versus "I'm staying out because I've examined the risk/reward profile, I've analysed the technological and regulatory dependencies, and I've concluded that the current state of the market doesn't justify a position." This distinction matters. Conviction empowers investors not just to act, but to *feel peace in their restraint*—even as the headlines scream otherwise.

The journey toward conviction starts with sharpening your lens. Ask not just *what* the crypto markets are doing, but *why* you're watching them. What is it you're hoping to learn? Are you intrigued by decentralisation as a governance experiment? Are you exploring Bitcoin as an inflation hedge or a geopolitical asset? Are you curious about Ethereum because of its programmable finance implications? Or are you simply trying to figure out why everyone seems to care? Each of these motivations leads to a different set of questions—and thus, a different process for developing conviction.

There is no universal thesis, and there shouldn't be. A thirty-year-old software engineer living in a country with capital controls will approach crypto very differently from a sixty-year-old retiree in a regulated market with defined pension benefits. One might see crypto as a tool for freedom; the other as a threat to capital preservation. Both can be rational. *The key is not consensus—it is coherence.* Does your stance on crypto reflect your needs, beliefs, and strategic objectives? Or are you outsourcing your logic to the loudest voices in your feed?

Consider, for instance, the common narrative that "crypto is early, so you need to get in now." This framing trades on a mixture of urgency and inevitability. But "early" is not the same as "underpriced," and inevitability is not a substitute for value. A mature investor doesn't just ask *when* to enter—but *whether* entering adds value to their portfolio at all. Conviction doesn't demand being first. It demands being aligned.

One of the most reliable indicators of genuine conviction is the ability to hold steady when narratives shift. During bull markets, restraint feels like a flaw. During bear markets, panic masquerades as realism. The investor with conviction doesn't ignore these emotional swings—they acknowledge them, then return to their thesis. If that thesis is built on solid ground, it will hold. If it was built on borrowed excitement, it will crumble. *This is why conviction must be earned, not assumed.*

To reach conviction, build your own internal research funnel. Start wide, but filter aggressively. Learn about the history of money, the nature of distributed systems, the incentive structures of tokenomics, and the mechanics of cryptographic consensus. But don't stop at technical curiosity. Ask economic questions: How does this protocol generate value? Who pays for it? What problem does it solve that cannot be solved more efficiently by existing systems? Then move to philosophical and geopolitical considerations: What does it mean to shift trust from institutions to code? What risks does that create? What protections does it eliminate? Conviction emerges not from accumulating answers, but from refining your questions.

This process is slow, and that's the point. Markets will move faster than you can read. New tokens will launch while you're still on chapter two of a white paper. Your inbox will overflow with predictions from people who don't know your risk profile, your financial goals, or your threshold for regret. Ignore them. Conviction cannot be crowdsourced. It must be constructed internally—and updated deliberately.

And sometimes, conviction means concluding that crypto is *not* for you, at least not right now. That conclusion is not an intellectual failure. It is a strategic clarity. It means you've considered the volatility, the lack of regulation, the incomplete infrastructure, the behaviour of the community, and you've decided that this domain currently offers more risk than reward, more confusion than clarity, more spectacle than substance. That is not cowardice. That is wisdom. *The rational investor knows when to sit out—and when to revisit that decision with new information.*

This is especially important in a field driven by cycles. Curiosity often spikes during bull markets, when prices soar and media attention intensifies. But this is the worst time to form opinions. Everything is noisy, and nuance disappears under layers of meme logic and profit-fuelled storytelling. Better to use bear markets—when the glamour fades—as your environment for thinking. What survives when speculation dies is often what matters. If your thesis still makes sense when the market is down 70%, it's likely built on more than hype.

Over time, your thesis may evolve—and it should. Perhaps you begin as a sceptic, drawn in by macroeconomic uncertainty. You study Bitcoin. You read the history of fiat currency collapse. You consider tail risks. Then you learn about Ethereum and programmable money. You compare it to existing systems like SWIFT or ACH. You note inefficiencies. You become interested in smart contract auditing, or decentralised identity, or on-chain governance. Slowly, you shift from observation to participation—not because the market told you to, but because your logic demanded it. This is the architecture of conviction. *It grows slowly, survives scrutiny, and stands independent of market cycles.*

The goal is not to arrive at the "right" opinion about crypto. The goal is to arrive at *your* opinion—and to own it fully. With enough clarity, you can listen without reacting, read without rushing, and act without regret. Whether you end up allocating 10% of your portfolio or none at all, your choice will be anchored in analysis, not emotion. That's what separates the thoughtful investor from the reactive one. That's what turns curiosity into conviction—and speculation into strategy.

Principles to Revisit in Every Cycle

Markets don't just move—they teach. But the lessons are often misunderstood, misapplied, or forgotten. In crypto, where volatility is the price of admission and euphoria is routinely mistaken for insight, the risk of confusion compounds with each bull and bear cycle. Yet across the wreckage of token collapses, parabolic surges, and short-lived narratives, certain decision principles remain—not as predictions, but as guardrails. These principles aren't designed to help you guess the future. They're designed to help you survive it, interpret it, and act with clarity regardless of its direction.

What makes a principle worth revisiting is not its novelty, but its *resilience* under stress. Anyone can sound wise in a white paper. But when liquidity dries up, headlines scream collapse, and sentiment turns from euphoric to contemptuous, what remains? Only what's been tested—often painfully. Crypto is a domain where technological ambition collides with financial speculation. That's not inherently bad, but it demands decision-making tools that are uncorrelated to price. *Your compass should not swing with the market.*

The first principle is this: *volatility is not a verdict*. It is not proof that something is broken, nor confirmation that something is destined to win. Volatility is intrinsic to early-stage innovation combined with liquid markets. The fact that crypto can rise or fall by double digits in a day is not, in itself, a signal. It is a setting. If you interpret every sharp move as either vindication or disaster, you are not investing—you are reacting. Treat volatility like turbulence on a flight: uncomfortable, sometimes scary, but expected if you understand the environment.

Second: *price and value are often decoupled—and more so in crypto than in almost any other asset class*. A project can have a rapidly appreciating token and yet no viable use case. Another may be building real infrastructure but receive no market recognition for years. Prices are driven not just by fundamentals, but by narrative gravity, trading psychology, and the internal dynamics of token design. Don't conflate motion with merit. When in doubt, ask: *who benefits from this token increasing in price, and what is their incentive to sustain it?*

Third: *your risk tolerance is not fixed; it is situational*. You may feel composed when reading white papers on a Sunday afternoon. But will that same version of you make calm, coherent decisions when a major exchange halts withdrawals or when regulatory agencies target the project you've backed? It's easy to overestimate your risk appetite during calm periods. Stress-test your assumptions. Don't just ask "What do I think about this asset?"—ask "What would I *do* if it dropped 70% and stayed there for two years?" If the answer is "sell in panic," then your conviction was not conviction. It was proximity to convenience.

Fourth: *time horizon determines strategy*. If you're evaluating tokens based on this week's price action but claiming to have a five-year thesis, you're engaging in performative investing. Clarity comes from alignment. If you're long-term by claim, then your evaluation criteria must reflect that. Are you tracking developer activity? Regulatory trends? Adoption metrics? Or are you simply watching charts in disguise, seeking emotional comfort from daily confirmation? Long-term conviction without long-term perspective is theatre.

Fifth: *cash is a position.* In bull markets, cash feels like missed opportunity. In bear markets, it feels like safety. But in both cases, it is power—power to observe, to re-enter with clarity, to act when others are forced to react. Many of the most disciplined investors in crypto spend more time *not* invested than invested. This doesn't reflect indecision. It reflects a principled refusal to chase momentum or confuse activity with progress. Holding cash is not "sitting out." It is preparing. It is reserving optionality.

Sixth: *narratives are seductive, but they are not evidence.* "Decentralised" does not mean functional. "Web3" does not mean equitable. "Tokenised" does not mean useful. Crypto thrives on story because it's hard to explain and easy to reframe. But rational investors distinguish between compelling language and compelling logic. When a new idea captures attention—whether it's DAOs, DeFi, NFTs, or decentralised social media—the smart question isn't "What if this works?" but "What needs to be true for this to work, *and is that happening?*"

Seventh: *ask who is underwriting the risk you're being paid to take.* In traditional finance, yield is generally tied to identifiable risk: credit, duration, volatility. In crypto, yield is often abstracted—fuelled by token inflation, subsidised by venture capital, or dependent on fragile mechanisms. If you don't understand where the yield comes from, you *are* the yield. This principle matters most when yields are unusually high. Don't be surprised by the collapse of something you never understood in the first place.

Eighth: *regulation is not an externality—it is a variable.* Many crypto participants treat law as something to be ignored until enforced. This is not prudent, it is naïve. Regulation is not always hostile, but it is always present—whether formally written or informally enforced. When building a thesis around a protocol or sector, ask not only "what is technically possible?" but "what is legally permissible, sustainably?" Some of the loudest innovations of the last cycle—yield farming, token launches, synthetic derivatives—hit a wall not because they failed technically, but because they became regulatory targets. *A rational thesis anticipates friction.*

Ninth: *liquidity hides risk—and reveals it suddenly.* Many crypto assets appear more stable than they are simply because the market is deep during uptrends. But when cycles reverse, depth disappears. Slippage rises. Market makers pull back. What looked like a liquid asset becomes illiquid overnight. When assessing any crypto investment, ask: *how would I exit this position if I needed to?*—and don't assume you'll always get the price on your screen. Risk is not just what you hold. It's what you might not be able to sell.

Tenth: *personal incentives distort perception.* Are you evaluating a project because you believe in its architecture—or because you've already invested in it and now feel the need to defend it? Are you promoting an idea because it's logical—or because your reputation is tied to it? Human beings are not neutral evaluators. Once money, ego, or social identity enter the frame, clarity diminishes. One of the most powerful habits an investor can cultivate is intellectual detachment: the ability to examine a position with the same scrutiny regardless of ownership. *Ask yourself: would I buy this today? If not, why am I still holding it?*

These principles are not a checklist. They are a mindset. They do not offer a map, but a compass—one that can help you navigate uncertainty without collapsing under it. Markets will always test you. Sometimes slowly, through erosion of patience. Sometimes violently, through sharp corrections. But the principles that endure are not those that predict the outcome. They are those that help you think clearly *through* it.

Cycles will continue. Hype will return. And the temptation to believe that "this time is different" will reassert itself, just as it has in every asset class, in every decade. But the disciplined investor doesn't need clairvoyance. They need filters. Filters that outlast the season. Filters that make you stronger the more they are applied. That's what these principles are. Not magic. Not secrets. Just clarity—earned through repetition, reaffirmed through doubt, and made durable by time.

A Framework, Not a Forecast

Predictions sell. They always have. Humans are irresistibly drawn to those who claim to see the future—whether in stock tickers, tarot cards, or token price charts. In the crypto space, this impulse is amplified. The velocity of change, the scale of disruption, the intoxicating potential of "what if"—all encourage us to look for someone, or something, to tell us what's coming next. But here's the essential truth: no one knows. Not the traders, not the technologists, not the thought leaders, not even the protocols themselves. The future of crypto—its winners, use cases, regulatory shape, social meaning—is not knowable in advance. And yet, the fact that we can't predict the future doesn't mean we shouldn't prepare for it. It means we must *approach it differently*.

The purpose of this book has not been to forecast where crypto is headed, but to help you think more clearly no matter where it goes. That distinction is subtle, but profound. Forecasts make you dependent—on the pundit, the model, the trendline. Frameworks, by contrast, make you resilient. They give you tools to evaluate, adapt, and decide with consistency—even as the environment changes around you. This difference is especially urgent in a domain like crypto, where hype cycles can reverse in weeks, technological breakthroughs emerge unexpectedly, and market structure itself can mutate mid-cycle. *In crypto, time compresses and narratives distort. The only constant is your capacity to reason through it all.*

To build that capacity, we need something sturdier than market opinion. We need clarity of thought, robustness of process, and a philosophy that holds its shape even when the data doesn't. A good framework does not offer easy answers. Instead, it sharpens the questions you ask and aligns your actions with what you actually believe—not just what you feel pressured to believe. It helps you distinguish between signals and noise, between a passing trend and a durable thesis, between your own convictions and the ambient confidence of the crowd.

This is not unique to crypto. But crypto makes the need for it more visible. In traditional markets, decades of institutional guardrails—standardised disclosures, audited statements, regulatory protections—provide a kind of cognitive scaffolding. Crypto strips that away. It replaces familiar metrics with unfamiliar jargon, stable hierarchies with decentralised communities, and linear growth with exponential narratives. In this environment, the lack of a decision framework is not a minor oversight. It's a structural liability. Without it, you're not investing—you're improvising.

Consider how this plays out in the typical investor cycle. At first, there's curiosity. You hear about a new token or protocol. Maybe someone you trust shares a success story. You start reading. Terms like "DeFi," "staking," and "L2 scaling" become part of your lexicon. Then comes experimentation—setting up a wallet, transferring funds, trying out a decentralised exchange. And perhaps, early on, you see positive returns. This feels like validation. You believe you understand the space. You increase your exposure. And then, at some point—perhaps during a market correction, a protocol exploit, or a regulatory shock—you lose money. Confidence wavers. You begin to question what you're really participating in.

This pattern is not new. But what distinguishes mature investors from reactive ones is not how they *feel* during this cycle—it's how they *decide*. A mature investor doesn't ask, "Is this going up?" They ask, "What assumptions is this investment based on, and are those assumptions still true?" They don't cling to narratives because they're popular. They interrogate narratives based on evidence. They don't panic when price drops. They reassess, reframe, and act with proportion. In short, they operate from a framework. They know *why* they own what they own, *what would make them change their mind*, and *how much of their capital this position deserves*. This isn't just intellectual hygiene. It's financial survival.

So what does a robust framework look like? It begins with principles. Not slogans or preferences, but actual operating tenets—statements you can test and apply. For example:

– I only invest in technologies I understand at the architectural level—or am willing to invest time to understand.
– I distinguish between utility tokens, governance tokens, and speculative assets.

– I cap my exposure to unregulated platforms at X% of my portfolio.
– I assume that high yields require high scrutiny and are rarely sustainable.
– I prioritise decentralisation not as a philosophical ideal but as a vector of resilience.
– I diversify across use cases, not just names.
– I reevaluate positions quarterly—not based on price, but on progress.

These principles act as filters. They won't guarantee success, but they reduce the odds of being misled by hype, panic, or false certainty. They also give you a basis to talk to others—not to debate price predictions, but to compare strategies, spot blind spots, and learn collectively. This last point is underrated: crypto may be decentralised, but understanding it is inherently social. If you can't explain your framework to someone else—and hear theirs in return—you're likely mistaking conviction for insulation.

One of the most damaging myths in crypto is that conviction must mean maximalism—that to truly believe in the space, you must bet big, dismiss sceptics, and treat volatility as a badge of honour. But true conviction is *measured,* not loud. It is built slowly, from repeated observation and internal coherence, not from watching influencers or timing memes. Conviction is compatible with doubt. It even welcomes it. Because a framework isn't a fixed belief—it's a method for revising beliefs intelligently.

This is especially important when external conditions change. What happens when regulatory clarity arrives—either opening new avenues or closing existing ones? What happens when interoperability improves, or when infrastructure failures erode trust? What happens if a single chain begins to dominate, or if the concept of chains itself becomes abstracted by new architectures? Each of these shifts has implications. A good framework helps you absorb them without collapsing your worldview. It makes you adaptive, not dogmatic.

It also prevents overreach. One of the quieter benefits of operating from a framework is that it constrains enthusiasm within rational bounds. It reminds you that *not investing is also a decision*—and often, a wise one. Crypto is not an IQ test, nor a moral referendum. You don't "fail" if you decide that it doesn't fit your goals. The purpose of a framework is not to lure you in. It's to give you the tools to decide if you *should* be in. And if the answer is no—or not yet—that is not indecision. It is discipline.

This is where the temptation to forecast reappears. When you tell others you're not invested, they may challenge you. "But don't you see where this is going?" "Don't you realise how big this could be?" These questions are often posed with urgency, even moral overtones. But they are built on the assumption that foresight equals wisdom. It doesn't. What matters more is clarity, alignment, and intentionality. Are you acting from a forecast—or from a framework? Because if it's the former, you are hostage to your own confidence. But if it's the latter, you're free to adapt, to wait, to act from knowledge rather than noise.

A forecast, even a well-informed one, can be invalidated by a single unexpected variable. A framework, if well constructed, remains useful even when its specific expectations are wrong. That is its power. It doesn't depend on being right. It depends on being robust. This book was not written to tell you what will happen. It was written to help you think better—so that whatever *does* happen, your decisions are not outsourced to chance or crowd sentiment. Whether crypto fulfils its promise, falters, fragments, or transforms, your role is not to *guess*. It is to *engage wisely*.

That is what makes a framework enduring. It respects your agency. It scales with your understanding. It invites revision, not rigidity. And most of all, it allows you to participate in the future—not as a passenger, but as an interpreter. A rational actor, not a reactive one. A student of patterns, not a servant of hype. This isn't about predicting what comes next. It's about being ready—mentally, strategically, and philosophically—*for whatever does*.

About the Author

Daniel R. Hale is a lifelong student of systems—economic, digital, and psychological. Over two decades, he has built a reputation for making complex, volatile topics digestible for grounded, real-world decision-makers. From early skepticism to cautious participation, Daniel's path through the world of crypto mirrors that of many of his readers: curious but cautious, informed but independent. He writes for those who seek clarity over hype and resilience over risk-chasing. Through his writing, Daniel champions a rational, risk-aware approach to new technologies, helping investors of all levels think critically in a world where volatility is often mistaken for value. When he's not writing, he's studying the quiet patterns that separate fads from fundamentals.

www.ingramcontent.com/pod-product-compliance
Lightning Source LLC
Chambersburg PA
CBHW031336230926
51848CB00002B/258
* 9 7 8 9 3 7 1 7 7 5 0 6 9 *